Working with
Suicidal Individuals

of related interest

New Approaches to Preventing Suicide
A Manual for Practitioners
Edited by David Duffy and Tony Ryan
Foreword by Louis Appleby
ISBN 978 1 84310 221 2

Silent Grief
Living in the Wake of Suicide
Revised Edition
Christopher Lukas and Henry M. Seiden
ISBN 978 1 84310 847 4

By Their Own Young Hand
Deliberate Self-Harm and Suicidal Ideas in Adolescents
Keith Hawton and Karen Rodham
With Emma Evans
ISBN 978 1 84310 230 4

Deliberate Self-Harm in Adolescence
Claudine Fox and Keith Hawton
Child and Adolescent Mental Health Series
ISBN 978 1 84310 237 3

Cutting it Out
A Journey Through Psychotherapy and Self-Harm
Carolyn Smith
Foreword by Maggie Turp
ISBN 978 1 84310 266 3

Working with Suicidal Individuals

A Guide to Providing Understanding,
Assessment and Support

Tony White

Jessica Kingsley *Publishers*
London and Philadelphia

First published in 2011
by Jessica Kingsley Publishers
116 Pentonville Road
London N1 9JB, UK
and
400 Market Street, Suite 400
Philadelphia, PA 19106, USA
www.jkp.com

Library of Congress Cataloging in Publication Data
White, Tony, 1957-
Working with suicidal individuals : a guide to providing
understanding, assessment, and support / Tony White.
       p. ; cm.
Includes bibliographical references and index.
ISBN 978-1-84905-115-6 (alk. paper)
1. Suicidal behavior. 2. Suicidal behavior--Treatment. 3. Suicide--Risk factors. I. Title.
[DNLM: 1. Suicide--psychology. 2. Risk Assessment. 3. Self-Injurious
Behavior--therapy. 4. Transactional Analysis--methods. WM 165]
RC569.W478 2011
616.85'8445--dc22
                          2010026168

British Library Cataloguing in Publication Data
A CIP catalogue record for this book is available from the British Library

ISBN 978 1 84905 115 6

Printed and bound in Great Britain by
MPG Books Group

Contents

Part 1 Understanding Suicide — 7

1. Introduction — 9
2. What is Suicide? — 14
3. Transactional Analysis — 21
4. The Suicide Decision — 35
5. Modeling Suicidal Behavior — 58
6. Reactions to High Stress — 68
7. Suicide and Self-Harm — 74

Part 2 Assessing Suicide Risk — 93

8. Quantitative Measures of Assessing Suicide Risk — 95
9. Qualitative Measures of Assessing Suicide Risk — 150

Part 3 Supporting the Suicidal Individual — 181

10. The Suicide Secret and the Deliberate Suicide Risk — 183
11. Pseudo-Suicide, Suicide and Teenage Suicide — 191
12. Suicidal Ambivalence — 204
13. Suicide Timelines — 215
14. The No-Suicide Contract — 222
15. Redecision Therapy — 243

Epilogue — 254

Appendix A: Stopper Analysis — 255

References — 258

Further Reading — 263

Subject Index — 264

Author Index — 270

Part 1

Understanding Suicide

Chapter 1

Introduction

The statistics

The statistics on suicide are clear and unequivocal. The World Health Organization (2009) notes that every year almost one million people die from suicide. Hawton and Heeringen (2009) agree with this, stating that this equates to one suicide every 40 seconds. They also note that suicide is the tenth leading cause of death, accounting for 1.5 percent of all deaths worldwide. In the last 45 years, suicide rates have increased 60 percent worldwide. Suicide is now one of the three leading causes of death among those aged between 15 and 44 years. These figures do not include suicide attempts which are 20–40 times more frequent than a completed suicide.

A major factor in suicide is mental health problems; it is estimated that 90 percent of people who end their life by their own hand have some degree of psychiatric disorder. Depression is one particular mental health problem that is correlated with suicide, particularly when the depressed person shows symptoms of previous self-harm, hopelessness, suicidal urges and thoughts. Other common mental health problems are bipolar disorder, schizophrenia, anorexia nervosa and body dismorphic disorder. This last disorder may partly explain why suicide risk increases in females after breast augmentation surgery. Other causes of increased suicide risk can be physical and sexual abuse throughout childhood, as well as world events—for example, natural disasters and sudden deaths of high-profile people such as Michael Jackson.

In Europe, Serbia—and especially its northern province of Vojvodina—has the highest rate of suicide in Europe, with 19 out of 100,000 people opting to kill themselves, compared to a European average of 13 per 100,000. Interestingly enough, a number of sources have noted that suicide rates tend to drop during wars but jump in times of crisis. For example, in Serbia the highest rate of suicides recorded was during the hyper-inflation period and the lowest during the NATO bombing in 1999. It is hypothesized that, during times of war, suicide rates decrease due to the social cohesion that war can create in communities.

Hawton and Heeringen (2009) also state of the statistics, it is "suspected [that] under-reporting in many countries means this is probably a big under-estimate" (p.1372). Governments tend to put the statistics of suicide lower than they actually are. High rates of suicide do not look good for a country as they imply the population is very unhappy, dissatisfied and not being properly governed. The recording of suicides for statistical purposes can be oriented so that the rates of suicide are likely to be lowered. A prime example of this is with fatal car accidents. I have had clients report directly to me that, should they attempt a suicide, they intend to make it look like an accident, and one of the easiest ways of doing that is with a car accident. Not uncommonly, they plan to drink a bottle of alcohol and then drive at very high speed into a tree, bridge or similar structure. It is highly likely that official statistics will record this as a car accident due to alcohol and high speed, rather than a suicide.

The usual reasons given by suicidal people for making it look like an accident are threefold. First, they do not want to leave behind a stigma for their loved ones. There is less stigma attached to a person who dies by accident than one who dies by suicide. Second, they do not want their loved ones to be guilt-ridden and questioning of self as to whether they should have done more or seen the suicide coming. Third, they may be concerned that their insurance company may not pay out on the life insurance policy if their death is deemed to be suicidal.

Goal of the book

Statistics like these obviously show there is a great need to study and understand why so many people choose to die by their own hand. This book seeks to add to the field in the assessment, management and understanding of the suicidal person. A problem with the study of suicide in recent years has been a distinct lack of new material. For the past twenty years the literature has essentially been picture-straightening, with theorists and practitioners restating or reorganizing what has been said before. This book offers considerable new material on both the theory of suicidal behavior and the treatment of such individuals. For example, the assessment of suicide risk has been discussed in many books over the years, but these studies tend to be one-dimensional in that they only look at the quantitative methods of risk assessment. This book will introduce qualitative methods of suicide risk assessment which isolate the crucial factor of the suicidal person and provide a much more complete assessment of suicide risk.

The overall structure of the book is threefold. First, it offers a theoretical understanding of the suicidal individual and an explanation of why some people are suicidal and others do not consider suicide. It will examine the different motivations of suicidal behavior, even by those who are not suicidal in the first instance. Second, this book will provide a comprehensive system for the assessment of suicide risk, including both quantitative and qualitative approaches. This provides a much more robust framework by which to make assessments of suicide risk. Third, once the assessment has been made and those who are potentially suicidal have been identified, this book will cover ways in which these people can be managed—for example, with a no-suicide contract—and how they can be treated so that suicide is no longer seen as an option for them. Case studies will be provided in all three sections of this book to demonstrate the theory and practice described.

The author's background

I have worked for 30 years as a counselor and psychologist in private practice, in drug rehabilitation, with the chronically mentally ill and in a prison. In that time I have come across many suicidal people, including some who have been at considerable risk. At the time of writing this book, I have never had a client complete a suicide, at least that I am aware of. However, as I remain working in the helping professions, it is a possibility that one day such an event will occur.

While working in the prison system, in particular, I learned a great deal about the suicidal individual. I got to speak with and know literally hundreds of suicidal and pseudo-suicidal individuals. My principal task was to coordinate and oversee the system used by the prison to identify and manage suicidal and self-harming inmates. This provided an exponential learning curve as I was dealing with suicidal people day in and day out. I truly learned how they think and operate. I have also been touched personally by suicide. As a teenager, I attempted suicide twice. That personal experience has afforded me a more profound understanding of the area of suicide, particularly in the area of teenage suicide.

Terminology

Sometimes one hears the phrase "He successfully committed suicide". Generally, in the field one does not use the word "success" as to kill oneself is hardly a successful act. Also it is generally a misnomer to say that a person has *committed* suicide. In Australia, suicide and attempted suicide are no longer a crime in all states except one. This is also the case in most westernized societies. The term "committed" goes back to the days when suicide was illegal. To complete a suicide was an illegal act, just as it is to *commit* a robbery. In most countries, it is no longer illegal to attempt suicide or to complete a suicide, so the term "commit" is a misnomer as it carries the connotation of an illegal act where there is none. The more correct terminology used in this book will be: the person attempted suicide, the person completed a suicide attempt or the person completed a suicide.

The personal level for practitioners

It is hoped that this book will also assist practitioners and others who deal with suicidal people to gain some understanding of their own attitudes to suicide. Suicide is a instance of death that usually elicits a stronger emotional response. If a loved one dies through illness or by accident, that can effect us profoundly. However, if a loved one dies by killing self, that usually creates more of an emotional reaction. Death through illness or by accident is in some ways more understandable and acceptable than a death by suicide. Indeed, if a loved one dies by suicide, perhaps that also reminds us that we are all capable of taking our own lives and it may be this that frightens us all at some level. A death by illness or accident requires some level of bad luck, but a death through suicide requires no such bad luck. It demonstrates that we are all in control of whether we live or die and that some choose to die. If they can do that, it shows to each of us that we also can.

The statistics cited above mean that suicide is an event that can easily come into our own personal world. Many, if not most, people know someone who knows a person who has completed a suicide or has been seriously suicidal. Many even know such a person first-hand. Most people know someone who is in the higher risk groups, such as those with a mental illness, those with alcohol or drug problems, the prison population, the seriously depressed and so on. With regard to our very selves, 66 percent of the general population have at some time thought about suicide and 32 percent have considered suicide in a significant way (Steele and McLennan 1995). Suicide is something that touches us personally, either by knowing someone who is suicidal or by feeling that way ourselves, and therefore we need to be prepared for how to deal with that. This is especially so for those in the helping professions who tend to deal with emotionally unstable people. Sooner or later they will have to deal with someone who completes a suicide or makes a significant attempt.

Of course, there is no right way or wrong way to respond emotionally. There can be a variety of responses:

- Some respond with anger and see the suicidal as selfish for hurting the ones they left behind.
- Some feel sad and despondent at the waste of human life.
- Some respond in a contemplative way and ask the question "why"?
- Some take the philosophical view and say that everyone has the right to choose when to die.
- Some find it frightening because the person seemed so happy and full of life.
- Some see it as a courageous act.

Then there is the whole area of responsibility, which again is especially relevant to the healthcare practitioner. If a client suicides, some practitioners can start to feel they were in some way responsible. They may think their suicide risk assessment was poor or that they should have done more to help the person. I have known practitioners who have felt precisely these things and have been deeply affected. It is hoped that this book will assist readers to come to some understanding of themselves in these ways. It aims to give them information about the suicidal so that they can begin to define their personal view of the suicide act and how they view their responsibility while working with the suicidal individual.

Throughout the book, the word "child" is used to describe children of both genders. For reasons of convenience, both boys and girls are referred to using the pronouns "he" and "him", as are adults of both genders.

Unless otherwise indicated, all case studies mentioned in this book are fictional composites created to highlight an issue.

Chapter 2

What is Suicide?

This chapter seeks to define what constitutes suicide and suicidal actions. One can find a common definition of suicide as *the act of intentionally taking one's own life*. The key part of this definition is the word "intentionally". This definition seems quite simple and clear. However, upon closer examination, one finds there are various aspects and permutations that leave us with less clarity. These are addressed below.

What constitutes a suicide?

A lot is said about suicide bombers in these turbulent days and one hears the term used regularly. However, is the suicide bomber actually suicidal? This is questionable if one considers the *intent* of the suicide bomber. To be suicidal, the suicide bomber's primary intent must be to kill self. However, one could reasonably argue that the primary intent of the suicide bomber is to kill others rather than to kill self. The death of the bomber in this sense is only a side effect of the primary intention to kill others, and thus one could say that the suicide bomber does not meet the definition of what constitutes suicide.

In historical accounts of the First World War, one hears of the horrifying trench warfare. In these battles there were very few significant victories, and the soldiers at times had to climb out of the trenches and simply run at the enemy. They knew as soon as they did so that there was a high probability they would be killed by gunfire. I think most would say that these young men were not suicidal. However, looking at it from a purely behavioral point of view, these men were putting themselves in a situation in which there was a high probability they would die. Is that a suicidal act? Their intent was not to die but to overpower the enemy. Such behavior could not therefore be defined as suicidal.

These wartime examples raise other questions about the definition of suicide. The fact that the soldiers in the trenches were ordered to storm the enemy raises an interesting question. If someone is ordered to kill self, is that a suicide? The suicide bomber may not be taking an order from an officer in the trenches but from some kind of religious instructor. Perhaps this is further evidence that the suicide bomber does not meet the definition cited at the beginning of this chapter.

Then there is the question of the status obtained by a person who kills self. We are told that the suicide bomber can often be seen as a martyr after killing self and others. This raises another question. If one kills self to become a martyr, is that a suicide? If the intent is to become a martyr and the killing of self is a way to achieve that status, then it would seem not to meet the definition of suicide.

CASE STUDY 2.1: SUICIDE TO ACHIEVE STATUS

A 35-year-old man attempts to end his life by cutting an artery in his neck. He uses a razor blade and very nearly dies, but is found at the last moment and revived. Subsequent discussion with him shows that he suffers from chronic schizophrenia and is on regular antipsychotic medication. One month prior to the attempt to end his life, he stopped taking his medication because he felt that he was well and did not need it anymore. After stopping the medication he began to develop hallucinations and strong delusions. One of his delusions was talking with God. God started to tell him that he wanted him to come and be with him, and to do that he had to go to heaven. To get to heaven, the man attempted to kill himself.

In the technical sense, this does not meet the definition of suicide. The man's goal was to be with God and thus achieve a certain status. His primary goal was not to kill self; he viewed killing self as a means to achieve a particular status.

It seems, therefore, that there are three factors to consider regarding the definition of suicide:

1. Killing self is the primary intention.

2. The individual was not following an order from some superior.

3. The individual was not trying to achieve some kind of status after death.

Accidents and suicide

Freud originally postulated that we all have two basic drives, which he called Eros and Thanatos. Eros, or the life force, is the drive to create, develop and grow, whereas Thanatos is the death instinct or the destructive part of ourselves. These destructive urges can be directed out at others or in towards self with the ultimate expression being either murder or suicide.

As a result of the urges provided by Thanatos, everyone engages in behavior from time to time that is self-defeating or self-destructive. This can range from smoking cigarettes, drinking too much or not exercising enough, to repetitively playing psychological games with others that we know will damage our relationships. For most of us these urges are not too strong and do not cause too much damage in our lives. For others, such as the suicidal, the urges can be quite strong at times because the person made the suicidal decision in childhood as well. People are aware of these self-destructive urges in varying degrees. Some are quite aware of their desire to damage self, whereas others may be almost oblivious to these urges and feelings. When an individual is not aware, it means the self-destruction will be expressed in ways of which they are not aware. They will engage in behavior that is self-destructive without even realizing it.

Thus we are provided with the link between accidents and suicide. Sometimes accidents are precisely that: accidents. Some get killed because they were in the wrong place at the wrong time—for example, in a plane crash or an earthquake. At other times accidents can be much less "accidental". Some people, without being aware of it, place themselves in high-risk circumstances where they can get hurt. They may feel it was an accident, when, in fact, it was their self-destructive urges working. Figure 2.1 shows this relationship between accidents and suicide.

In some circumstances, accidents are clearly accidents and, in some situations, suicides are clearly suicides, but there is also a gray area in the middle. Car accidents are a good example of this. Take the person who drinks to significant intoxication, then drives his car at high speed. What is this person saying with his behavior, especially if he does it repeatedly? At some level he knows he is taking risks and placing himself into a situation in which he could be killed. Other people may be quite unaware of this, and should he crash, they will

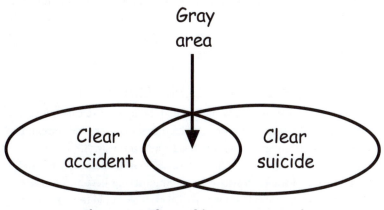

**Figure 2.1 The ambiguous nature of
some accidents and suicides**

view it as a car accident when it may be more accurately described
as a "car suicide".

Any person who goes into a war zone voluntarily, who becomes
a racing car driver, who takes up extreme sports or who works with
wild animals is placing self in a situation in which the possibility of
getting killed is significantly increased. In one sense, this can be seen
as an expression of their Thanatos or drive to self-destruct. When
asked if they are feeling suicidal, most people in these situations
will say they are definitely not and add that they feel they have
everything to live for and are quite happy. They will say they are
taking calculated risks when they engage in such activities. This is
the key point. How much risk do they take and how aware are they
of their self-destructive urges or the suicide decision they may have
made in childhood? Some of them will not be aware of such urges,
and should they die, it will be less of an accident and more of a
suicide, but it is in the gray area. How much it was an accident and
how much it was a suicide can never be determined.

Interestingly enough, in surveying the literature one finds similar
comments—for example, from the renowned Aaron Beck (1967). In
discussing the suicidal wishes of some of his depressed patients, he
states: "A suicidal wish may be manifested by the patient's taking
unnecessary risks. A number of patients drove their cars at excessive
rates of speed in the hope that something might happen" (p.31). If

something did happen, would it be a suicide or an accident? The answer is unclear.

Case study 2.2 provides an example of the vague line that sometimes exists between suicide and accidents.

CASE STUDY 2.2: *RECKLESS BEHAVIOR AND SUICIDE*

A 30-year-old man states that he has had thoughts of suicide but says that he could never actually do it. He has never made a suicide attempt. Instead, he describes his reckless behavior in this way: "It's in the bad times when all the controls I have on myself I just let go of and it's 'I will just do what I want'. This is when my drug-taking becomes reckless. Also it's in those times that I can get full of drink, get in the car and go driving recklessly." When he is in this frame of mind, the intravenous amphetamine use becomes reckless and there have been a number of hospitalizations due to overdose.

He also recounts a time when he attacked the police with a knife during their attendance at his home due to a domestic dispute. He states that it was a very volatile situation and he nearly got himself killed by the police who had guns drawn and were insisting that he put the knife down.

This case study shows that he does not actually engage in suicide attempts, but he does behave in ways in which he could be killed. His level of awareness of what he is doing varies from situation to situation. At times he is quite aware that his reckless behavior could result in being killed; at other times he has little awareness of it. The lack of awareness of his motivation to die (or be killed) results in behavior that could be considered partially suicidal and partially just reckless.

Suicide by being killed

Case study 2.2 illustrates another point that one hears mentioned from time to time by suicidal individuals. Some people are just too scared or simply cannot ever imagine themselves going through with the actual act of killing self. They do not see it as a thing they could ever do, while at the same time they have quite strong self-destructive urges. The man in the case study reports precisely this. However, the self-destructive urges will continue to demand to be expressed regardless, so he has to find another way of expressing them. One way is to have an "accident" or, alternatively, to have someone else kill you, sometimes colloquially referred to as "death by cop". This phenomenon has been discussed many times in forensic and police journals (see Jenet and Segal 1985). It involves behaving in such a way that the police will kill you—which almost happened in Case study 2.2. Some murders in domestic violence could also be this kind of suicidal act.

There is a insightful article entitled "The Psychology of Suicide-Murder and the Death Penalty" by van Wormer and Odiah (1999). These writers describe a phenomenon called "suicide-murder" (not the usual "murder-suicide"). They cite research evidence based on case studies done in prisons with males who committed murders in states where the death penalty existed for such crimes. They suggest that, in some instances, part of the motivation of the murderers to commit the crime was so that the state would kill them by execution. They were motivated at least in part by suicidal urges but felt they could never actually go through with the suicidal act, so they behaved in such a way that the state would kill them. Many of the men presented in the case studies were clearly suicidal, and some demonstrated they had clearly plotted their deaths long before arriving on death row.

In addition, van Wormer and Odiah discuss what they term "voluntary executions". In the United States, there were 223 executions between 1976 and 1993. Twenty-nine of those were consensual or at the inmates' request. In another study, they report 16 examples of men on death row who volunteered for the death penalty, usually by refusing to fight appeals of their cases. Indeed, another two individuals who had requested an execution were subsequently found innocent and released! Each of these men chose death as a solution to their problems. They did not die by their own hand but chose to die by having the state kill them. These cases involved a conscious decision to die that persisted over a significant length of time and was eventually carried out. This is a strong indicator that these men had made the suicidal decision early in their lives and it remained in their psyche until circumstances they created resulted in them enacting that solution to solve their problems.

Conclusion

This chapter has sought to define suicide, but that it is not as clear as simply identifying the person who kills self. People kill self, particularly in wartime, for a variety of reasons, some with the primary intention to die and some not. The gray area of accidents and suicide has also been discussed. It was postulated that some find the idea of actually going through with the act of killing self simply too dreadful. However, in such people the urge to die still remains so that they behave in ways that increase the possibility of them being killed by accident. The same notion was also presented with the idea of "death by cop" whereby the suicidal individual gets others or the state to kill him. If one has made the suicide decision, there is a variety of ways in which that decision can be carried out that do not involve the individual actually taking his own life by his own hand.

Chapter 3
Transactional Analysis

Transactional analysis was developed by Eric Berne, who is most widely know for his 1964 book, *Games People Play*. It is a comprehensive theory of personality, human communication, relationships and psychotherapy. This chapter provides an introduction to the theory so that it can be used in understanding, assessing and supporting suicidal individuals. The concepts of ego states and transactions are presented because they are necessary to understand the book at hand. Of course, there is much more to the theory of transactional analysis such a psychological games and life scripts. For a good introduction to the theory, read *TA Today* (Stewart and Joines 1987).

Theory of personality

Berne proposed three aspects of the personality, which he called ego states. The Parent ego state, the Adult ego state and the Child ego state are represented by three circles and labeled P, A and C in Figure 3.1.

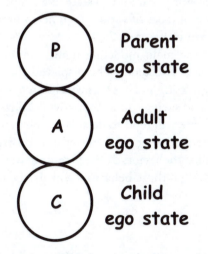

Figure 3.1 The three ego states of personality

In this book, following Berne's convention, a capital letter is used when referring to a Parent, Adult or Child ego state rather than an actual parent, adult or child.

The Parent ego state

The Parent ego state is that part of the personality that represents the prominent figures in life on whom the person has modeled. It is a historical record of those who have made an impression on the individual such that they have been imitated. This usually includes the mother and father, perhaps older siblings, significant peers, teachers and so on. The modeling into the Parent ego state continues for an individual's entire life from birth until death. For instance, husbands and wives model quite significantly from each other and pick up each other's traits and behaviors. However, usually the most important and powerful modeling occurs in childhood, with the parents or parent-type figures being the principal models.

Such modeling is inevitable and will continue to happen whether one wants it to or not. This is sometimes called the imitative instinct. People will instinctively copy others, often quite unaware that they are doing so. The modeling is indiscriminate and the child will model both the healthy behaviors and unhealthy behaviors of the parents. If the child sees his mother drinking alcohol, then he will model her on that and it is stored in the Parent ego state like a tape. The Parent ego state is a collection of tapes of various significant others and can be represented as shown in Figure 3.2.

Figure 3.2 shows the main modeling figures of the individual. These modeled behaviors will tend to be displayed throughout life. When the youngster grows up and has his own children, sometimes he finds that he is doing and saying things to his own children that were said to him as a child. He will tend to do this automatically without even realizing it. If the parenting was healthy and constructive, then the child will model those behaviors. If the parenting was not healthy or growth-promoting, then those behaviors will also be modeled.

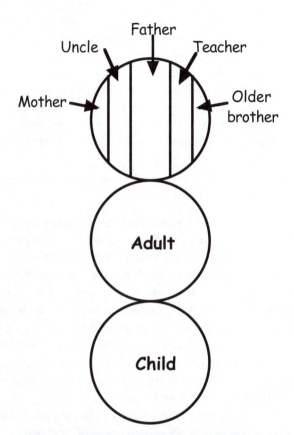

**Figure 3.2 The Parent ego state illustrated as a
collection of tapes collected by the child**

CASE STUDY 3.1: *MODELING PARENTAL BEHAVIOR*

A 33-year-old man lived most of his childhood and teenage years on
farms. He reports many instances of his father threatening suicide. He
can recall these happening when he was as young as six or seven years
old and persisting until he was about 14 years old when his family left
farming and moved to the city. Typically, his father would begin drinking
in the afternoon and would continue until late into the night. When he
had been drinking for some time, he would get very morose, and on
some occasions would state that he did not want to live anymore. He
would then get a rifle from the gun cabinet, load it and place it next to
the chair he was sitting in as he continued to drink.

As a child, this man would watch this happening in his home many times. He would spend most of the time hiding in his bedroom, listening to all the goings on, but from time to time he would come out of his room to see what was happening. He never intervened in any way. His mother would be crying and trying to convince her husband not to do anything and to put the gun away. They would argue for hours on end. His father never threatened to shoot anyone else and was never physically violent. He simply repeatedly threatened to shoot himself in the head and had a loaded gun next to him as he got more and more intoxicated. He never carried out his threat.

As a child, this man would have modeled this behavior and it would form one of the tapes in his Parent ego state. This is especially so because it occurred when he was young, it happened many times, the modeling figure was father and it was an emotionally charged situation. It becomes part of his personality whether he likes it or not. This does not mean he will display the same behavior because he has other tapes in his Parent ego state, and his Adult and Child ego states also have a strong determining influence on how this man behaves. However, the Parent ego state tape is there in his personality and therefore he has more potential to show such behavior than someone who never modeled such things.

In addition to these tapes, the Parent ego state also contains all the morals, values and beliefs about what is good and bad behavior. These are also copied from parent-type figures in life. The Parent ego state is therefore important in that it makes us behave in a socialized way. Without the Parent ego state, we would not have any guilt, and thus we could never have a society because anarchy would rein. The Parent ego state keeps the more primal urges found in the Child ego state in check. As a result, those who form the criminal population often have a dysfunctional Parent ego state: the person is undersocialized and thus commits crimes. It also works the other way as well, when the Parent ego state is too big and the person becomes oversocialized and thus can develop conditions such as anxiety and depression.

The Adult ego state

The Adult ego state represents that part of the personality that processes reality, makes decisions and understands what was going on. Sometimes it is seen as the computer of the personality. It receives information from each of the five senses and then processes that information in an organized and rational way. The early beginnings of Adult thinking begin around the end of the second year of life as the infant's verbal abilities increase. The Adult ego state continues to develop through childhood, especially at school, until puberty, when abstract and logical thinking becomes fully available (Piaget and Inhelder 1969). It collects, stores and uses information in a factual kind of way without feeling (much like a computer) which separates it from the Child ego state that has lots of feelings. It uses information to make assessments and calculate probabilities. For instance, in making a suicide risk assessment, the Adult ego state should be used to calculate the probabilities of risk. It does not make opinions, which are the function of the Parent ego state, and Adult thinking is seen to occur in the left hemisphere of the brain.

The Adult ego state is crucial for normal psychological functioning. The stronger it is, the better the person will make accurate decisions. For instance, a person may feel worthless and that things would be better if he was not here. This is a Child ego state feeling and not an Adult ego state assessment. His Adult ego state knows he is not worthless and that he is a valuable person who has every right to live a full life like everyone else. The stronger the Adult, the less impact the faulty belief of the Child ego state will have on his behavior.

The Child ego state

The Child ego state is where the feelings, primal drives and childlike aspects of us remain. In all of us there is an "inner child" that remains with us to our dying day. Sometimes it remains unchanged, with the feelings and thoughts we had in childhood staying with us and interfering with our everyday life in adulthood. If, as a child, life was scary and frightening, then in adulthood the person may develop anxiety conditions such as phobias or repetitive nightmares. Feelings such as anger, sadness, shame, hunger, thirst, sexual desire and joy are all part of the Child ego state. Whereas the Parent ego state is copying, the Child ego state is reacting.

CASE STUDY 3.2: *THE CHILD EGO STATE*

A 25-year-old female, raised in England, reports how she always hated boarding school. Much of her primary and secondary schooling was in boarding school. She also notes that her parents only lived a 15-minute drive from the school. She could have easily commuted to and from school each day but she was made a boarder and states that she hated it and always wanted to go home to her parents. It puzzled her why she had to be a boarder when other children who also lived nearby did not. Every day she hated being there. The food was horrible and she just wanted to be at home with her parents.

Her Child ego state will inevitably react to being placed in boarding school and make some kind of sense of it. She concluded that there must be something wrong with her because her parents did not want her at home and that they would be better off if she was dead. The Child ego state reacted by making the suicide decision. As a young child, she could not make an Adult ego state decision because her Adult ego state was not properly formed. The Child ego state reacted in the way it did and those feelings of anger and not being wanted remained with her until she entered counseling at age 25.

Ego states and the newborn child

When a child is born, it only has the Child ego state part of the personality. The Adult and Parent ego states are not formed so the newborn can only react to the world with this aspect of the personality. However, the Child ego state is actually subdivided into three separate ego states:

1. the Child in the Child ego state (C1) also known as the Somatic Child

2. the Adult in the Child ego state (A1) also known as the Little Professor

3. the Parent in the Child ego state (P1) also known as the Electrode.

(Modified from Woollams and Brown 1978)

These ego states are shown in Figure 3.3. This theory is essential to the understanding how the suicide decision occurs.

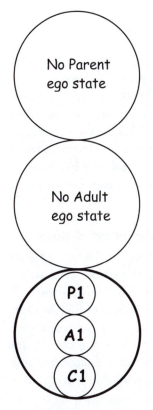

Newborn child

Figure 3.3 The three ego states within the Child ego state

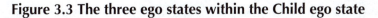

The CI or Somatic Child ego state

The C1 or Somatic Child ego state is what the newborn brings into the world from its experiences in the womb, combined with its natural temperament qualities. It contains all the feelings and urges, along with the other needs for food, warmth, affection, security and so on. It is called the Somatic Child because it is focussed on the body and bodily needs. The very young child has very little verbal capacity and thus the body does the talking for it—pleasure and pain, bodily feelings of frustration or feelings of warmth, colic, joy and tiredness.

Adults who are said to have preverbal issues had problems at this very early stage of life in their attachment with the main parenting figures. With a disrupted attachment, the newborn will have bodily reactions to it and these remain in the body of the person.

For instance, if the infant feels hungry and cries, but no one comes, then it begins to cry less and remembers those experiences in its body. In adulthood, this person can become a compulsive eater because of the unmet needs all those years ago. They have a constant feeling of hunger in their body which is the Somatic Child ego state remembering that unmet need. When asked to describe it or talk about it, the person will have difficulty because it is a bodily memory that is preverbal. The person will report that he cannot find the words to explain it but he can feel it in his body. These experiences of the Somatic Child can be recalled many years later because they remain with us all our lives.

The A1 or Little Professor ego state

The A1 or the Adult in the Child ego state is sometimes known as the Little Professor ego state because it is the little thinker in the young child. Research tends to show that conscious thinking begins about the third month of life. At that point, the child begins thinking which tends to be immature, magical, intuitive, creative and curious. He displays an interest in himself and the world and begins his Little Professor thinking about what he sees, hears and touches. Such young children can become quite engrossed in thinking and learning about toys and their bodies. When they develop the beginnings of speech, they ask many, many questions. This shows their thinking ability.

However, the thinking is not like the grown-up Adult ego state described before. This is prelogical thinking that tends to occur on the right side of the brain, and thus the youngster can make some quite odd conclusions because he does not think in a logical, systematic way. For instance, the A1 will demonstrate magical thinking as is shown in Case study 3.2 above. The young girl concluded that her parents would be better off if she was dead. Obviously, this would not be true when understood from the grown-up Adult ego state. She believed magically that she could make her parents happier by being dead. This is the sort of thinking that can occur in the Little Professor ego state.

Indeed, in psychoses such as schizophrenia, many of the thought disorders are precisely this. The Adult ego state is non-functioning, so the psychotic is only left with Little Professor thinking. Hence one gets symptoms such as magical thinking, ideas of reference, loosening of association and tangentiality. All these can occur when the Little Professor is processing information and the grown-up Adult ego state is not available, as is the case with young children. The problem with this is that people make most of their major life decisions about the value of self and others when they only have Little Professor information processing and very little Adult ego state thinking. Therefore, they can make unfortunate decisions, as is shown in Case study 3.2.

In subsequent counseling, the woman in Case study 3.2 came to the realization that her mother was a narcissistic woman. She was sent to boarding school because her mother wanted to have a life that was largely free of any child-rearing responsibilities. She could achieve this by sending the daughter to boarding school under the guise of doing it because she wanted her daughter to get a good education, thus maintaining respect among her peers. The grown-up Adult ego state could understand that, whereas the Little Professor ego state was simply not capable of such sophisticated thinking and thus she ended up making the suicide decision instead.

The P1 or Electrode ego state

The P1 or the Parent in the Child ego state is sometimes known as the Electrode. The two case studies presented above are just examples of what happens many times in a child's life. Parents relate in consistent patterns to their children, and thus the child will tend to make the same sort of decisions over and over again. When the Little Professor makes a decision, it is stored away in the P1 or Electrode. As the same sort of decisions are made, they are reinforced over and over, until eventually the child does not need to make new decisions and will react automatically based on the decisions that are already in place in the Electrode ego state.

That is why it is called the Electrode, to indicate the automatic nature of the process. By the time the child is six years old, he does not need to make new decisions and will simply respond automatically to new distressing events based on what is stored in the Electrode. For example, in Case study 3.2, the girl decided that she was placed in the boarding school because there was something wrong with her. She concluded that her parents put her there because of some failing in her and this decision was placed in the Electrode. When she grows into an adult woman, she takes all these early decisions with her, most often without being aware she is doing so. Most people are not even aware of the decisions they have in the Electrode.

At age 30, she is told one day by her boss that she is going to be shifted to a new department, which in essence is a demotion. The boss is doing this because of office politics and he has to put a new person into her current role so as to satisfy his superiors. He does not want to move her as she is a good worker. However, in her mind she has an automatic response from the decision in the Electrode. She automatically concludes that she is being moved because of some failing in her, because there is something wrong with her and she has not done the right things at work. This will be her automatic response and demonstrates the way the Electrode functions.

The functional ego states

The descriptions above show how the ego states are structured. This section will describe how the three ego states function. The ego states can be divided into six main functional ego states as shown in Figure 3.4.

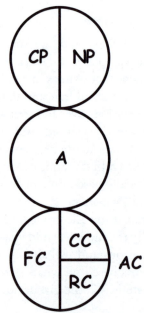

Figure 3.4 The functional ego states of the personality

The Parent ego state

The Parent ego state can be divided into two parts:

1. The Critical Parent ego state (CP) blames, attacks, criticises, set limits and takes control. It tends to be judgmental and moralistic, and uses words such as "must", "should", "ought to" and "bad". It's like the critical father telling off the children for their bad behavior.

2. The Nurturing Parent ego state (NP) is helpful and caring, and comforts and rescues others. It tends to be giving and accepting, and uses words such as "I love you", "nice" and "cute". It's like the nurturing mother who is caring for a distressed child.

The Adult ego state

The Adult ego state (A) listens, observes, is objective, organizes and solves problems. It tends to be observant and evaluative, and uses words such as "why", "what", "how", "correct" and "incorrect".

The Child ego state

The Child ego state is divided into two parts—the Free Child ego state and the Adapted Child ego state. The Adapted Child ego state can then be further subdivided into the Conforming Child ego state and the Rebellious Child ego state.

1. The Free Child ego state (FC) has feelings and wants, and is spontaneous, intuitive, intimate. It tends to be curious and uninhibited, and uses words such as "I'm angry", "wow", "fun" and "ouch". It's like a young child running free on the beach or the child crying because his goldfish just died.

2. The Adapted Child ego state (AC) is the part of us that adapts to authority. It can do this in one of two ways as shown by the Conforming and Rebellious ego states.

   (a) The Conforming Child ego state (CC) pleases others, conforms, obeys. It tends to be compliant and do what it is told, is pleasing, innocent, and uses words such as "please", "thank you", "yes" and "may I". It's like the young child who is cleaning up its room or sitting quietly waiting for Mummy to finish what she is doing.

(b) The Rebellious Child ego state (RC) is oppositional, defiant, naughty, anti-authority. It tends to be demanding, pouting and sulky, and uses words such as "no", "get away", "I won't do it, try and make me". It's like the child sitting at the dinner table with its lips tightly closed and refusing to eat its food.

The RC is seen as an adaption to authority because it is adapting by doing the opposite. It's still not doing what it wants like the FC does, and is just doing the opposite to what it is being told to do. For example, the RC will refuse to eat its dinner even if it is hungry, whereas the FC would eat the food.

Transactions

Whereas ego states provide a theory of personality, transactions provides a theory of human communication and relationships. A transaction consists of two communications, a stimulus and a response, as shown in Figure 3.5.

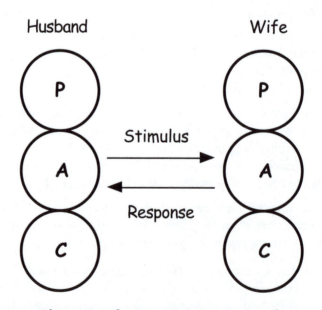

Figure 3.5 The two parts to a transaction

In Figure 3.5, we have two people—a husband and wife. The husband starts the first part of the transaction with the stimulus "What is the time?" He is stating the question from his Adult ego state and is directing it at her Adult ego state. She responds with "It is 9.30 a.m." She gives her response from her Adult to his Adult, and the transaction is complete. Transactions can be sent from any ego state and be directed to any ego state as shown in Figure 3.6.

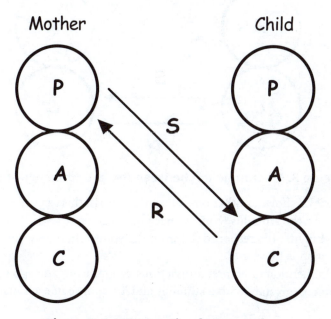

Figure 3.6 A transaction between the Parent and Child ego states

In Figure 3.6, the stimulus (S) is made by the mother from her Parent ego state as she is trying to get the young child to eat dinner: "You are a naughty boy. Open your mouth and eat your food."

The response (R) from the child is from his RC ego state: he has his lips closed and grunts "No!"

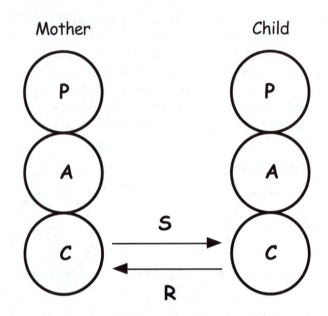

Figure 3.7 A transaction between the two Child ego states

Figure 3.7 shows another type of transaction. In this case, the mother may give the stimulus (S) from her Child ego state with "Let's have a food fight!" The response (R) from the young child may be "Yaaay! That sounds like fun."

As mentioned before, transactions can go from any ego state to any other ego state with a stimulus and a response in each instance.

Conclusion

This chapter has been a brief introduction to the theory of ego states and transactions. For the purposes of this book, that is sufficient theory in order to explain the concepts necessary for assessing and understanding the suicidal individual. As will become apparent in later chapters, the concepts of the Little Professor, Electrode and the Somatic Child ego states are of considerable importance, particularly in the chapters on the suicide decision (Chapter 4) and redecision therapy (Chapter 15). In those chapters, more detail will be added to the theory.

The Suicide Decision

Introduction

There is a great deal written in the literature about the causes of suicide, with the vast majority coming from correlational studies. Over the years there has been a very determined search to find the definitive factors of the suicidal person. This has usually been done by identifying high-risk groups. For instance, Hassan (1996) cites research which shows that marital problems, unemployment and health problems are found to precede suicide. George (2008) notes the research which suggests a link between suicide and mental illness, especially depression. In other cases, the prison population is reported to be ten times more liable to suicide than the general population. Finally, Cooper and Kapur (2004) state that suicide is more common in males, that approximately half of suicidal individuals have a history of self-harm and that adverse life events can trigger suicidal behavior in vulnerable individuals.

In this last sentence, the key words are "can trigger suicidal behavior". The statistics, although useful, do not actually tell you anything when you are dealing with the individual client. They cannot tell you if that individual sitting in front of you is suicidal or not. There are plenty of people who are depressed but are not suicidal at all, just as are there plenty of unemployed people who are not suicidal. Depression and unemployment can trigger suicidal behavior in some and not in others. It is necessary to discover why this is so.

Decisions

A recent article by Carr and Francis (2009) provides a very extensive literature review on the effects of childhood mistreatment and its relationship to adult psychological dysfunction. They state that both retrospective and longitudinal studies provide a large body of evidence that the maltreatment of children in childhood is associated with later adult psychopathology. Someone who is mistreated as a child will tend to suffer emotional problems in adulthood. Being suicidal in adulthood can be due to mistreatment in childhood. Transactional analysis explains this link theoretically with the concept of early decisions.

This concept asserts that suicidal thoughts and actions are based on early decisions by the person. Most suicidal individuals have made the suicide decision, sometimes referred to as the "don't exist" decision, early in life. Although there are some—for example, teenagers—who can suicide and not have made the suicide decision, the vast majority of suicidal individuals will have made such a decision early in life. The suicidal decision is the defining factor of the suicidal person and it can be seen as the trigger of most suicidal behavior. It can explain why one depressed person suicides and the other depressed person does not.

In his penetrating book *Man's Search for Meaning* (1959), Viktor Frankl discusses the psychological consequences for those who were imprisoned in the Auschwitz concentration camp. He notes that the vast majority of inmates were suicidal or at least thought of suicide at some point during their incarceration. This seems understandable due to the circumstances of their imprisonment, which included the ever present possibility of their own death and indeed the death and pain of those around them each and every day. Whilst almost everyone thought of suicide, he states that when he first entered the camp he made a promise to himself that he would not suicide. Although some did suicide soon after entering the camp, he was able to make the decision not to and he remarks that it was not a difficult decision for him to make.

Here we have a situation that could not get any worse. The Auschwitz inmates were placed into circumstances that could not have been worse in terms of day-to-day living conditions. Some chose to suicide; for others, such as Viktor Frankl, the question was never entertained in any serious way. My observations have been the same. Some people will endure terrible depression or lose everything they had in life, but suicide is never really considered as an option. Others need only a slight set of unlucky circumstances to arise and they will seriously contemplate suicide. Where does this decision come from and what form does it take? The truly suicidal person has made the suicide decision. This is the decisive feature of the suicidal person that places them apart from the non-suicidal, and thus it seems important to understand the key features of early decision-making by the young child.

The suicide decision

The suicide decision made by children actually includes a group of seven different suicide decisions. One thing any observer of human nature knows, since Freud began his crucial observations many years ago, is that humans behave in patterns. They tend to do the same things over and over again. This includes the same behaviors, feelings and even thoughts. In addition, people also tend to have the same patterns in relationships. They tend to relate to the same types of people, and within those relationships they tend to get into the same types of situations. Humans tend to do the same sort of things over and over.

There have been many explanations for this "repetition compulsion" over the years, one of the most prominent being Goulding and Goulding (1978) who talk about early decisions. They suggests that every person in childhood makes enduring choices about his life. These decisions dictate how the person thinks, feels and acts in whole variety of situations and relationships over his life span.

Examples of this are found in cognitive behavioral therapy (CBT). This therapy uses techniques such as cognitive restructuring and thought stopping. The person identifies the habitual thoughts that keep getting them into trouble—for example, excessive anger—and then uses techniques like the A-B-C-D model to change them (Reilly and Shopshire 2002). These habitual thoughts come from childhood where the youngster first created them with their early decisions. The child makes decisions about himself and others which then become habitual thought patterns for the rest of life, or "thinking errors" as they are sometimes called in CBT.

The child makes such early decisions in order to survive psychologically and physically in the early environment into which he is thrust. As the child grows, his environment changes slowly as he becomes more competent and powerful. When a teenager, he has much more control and power over who does what to him, compared to when he was six years old. Finally, when the individual becomes a full grown adult, he can have full control of what happens to him.

Even though the person grows up and becomes more potent in commanding his physical environment, the early decisions made as a young child live on. Most often they do not change and the majority of people will take those same early decisions with them to the grave, usually without even being aware of what they are. Although we can change our physical environment easily, changing our internal psychological environment or the early decisions is much more difficult.

In the histories of suicidal individuals, one finds that parents can say many things which imply the suicidal message. For instance, parents can say to the child:

- "He's our little accident."

- "If it wasn't for you, I wouldn't have had to marry your mother."

- "We only stayed together for the kids."

- "When you were born, you tore your mother apart."

- "You're always hanging around me, Jenny. Why don't you go and play on the freeway? Ha, ha, ha."

If a child hears these types of things many times over, he can come to the decision that it would be better if he was dead, so he decides that his death is a viable solution to a problem. Parents can give a suicidal message in many ways. They can do this directly and overtly with murderous actions and comments to a child. They may give such a message by acts of abandonment, such as giving the child out to friends and relatives, orphanages or boarding schools. Alternatively, the suicidal message can be implied by physical brutality to the child or by indifference from the parents.

The potential suicide decisions a child can make vary. As a result, there is a group of suicide decisions all of which have some kind of suicidal intent. Seven such decisions have been identified:

- "If you don't change, I will kill myself."

- "If things get too bad, I will kill myself."

- "I will show you even if it kills me."

- "I will get you to kill me."

- "I will kill myself by accident."

- "I will almost die (over and over) to get you to love me."
- "I will kill myself to hurt you."

(Modified from Goulding and Goulding 1979)

These give some idea as to the life circumstances that a person will need to have before acting on their internalized suicide decision.

Decision 1: "If you don't change, I will kill myself."

This decision can made by the person who tries to use suicide as a means to manipulate others. However, that does not mean he will not carry though with a suicide attempt. He may make suicide threats in an attempt to get the other to change, but it is still a suicide decision, and therefore the person views suicide as a means to solving a problem. The rationale used to act on the decision is that they are not getting something important they want. An example would be the woman who has an affair with the married man who keeps promising to leave his wife and never does. She keeps picking unavailable men who won't change, and thus she can finally come to the conclusion of the suicide decision and act upon that. In this way, it is also an angry, punishing kind of suicidal act because she is trying to get the other party to feel bad that he did not leave his wife when she has suicided. In monitoring such a person, one would examine the current relationship, looking for a situation where some change in others is wanted. Then one can specifically address that situation with the individual.

Decision 2: "If things get too bad, I will kill myself."

This is probably the most common of the seven decisions. With such people, one would be questioning them as to what they mean by "If things get too bad". It may be related to the loss of money, marriage or even reputation. Once identified, one can begin to understand and make predictions about when this person will act on the suicide decision. For example, in stock market crashes one hears of an increase in suicide rates, presumably due to a loss of money. Such a person would have concluded that, with the drop in share prices, things have gotten too bad and thus suicide can be used as a solution. In monitoring such a person, one would be looking at how the individual is setting himself up—for example, how much money they are risking on share trading.

Decision 3: "I will show you even if it kills me."

This involves suicide from a rebellious position where the individual is hitting out at someone he feels has mistreated him. With this decision, one would be seeking information about the person's current relationships, including who he wants to "show", and about the relationships in which he tends to adopt the rebellious position. There may also be magical thinking around death. The person has a pre-suicide fantasy of being able to be present at his own funeral and able to watch others suffering because they have been "shown".

Decision 4: "I will get you to kill me."

This can happen in domestic violence situations or when the person threatens the police to such a degree that they open fire on him (death by cop). It may also be present in some soldiers who enter a theatre of war voluntarily. Alternatively, some people on death row have made the suicide decision early in life and they get the state to kill them. This individual indicates the presence of a suicide decision but says he could never imagine himself doing it; he just does not have it in his behavioral repertoire.

Decision 5: "I will kill myself by accident."

In this instance, the individual repeatedly takes excessive risks so that at some point an "accident" may occur in which he is killed. One would enquire into the individual's life to discover what he is doing that is risky and to look for any Child ego state magical thinking about the risks he is taking. Does he present as being overly confident or have a sense of himself being invulnerable, as can happen with teenagers and narcissistic individuals?

Decision 6 "I will almost die (over and over) to get you to love me."

This is somewhat similar to Decision 1 in which the person makes suicidal gestures in order to get someone else to change his behavior. In dealing with this type of person, one would assess who is the person that he is wanting the "love" from. Then he has the opportunity to seek the love in other ways. Alternatively, how is he setting self up so he does not get the love he wants. An example of this decision is shown in Case study 4.1.

CASE STUDY 4.1: SUICIDAL GESTURES TO MAKE ANOTHER CHANGE

A 23-year-old woman, who had previously been a client of mine, articulated suicidal thoughts on many occasions. Her common pattern was to take medication and then contact her boyfriend who would come and save her by getting medical assistance. On this occasion, she contacted him by sending an email that she knew he was very likely to get. There was a one-in-a-hundred chance he would not get it. As it turned out, he never got the email and she died from the overdose.

Decision 7: "I will kill myself to hurt you."

This is similar to Decision 3 in that it is kind of a "payback". The suicide is designed to hurt someone. Again, one is investigating the relationships in the person's current life and identifying those whom he may wish to try and hurt. Directly addressing the suicidal person with these relationships can assist in his management. Case study 4.2 shows how a woman wanted to hurt her husband by her own death. Suicide notes can be especially instructive as to the type of suicide decision made. One is also seeking to find if there is magical thinking about being able to view one's own funeral to see the hurt people.

CASE STUDY 4.2: SUICIDE TO HURT ANOTHER

A 32-year-old woman had made many statements about suicide over the years. In more recent times there had been considerable marital disharmony and she felt unfairly treated by her husband. This resulted in many fights and arguments, also over a long period of time. In the end she finally hanged herself in a well-planned suicide. She left two suicide notes that openly attacked her husband, stating how she was unfairly treated by him and saying that she had hanged herself because of his mistreatment.

The process of early decision making

How early decisions are made can be explained with ego state diagrams. The decision-making process is a three-step process as shown in Figure 4.1.

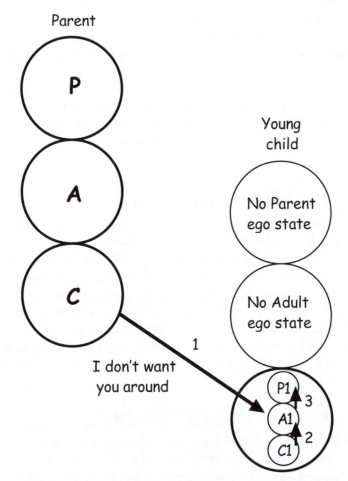

Figure 4.1 The three steps in making an early decision

Although parents may show a child through neglect that he is not wanted, it is still up to the individual child to make his own interpretation of such messages. Each child will make his own unique decision in reaction to what the parents are doing and saying. As was mentioned in Chapter 3, when a child is born, he does not have an Adult or Parent ego state; he only has a Child ego state. However, within the Child ego state there are three other ego states—the P1 or Electrode, A1 or Little Professor, and the C1 or Somatic Child.

The first step of the process occurs when the parents send the "don't exist" message to the child in a variety of different verbal and non-verbal forms. This is indicated as step 1 in Figure 4.1 where the parents tell the child he is not wanted. The message is directed to the A1 or Little Professor ego state because that is the cognitive or thinking part of the Child ego state that will seek to comprehend the message and then make sense of it. If a child is hit or ignored, then he has to make some sense out of that. He has to come to some conclusion about why such a thing has happened. It is the Little Professor that decides what those conclusions are, and they will be about what this means for self, others and life in general. For example, if a child is repeatedly neglected, the Little Professor has to decide if it is OK or not OK, and if others are OK or not OK. The Little Professor will make a decision as to the worth of self and others.

Unfortunately, the Little Professor does not think in the grown-up logical way of the Adult ego state, and therefore the child can come to some odd and even bizarre conclusions. He will think in illogical and magical ways. For instance, sometimes the suicide decision can be "Mommy and Daddy will love me if I am not here". The Little Professor conclusion is that, in order to get the parental love, the youngster has to kill himself. As grown-ups, we know from our Adult ego states that this is clearly an illogical decision, but that is how the Little Professor thinks at times.

In addition to this illogical thinking, the Little Professor makes decisions based on two pieces of information. The first of these is its comprehension of the message being sent by the parents and the second is the comprehension of its own emotional reaction to the message. The emotional reaction is felt by the C1 or Somatic Child and this is communicated to the Little Professor in step 2 of the process in Figure 4.1. The Little Professor listens to the message coming from the parents and listens to its own emotional reactions to the message and then makes its decision.

For instance, if a child is hit by a parent, it can respond in a sad way and cry. Another child may respond in an angry way and shout back at the parent. These children are likely to make different decisions because their emotional reactions are quite different. In the first case, the Little Professor comprehends being hit and also knows it feels a sad reaction. This child is more likely to conclude that he is less worth. In the second case, the Little Professor comprehends being hit and also knows it is angry and defiant in response. This child is more likely to conclude that he is OK and that the parent is the bad one.

At other times, the different emotional reactions can lead to the same decision being made but in different forms, as can be seen in the seven types of suicide decisions. The child who is sad may decide "If things get too bad, I will kill myself" or "I will kill myself by accident". The child who has an angry response to being hit may also make the suicide decision, but it will tend to be of a different form, such as "I will kill myself to hurt you" or "I will show you even if it kills me". The Little Professor of the child will tend to make different suicide decisions, depending on how the C1 or Somatic Child is feeling in response to the parental message coming in.

Once the decision is made, then it is placed in the P1 ego state as part 3 of the decision process. This same decision will then be reinforced many times until it becomes a habitual thinking error (as it is called in CBT). It then sits there, most often until the day the person dies, usually without being aware of it. As the person goes through life and comes upon different events, the way he reacts will depend on which decision he uses at the time. It will seem like an automatic reaction because the decisions in the Electrode are automatically called upon without the person even being aware of it.

An interesting feature of early decision theory is that a youngster is not a passive receptacle that just accumulates the parental messages given to him. He hears the demands made by the parents and then makes his own decisions based on what he perceives the parents are saying and his own emotional reactions to those perceptions. Sometimes the decision is quite contrary to what the parents are actually saying. However, this leaves the person in an empowered position. He is an integral part of the decision-making process and not just a victim. Case study 4.3 provides an example of the early decision-making process and how it results in suicidal behavior later in life.

CASE STUDY 4.3: *EARLY DECISION MAKING*

Juliette presents a childhood history of living in a home with her mother, father and younger sister. As all children do, she sought approval from mother and father but was given little; instead, she was told she useless, worthless, not wanted, good at nothing, and the younger sister was favored. As they grew, the younger sister also started to contribute to this. In most childhood domestic situations, parents who are so inclined will tend to say these things in a more camouflaged way, imply them or even just allude to them. The case of Juliette was unusual as there was no attempt to camouflage these statements at all. They were made clearly, openly and repeatedly, leaving her in no doubt that her partents thought she was vile, disgusting, unwanted, useless. The messages coming from the parents to Juliette's Little Professor ego state were clear and unequivocal.

Juliette's emotional response to these experiences was one of anger. Further investigation showed that when she was told these things she always tended to respond with anger. She would fight against them by disagreeing with her parents and arguing the point. One of her primary emotional responses to these messages was anger. Step 2 in her decision-making process had been defined. Her Somatic Child ego state felt anger and this was also communicated to the Little Professor.

From these experiences, Juliette made the decision "I will show you even if it kills me". She made the suicide decision which also incorporated her angry reactions, and thus it was one of the defiant suicide decisions. This decision was reinforced many times as similar events occurred throughout Juliette's childhood, and eventually the suicide decision ended up in the Electrode as one of her habitual responses to stress.

At age 25 she suffered the sudden loss of a very close friend through a car accident. At that time she also was in a relationship with a man who treated her well and with whom she was in love. However, her parents were continually undermining her, her boyfriend and the relationship. Eventually, this undermining took its toll and the relationship broke down. She recalls being extremely distressed at the loss of the relationship and the loss of her close friend, and stated that she did not know what to do. She felt totally confused and just could not make sense of it all. She also reports that, for the first time ever, she stopped directing her anger outwards and fighting her parents. She obtained a large quantity of medication, bought a bottle of vodka and went out to a secluded place in the country. She drank the alcohol and took the medication. Juliette, who had trained as a pharmacist for two years, states that she certainly took enough medication to end her life. This was a very serious suicide attempt. As it turned out, a man walking with his dog through the country came upon her, she was taken to hospital and survived. She was very lucky to have survived.

Since that time, ten years ago, Juliette reports that she has never made another attempt on her life, but there have been a few times when she has given it serious consideration. She describes two occasions once when she considered hanging herself and another time when she considered shooting herself in the head, but she has never actually made an attempt.

She reports now that she still hopes her parents will accept her and show her love. She still contacts them, but less frequently, and this contact usually leaves her with a feeling of disappointment and rejection and a sense of worthlessness. She states that usually she initially feels anger at them and their treatment of her, but after time the anger is turned inwards and she feels angry at self, then worthless and useless.

This case of Juliette is a good example of how the suicide decision is decided by the person in childhood and then just sit there in the back of the individual's mind. Juliette presents as a person who would be considered suicidal in the true psychological sense of the word. If she is again confronted with a very adverse set of life circumstances, then the suicide decision can again become operational and she will start to consider suicide as a serious option for solving her problems. When there are no distressing life circumstances present, there is little consideration of suicide.

Aspects of the decision-making process

Now we are left with the question as to why some children make the suicide decision and others do not. There are five main factors in the child's life which can result in a suicide decision being made and determine how strong that decision will be. These can be summarized as:

- the information available to the child from those doing the parenting
- the rational or irrational parental demands made on the child
- the interpretation the child makes of those demands

- the support received for those interpretations
- the personal resources of the child.

(Goulding and Goulding 1978)

The information available to the child from those doing the parenting

As a counselor, I have asked clients on many occasions questions such as "What did you think as your mother hit you?" Not uncommonly, one gets the response "I didn't know anything different. She had always done that, so I thought it was normal." Such a person has concluded that it was normal to get hit and therefore it must happen to most other children as well. The child concluded there was nothing unusual about being hit and made that decision as a result of the information provided by the parents.

The parents had never said to the child "I use corporal punishment in my parenting but there are many others who do not and they think it is quite wrong to hit a child". This lack of information is particularly influential in the decision-making process when the parents tend to isolate the child. The child is not allowed to go into other families and see how other parents respond to children being naughty without hitting them. This lack of information can also happen when families live in isolated areas such as in farming communities.

These circumstances will tend to firm up or make the suicide decision stronger because the child is not getting any contradictory information. For instance, a child may make the decision "If things get too bad, I will kill myself" because he is repeatedly hit by the parents. This will be a more powerful decision if he also sees his siblings being hit. If the child only views parents who use corporal punishment, he is not getting any contradictory information that may make the suicide decision less robust.

CASE STUDY 4.4: ABUSE AND THE SUICIDE DECISION

A 60-year-old man was abandoned by his mother as a young child and taken into an orphanage in the UK. As a young boy aged about five, he was transferred to Australia under the British Child Migrant Scheme along with a large group of boys about the same age. On arrival in Australia, he was taken directly to a boys' home in a rural area where the orphanage operated as both a school and a farm. He stayed at the boys' home until he was 16 years of age and he never went outside of its boundaries. He was completely isolated from the outside world for those years.

At the home there was extensive and severe physical, sexual and emotional abuse inflicted on him and many of the other boys. He was beaten regularly by the adults and he saw many other boys beaten as well. At times the older boys would also physically and sexually assault the younger boys. There was a complete lack of affection or emotional warmth from anyone. Eventually, he formed a gang of about four boys who would stay together to fight off sexual and physical attacks.

He developed a deep hatred of the adults there who were meant to be caring for him. He also reports a complete lack of confidence in himself and that he had zero feelings of self-worth or any sort of belief in himself. Eventually, he left and went into the outside world for the first time in many years. As he grew, he developed an alcohol problem and became an itinerant farm worker, moving from farm to farm doing manual work.

He also had a liking for high-performance cars and would drive them at great speed. By about age 25, he had been feeling quite suicidal for some time. He states that he found a stretch of road where he could get up to maximum speed. There was a large tree at the end of a straight section of the road. At that time he was particularly down and reported that he had "had enough" and just wanted "out of it all". He drove to the planned section of road and drove along it at great speed. He recalls seeing the tree get closer and closer and then he reports, "Something in my head just clicked and I could not go through with it." He did not crash the car. He still remains suicidal at times until this day.

This case study provides an example of a man who made the suicide decision as a reaction to the severe abuse he was subjected to. The decision in this case would have been particularly strong due to his very isolated childhood. He lived in the same environment for most of his childhood and did not get to see other families where children were treated well and with love. In his environment he was consistently abused, he saw other boys being abused and he saw some of the older boys also being the abusers. Thus the information given to him from the parent figures was very consistent and he saw no inconsistent information that may have weakened his conclusion: "If things get too bad, I will kill myself." In working with this man, I knew the suicide decision would be strong in his case.

It is quite likely he will make a serious suicide attempt in the future. As we know the type of suicide decision he made—"If things get too bad, I will kill myself"—we have some insight into predicting when he will be particularly vulnerable—that is, when he reports things are getting on top of him or when he feels life circumstances are just mounting up and up. Although treating the suicide decision he made would be a goal of counseling, due to his very damaged background and the strength of the decision, ongoing suicide monitoring is also required.

The rational or irrational parental demands made on the child

Of course, all parents were once children themselves and thus they also have their early decisions. They also have neurotic aspects to their personality. For instance, a father with paranoid thinking may openly tell his children that others cannot be trusted and those outside the family always have a hidden agenda. He starts to demand from his own Child ego state, from his own irrational fears, that his children be suspicious of others and not reveal personal information to others outside the family.

CASE STUDY 4.5: *IRRATIONAL PARENTAL BEHAVIOR*

A 24-year-old man recalled a game his father used to play with him. He was about five or six years of age and his father would get him to stand on a retaining wall in the back yard that was about a meter and a half high. His father would tell him to jump to him and that he would catch him. The child would jump, the father would quickly draw back, not catch him and the child would fall on to the grass below. The child would not be hurt from the fall, just surprised and shocked.

This game was used by the father to teach the boy to be careful whom you trust in the world and that most people cannot be trusted. The game came out of the father's own irrational mistrust and suspicion. The father learned as a child not to trust others and this was communicated down the line to his own children out of his own fears. If he was in his rational Adult ego state, he would communicate the rational information to the child that some people are trustworthy and some are not.

Another example could be the mother who, as a child, was physically abused by an angry father. As a consequence, she developed strong fear reactions to anyone who gets angry. When she perceives someone getting angry, she becomes anxious and immediately sets about trying to placate them and defuse the situation. Of course, all children get angry and when this mother sees her son start to feel anger, she feels the same anxiety and rushes around trying to placate him.

From this, the young child picks up mother's strong aversion to anger and thus can decide that anger is not OK. He may then set about denying or repressing his own anger. When he grows into an adult, the early decision endures and he continues to have trouble accepting and expressing his own anger. All of this can be done without any conscious awareness by the parents. Very few parents want their children to make a suicide decision but, irrationally, some may do. In some families, one child may be singled out because of his mother's or father's own irrational Child ego state beliefs. For instance, a boy's looks or temperament may remind the mother of her own father who was brutal to her and towards whom she has much anger. Over time she finds that she starts reacting to her son with some of the same feelings she had towards her father when she was a child. That may include a hatred of him and a wish for him to be dead. She may be aware of this but finds it difficult to conceal the feelings of hatred and loathing. Thus considerable pressure is being placed on the son to make the suicide decision as his mother actively promotes such a decision as a result of her own irrational feelings and thoughts.

This irrational response to a child can happen under other circumstances as well—for example, when a parent feels trapped by a child. Due to her own childhood difficulties, a mother may be very much a Child ego state herself—for instance, when a child is born to a 16-year-old emotionally immature mother. Over time the mother starts to feel she no longer has any sort of a life and sees herself as trapped by the child. She starts to communicate to the child, usually unaware that she is doing so, that he is not wanted and that he has wrecked her life. This is likely to promote a suicide decision by the child as a result of his mother's own emotional immaturity.

Similar to this is the situation of denied abortion, when a mother (or father) is denied access to aborting a fetus. This may be because it is illegal or because religious, cultural and familial pressures are put on the parents not to abort the child. There has been much research into the developmental effects of denied abortion and how a child is affected if the parents have been denied such a medical procedure. The concern is that the parents will not accept the child and, if this happens, the possibility of the child concluding he is bad or worthless increases significantly. Hence, the possibility of the child making the suicide decision increases. This rejection by the parents can be out of their awareness thus leading to irrational actions by them.

In surveying the research on denied abortion, White (1995) finds that, as a group, the parents' acceptance of such a child was "incomplete, ineffective, and ambivalent, leading to more or less deviant interactions, less empathy of the child's needs, less understanding of his/her behavioral signals, less warm emotional interchange of stimuli, etc." (p.10). It seems reasonable to conclude that a child could react to such a parental response by making the suicide decision.

One also finds the suicide decision being made by a child in the case of the hot potato. Mother has her own suicide decision that she made as a young child. She finds that she can avoid acting out the decision by placing it on to the child, again unaware that she is doing so. Hence she passes on the hot potato and this allows her to take the focus off her own suicidal urges. She subtly encourages the child to do dangerous things, be self-destructive, so that she can then look out for and worry about the child. The child can easily respond to such irrational encouragement by making the suicide decision.

At other times it is not irrational demands placed on the child, but instead the parents can be quite aware and "rational" in treating the child poorly. Alas, there is a small group of adults who overtly and consciously tell the child that he is worthless, of little value and that things would be better if he was dead. This may be a parent or step-parent who is devoid of any warmth or caring. Such people are themselves often from very poor backgrounds, where there is significant alcohol or drug use, or perhaps significant mental illness. Or they may be psychopathic in some way and thus lack any ability or desire to empathize or have warmth for the child. Often children in these environments suffer substantial physical and/or sexual abuse as well. An example of this is shown in Case study 4.4 above.

The point being made is that all parents have a Child ego state, which is why the suicide message to the child from the parents is diagramed as coming from the biological parent's own Child ego state (see Figure 4.1). Thus every parent will at times react and behave in a childlike way. In most instances, this is not too often and relatively benign. However, there are some parents who have emotional demons resulting from their own childhoods, and in these instances, the emotional problems will sooner or later be expressed to their own children. It is in such circumstances that the suicide message can be delivered to the child. With all clients, therefore, it is important to assess how emotionally damaged their own parent(s) were. The more damaged, the more potentially dangerous decisions were made, including the suicide decision.

The interpretation the child makes of those demands

This was mentioned previously in the section discussing the three-step process of early decision making. Parents can send any message they like to their offspring, but in the end it is the interpretation of those messages that is important. It is what the Little Professor ego state in the child decides about the message from the parents that is important.

A child who is hit by his mother may decide that such things are normal and thus there is something wrong with him. The youngster may conclude that, "She thinks I am bad and therefore it would be better if I was not here". Thus we have a potential suicidal decision. Another child who is hit by his mother may decide something quite different. It may decide that there is nothing wrong with him and that his mother's actions are quite unjust. This person is not making the suicide decision and may grow up to become a campaigner for children's rights rather than deciding to suicide one day.

The child's interpretation of the message from the parents makes it is a two-way process in which each child will make his own unique interpretation of what the parents are doing and saying. A brother and sister can stand side by side watching their father drink himself blind drunk night after night and make two quite different decisions. The sister may decide that, "The thing to do in life is destroy yourself", and thus we have a suicide decision where she ends up a heavy smoker for the rest of her days. The brother next to her may conclude that "He is being stupid and I am never going to do that" and he becomes a teetotaler throughout life.

Unfortunately, it works the other way as well. A young child can come from a family where he is loved and treated quite well and still makes some self-destructive decisions. He may pick up the wrong meaning from the parents, or there may be someone who is less prominent in the child's life—a sibling, for example—on whom he focusses. There is always going to be a child who does not listen to the main messages being delivered and thus makes unpredictable self-destructive conclusions.

The support received for those interpretations
Fritz Perls, the father of Gestalt therapy, is reported to have once said, "If one person calls you an elephant he is probably projecting. If ten people call you an elephant go buy a bag of peanuts." This illustrates the importance of the support there is in a young child's environment for the decisions he makes.

For instance, in some countries women are viewed as second-class citizens, which can be reflected in their level of pay, voting rights, legal rights to divorce and so on. A young girl raised in such a culture is more likely to decide that she is of less importance than males, compared to the girl raised in a less oppressive culture. Her decision is supported and reinforced by the vast majority of those who live in that society. If the young girl decides she is of equal importance, then she constantly has to battle with the attitudes and actions of most of those around her, especially her parents. If she decides she is of less importance, then she has no such ongoing psychological battle in her own mind.

Despite this, there still will be a small group of females who resist the outside pressure. The A1 or Little Professor will still believe she is of equal importance. However, generally speaking, the more a decision gets support from those around the child, the more likely that decision will remain and indeed increase in conviction. If a child makes a suicide decision and others in the family are promoting that decision, then it is more likely to take hold and persist. If the child is from a family where other members are telling him they want him to live and be happy, then the suicide decision, although still there, will be less robust. Hence in counseling the client with the suicide decision, one needs to find out what those in the environment nearby were saying to the child. If they were saying they wanted the child to live and enjoy life, then the suicide decision will be more amenable to change in counseling.

The personal resources of the child

This is one of the more influential features of the early decision-making process. One problem with the decision theory as presented by Goulding and Goulding (1978) is that it focusses on the "nurture" aspect alone. There is little weight given to the "nature" side of the child. Hence this aspect of the personality is added here.

All people are born with some kind of natural temperament. Some children are born with a strong will and some are not. Some children will naturally fight for their rights whereas others will not. One only has to observe young infants to see even at that very young age that children respond in quite different ways and with different amounts of vigor. In the 1950s there was a famous study done called the New York Longitudinal Study by Thomas, Chess and Birch (1968). These researchers followed 140 children from birth to adolescence. Their initial interest was in infant reactivity, but as the study progressed they began to realize that they were documenting differences in the young children's temperaments. Over time they found they could accurately identify six qualities of temperament and these remained consistent over time as the child grew:

1. Rhythmicity—regular or irregular

2. Approach/withdrawal—positive or negative

3. Adaptability—adaptive or non-adaptive

4. Intensity of reaction—mild or intense

5. Quality of mood—positive or negative

6. Activity level—low or high.

Of these six qualities, there are two in particular that will influence what kind of decisions a child will make. These are adaptability and intensity of reaction. Some common positive and negative features of these are listed below.

Adaptability

In this instance, the child is either adaptive to its environment or not.

- Adaptive (positive): fits in, accepts authority, flexible, versatile.

- Adaptive (negative): too conforming, lacks substance, does not initiate, lacks creativity.

- Non-adaptive (positive): determined, a natural leader, innovative.

- Non-adaptive (negative): inflexible, authority problems, argumentative.

Intensity of reaction

In this instance, the child will have strong and intense emotional reactions or not.

- Mild (positive): unflappable, calm, handles stress and crises, laid back.

- Mild (negative): shows little feeling, hard to get to know, shallow.

- Intense (positive): excitable, active, speaks up, know where you stand.

- Intense (negative): moody, wild, "small dose person", flies off the handle.

Some children are naturally born with a fighting spirit. Such a child will tend to have a non-adaptive temperament and be high in intensity of reaction. When such a child is told that he is bad, not wanted or not doing things right, his natural reaction is to fight against that. As a consequence, he will tend to make decisions such as "I am not bad; you are the bad one for saying that". It will be more rejecting of parental messages that tell the child he is worthless or bad in some way. It is less likely to make suicidal decisions, which most often require the young child to decide that he is of little worth.

Other children are born with more complacent temperaments. This child will tend to have a more adaptive temperament and have a milder intensity of reaction. When this child is hit or treated with neglect, he is more likely to conclude that such actions are being done because there is something wrong with him. He will fight less against the parental message delivered. He will make decisions such as "My parents are treating me badly because I am bad" and these will tend to lead to more suicidal-like decisions.

This can explain why depressed people are more prone to suicide. Depression does not make people suicidal; there are many depressives who are not suicidal at all. However, many depressives are sad, melancholic individuals who more prone to make the suicide decision. Depression is a sad and down state of mind which is the opposite to the active, angry, fighting state of mind. Depressives will tend to have natural temperaments that include adaptability and a low level of intensity of reaction. If their parents treated them with neglect, they will tend to naturally adapt to that and not have a strong angry rejection of the message. Hence more suicidal decisions are made as the child is more accepting of the parental message that there is something wrong with him and things would be better if he were dead.

It should be said, however, that there are two suicidal decisions which come from more of a fighting reaction:

- "I will kill myself to hurt you."

- "I will show you even if it kills me."

In this case, the person is approaching suicide from a fighting position. He is using suicide to hit out at others, which does carry some of the non-adaptive temperament and is high in intensity of reaction found in the more fighting-spirit type of person. These are particularly relevant in adolescent suicide. There are, of course, many ways to defy authority and to hit out angrily at others. To use suicidal actions or statements does indicate that the person has also made a suicide decision and thus has adapted to the parental messages in part. In this instance, one can have suicidal decisions made by those who are not of such a compliant temperament. These statements about temperament and the sort of decisions made need to be kept in context. They are only a general rule of thumb. However, it seems safe to assume that the child who naturally tends to fight for his rights will be less likely to make the suicide decision. The child who is more naturally passive and accepting will tend to make the suicide decision when the parents are saying that he is of little worth.

Conclusion

This chapter has examined in detail the concept of the suicide decision and highlighted the importance of the suicide decision in understanding and managing the suicidal individual. It is the defining factor in the suicidal person. There are other smaller groups who will suicide and have not made the suicide decision; however, in most cases by far such a decision will have been made.

This, of course, makes it important to be aware of the nature of such decisions and that has been the purpose of this chapter. If one can identify and understand such a decision, then the ability to make a suicide risk assessment will be enhanced. If one can identify what specific type of suicide decision was made, then the long-term management of the person will be more complete. If one understands the five different aspects of the decision-making process, then again the long-term management of the person will be more effective.

This theory of early decisions will be discussed again in Chapter 14 on the no-suicide contract and Chapter 16 on redecision therapy.

Chapter 5

Modeling Suicidal Behavior

Modeling and imitation

In Chapter 4, the content of the Child ego state was discussed and how early decisions were the product of it. In this chapter, we move up to the Parent ego state and find that imitation and modeling occur instead. As is extensively recorded in the literature, children (and adults) can acquire behavior by modeling or imitating those around them. When a child watches a parent exhibit a behavior, that behavior is recorded by them, and the likelihood of the child displaying similar behavior in the future is increased compared to the child who never observed such behavior. Children will model their parents indiscriminately and unconsciously. They will model parents and others around them whether they like it or not. They will model healthy behaviors and unhealthy behaviors. If the parents are displaying loving behavior to each other, the child will incorporate and model such loving behavior. Unfortunately, it works the other way as well, and if a child observes a parent displaying suicidal behavior, they will model on that also.

This modeling process can be explained in transactional analysis terms with the Parent ego state. As was shown in Chapter 3, the Parent ego state is a collection of tapes of those whom the child has modeled and imitated throughout life. This is shown in Figure 5.1.

If a parent is displaying suicidal behavior, the child literally takes in or introjects the parent's suicidal behavior so that it becomes part of its own personality. The modeling will be particularly strong when those behaviors are displayed directly in the relationship with the child. The modeling will also be strong when the behaviors occur in an emotionally charged state. If the father displayed suicidal behavior in front of the child, then that behavior will form the father tape of the person's Parent ego state as shown in Figure 5.1. One could say the child has incorporated the suicide decision of the father.

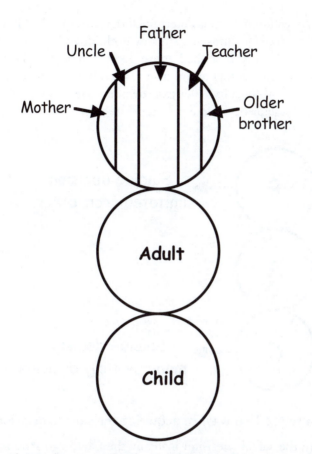

**Figure 5.1 How the Parent ego state is structured
as a collection of recorded tapes**

CASE STUDY 5.1: *SUICIDAL BEHAVIOR OF A PARENT*

A 30-year-old man's mother attempted suicide a number of times when he was in late childhood and a young teenager. None of the attempts was completed. On a number of occasions he found his mother slumped in a chair having taken a bottle of medicine and having drunk a bottle of vodka. He would call the ambulance and then keep her awake until it arrived. In addition, on many occasions his mother would talk about, almost boast about, past suicide attempts, such as trying to strangle herself with a coat hanger or how she got drunk and chose to go to sleep under a truck, hoping the driver would run her over. He reports one occasion when finding her slumped in the chair, he shouted at her in great anger, "I wish you would do it properly for once."

Through questioning, it was determined that this man had not made the suicide decision himself in his own childhood. However, as a result of his history described above, he had modeled the suicide decision from his mother and thus it resided in the Parent ego state aspect of his personality. This case demonstrates how a child can acquire the suicide decision in two separate ways as shown in Figure 5.2.

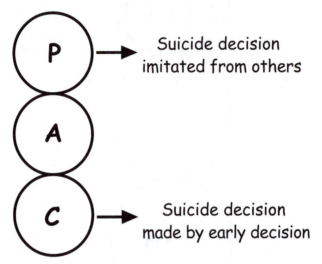

Figure 5.2 Two ways of acquiring the suicide decision

Typically, the suicide decision made by the Child ego state in early life is more influential in the personality. It is more potent and stronger than imitated behaviors that are acquired in the Parent ego state. However, they are both influences in the personality and thus both will have a determining role in the behavior displayed by the individual. If the person made the suicide decision in childhood, but his parents never modeled any suicidal or self-destructive behavior, then the Parent ego state modeling will make it less likely that he will actually make a suicide attempt. The influence from the Parent ego state will temper the early decision made by the Child ego state. Of course, the individual may still attempt suicide, but one could say that he is more protected by the influence from the Parent ego state.

The opposite situation can also exist, as indicated in Case study 5.1. The person described had not made the suicide decision in his Child ego state, but at the same time he had modeled suicidal behavior from his mother. Again we find the two ego states having opposite influences on the final behavior displayed. In these circumstances, the person is at even less risk of a completed suicide than the one just described above because the Child ego state is more influential. Indeed, this is what happened in Case study 5.1.

CASE STUDY 5.1 (CONTINUED): RECKLESS BEHAVIOR

The man states quite clearly that he has thought about suicide in the past but has never attempted and will never attempt. He states that suicidal acts are just not anywhere in his behavioral repertoire. However, he does display behavior which might result in him being killed by accident or by getting someone else to kill him.

For example, he describes his reckless behavior. "It's in the bad times when all the controls I have on myself I let go of and I will just do what I want. This is when my drug taking becomes reckless. Also it's in those times when I can get full of drink, get in the car and go driving recklessly." When he is in this frame of mind, his intravenous amphetamine use becomes reckless and there have been a number of hospitalizations due to overdose.

He also recounts a time when he took to the police with a knife during their attendance at his home due to a domestic dispute. He states that he very nearly got himself killed by the police. As a consequence, he will not actually engage in suicide attempts but he will behave in ways that could lead to him being killed. His level of awareness of what he is doing varies from situation to situation. At times he is quite aware that his reckless behavior could result in him being killed, and at other times he has little awareness of it at the time and only realizes after the event.

This case example shows what can happen when the Child and Parent ego states are operating contrary to each other. One of the ego states will have a negating effect on the suicidality of the person because such behavior was either not modeled from a parent figure or not decided upon in early childhood. However, some people have both influences. They made the suicide decision early in life *and* had suicidal behavior talked about and modeled to them in childhood. In this case, the influence of the Child and Parent ego states are in unison and the risk of suicide increases. This individual can be considered to be at a significant level of long-term suicide risk. It is quite likely that suicide will be seriously considered at some point in his life.

CASE STUDY 5.2: *PARENTAL MODEL OF SUICIDAL BEHAVIOR*

A 33-year-old man lived most of his childhood and teenage years on farms. He reports many instances of his father threatening suicide. He can recall these happening when he was as young as six or seven years old and persisted until he was about 14 years old when his family left farming and moved to the city. Typically, his father would begin drinking in the late afternoon and would continue until late into the night. When he had been drinking for some time, he would get very morose, and on some occasions would state that he did not want to live anymore. He would then get a rifle from the gun cabinet, load it, place it next to the chair in which he was sitting and continue to drink.

As a child, this man watched this happening in his home many times. He would spend most of the time hiding in his bedroom, listening to all the goings on, but from time to time he would come out of his room to see what was happening. He never intervened in any way. His mother would be crying, trying to convince her husband not to do anything and to put the gun away. They would argue for hours on end. His father never threatened to shoot anyone else and was never physically violent. He simply repeatedly threatened to shoot himself in the head and had a loaded gun next to him as he got more and more intoxicated. He never carried out his threat.

As with Case study 5.1, this man had been given a model of suicidal behavior. As a consequence, it will form part of his Parent ego state where it becomes one of the audio and video tapes that reside with the other tapes in his Parent. It will remain there for all time because one cannot "get rid" of such memories and models. However, the Parent ego state is constantly updating so that the various tapes change in how influential they are in the personality. Just because such a suicidal model exists does not mean the person will act on that. Children are not clones of their parents; they can make decisions from their Adult ego state, and their Child ego state early decisions will also be different. However, the suicidal model is in the personality.

The other thing that needs to be said about modeling is that the strength of the model is also dependent on how involved the child was with the parent figure at the time. In Case study 5.2, the young child was simply an observer. He stood on the sidelines and observed his father's and mother's behavior, thus taking in the model purely from an observation point of view. In Case study 5.1, the youngster was an observer as well as a participant. He observed his mother attempting to suicide and also became directly involved in stopping the attempt being completed. He was involved first-hand in her non-completed suicide attempt. She also spoke directly with him about some of her previous suicide attempts, and so it formed part of their relationship. This child was not only an observer of the suicidal behavior but was also involved first-hand in the behavior and talk of suicide. He had an experiential understanding of the suicidal behavior, not just an observational understanding. Such modeling is seen to be more profound and thus is likely to be more influential in the personality.

Modifying Parent ego state tapes

One way of dealing with Parent tapes that have some kind of suicidal model is to do counseling that involves the incorporation of new Parent ego state tapes, most often that of the counselor or a significant other. When any two people spend time together, they will automatically copy each other. The Parent ego state tapes are getting continual updates from current relationships. This affects how influential the past tapes will be in decision making. The more significant the relationship, the more introjection or Parent ego state tape formation there will be of the current person.

At times one hears clients say "I was talking with someone the other day and I suddenly realized that I sounded exactly like you". Or the client may adopt some behavioral idiosyncrasies of the therapist or adopt similar dress or other attitudes they have. In this case, the client has introjected the counselor. The client has started to include the counselor as one of his Parent ego state tapes. By introjecting the counselor, the client is introjecting beliefs that he is OK, worthwhile and important, which the counselor communicates to the client. As this new tape becomes more influential in the personality, it will dominate more, and thus the pre-existing tapes with the suicidal modeling become less prominent. This is sometimes called a transference "cure". See Figure 5.3.

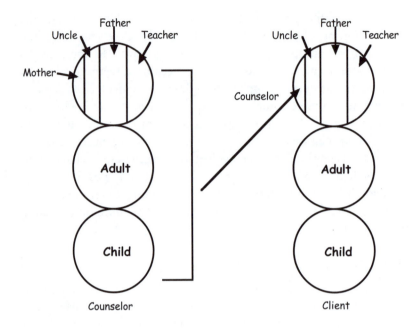

Figure 5.3 How transference by the client can result in new, non-suicidal tapes being adopted

In counseling situations where the therapeutic relationship or transference is allowed to develop, this kind of introjection will occur over time. Slowly, the counselor's personality will be modeled and taken into the client's Parent ego state as one of the tapes. The non-suicidal and healthy attitudes of the counselor literally become part of the personality of the client. If the client in Figure 5.3 modeled suicidal behavior and attitudes from the father, these are now countered to some degree by the non-suicidal attitudes of the counselor that have formed part of the Parent ego state. The client now has a choice over which tape to listen to.

The suicide pact and supported suicide

In the DSM-IV, the American Psychiatric Association (1994) discuss what is known as a *folie à deux* or shared psychotic disorder. In this case, two people who are in a close relationship over time develop the same delusional belief systems. This can include delusions that the government is tapping the phone line, beliefs about aliens coming to earth, beliefs about an explosive end to the world and so forth. Most often there tends to be one dominant party, and the other more submissive party takes on the delusions of the other. This usually means that, should the relationship end, the more submissive party will tend to drop the delusion over time, even though the submissive party probably has a tendency to have the same delusional beliefs anyway.

Figure 5.3 explains how this can happen. If we take a marital relationship, the more submissive party will introject and take on the delusional belief system of the other in his or her Parent ego state. When the relationship ends, that Parent ego state tape stops being reinforced and the other tapes become more prominent in the personality, making the submissive party drop the delusion over time. As the submissive party takes on the belief system, we have two like-minded individuals who will feed off each other. In their discussions, they discover they both believe the same things about the government, which further encourages them to see it as the truth. Indeed, to some extent, the more dominant party will also model on the other and thus his or her Parent ego state also develops such a tape. All in all, there is amplifying effect where both get support for their beliefs, thus making them more believable.

In one way, there is nothing odd about the process of a *folie à deux*. In every relationship that has a significant attachment, there will be Parent ego state tape incorporation by both parties. It is a natural and inevitable occurrence in all relationships. Over time, husbands and wives will develop some belief systems that are quite similar due to this process. These may be political views, religious views, views about life and so forth. As they do not contain psychotic delusions and do not interfere in their daily lives, they are rarely even noticed by others, but the same process is occurring. Of course, most couples are not clones of each other because both parties also have an Adult and Child ego state which can make them different from each other. However, upon more detailed inquiry, one will find some similar views that are based on this process of introjection, followed by an amplifying effect where two like-minded individuals get further support for their particular views from each other.

This also can happen with the idea of suicide. If the more dominant party views suicide as a reasonable solution to a problem, then the more submissive party may introject that into his or her own personality structure over time. As they discuss suicide, they find they agree with each other, creating the amplifying effect of two like-minded individuals and convincing each other of something that they already believe is true. In extreme circumstances, this can result in a suicide pact where two or more people will attempt suicide together. First, there is the introjection process between them, followed by the amplifying process about suicide. It could be argued that teenagers in particular are susceptible to this because their Parent ego states are still immature. Adolescence is a growth-spurt period for the Parent ego state during which it is actively incorporating tapes, more so than the fully grown adult. Hence, a *folie à deux* process between two teenagers can occur which views suicide as a viable solution. One does not have to search far on the internet to find reports of such teenage suicide pacts occurring.

In Chapter 9, a discussion of the quantitative measures of suicide risk and the protective factors of suicide risk is made. Protective factors are things such as receiving mental healthcare and family support. People with family around them are less likely to suicide because they feel supported and a sense of belonging. However, on closer examination, the protective quality of family may not be the case at all. Close family members may, in fact, support the suicidal person in his actions. The shared delusions about suicide develop over time as described above, followed by the subsequent amplifying effect. The suicidal person may be gaining support from close family members for his eventual suicide attempt. Thus, we have a derivative of the suicide pact where only one party suicides but that action is supported by others close to him.

Another derivation of the suicide pact comes out of desperation rather than the introjection process. An example of this is shown in Case study 5.1 of the young man whose life was made a living hell by his mother and her repetitive suicide attempts. This can happen particularly with the pseudo-suicidal individual who is using suicide as a way to obtain attention or manipulate others. Over time, close family members can get worn down and desperate by such behavior. It makes their lives very unpleasant and even tormented. Living with a person who is continually suicidal is very emotionally taxing and draining. As reported in Case study 5.1, at one point the young man shouted at his mother, "I wish you would do it properly for once." He was so desperate that he wished she would complete the suicide attempt. Such views by close family members would then further support the suicidal person in his attempts and illustrates another facet of the suicide pact phenomenon.

Conclusion

It is a basic tenet of psychology that people copy and model on each other. This is particularly so in childhood and adolescence. The imitating that occurs is inevitable, will occur unconsciously and is indiscriminate. The child will copy its parents in all ways, including their unhealthy behaviors, which can also include suicidal behaviors and statements. This allows the child to "obtain" a suicide decision by copying it from a parent.

In transactional analysis terms, that early decision is introjected into the personality as part of the Parent ego state. It is generally understood that an imitated suicide decision is not as potent as a person's own early suicide decision made from his own Child ego state. Having said that, an introjected suicide decision can still be influential in the personality and play a significant role in the decision making on later suicide attempts. Any person who has both an imitated suicide decision and a suicide decision made from their own Child ego state will usually be at significant risk of suicide at some time in his life. If the risk is not imminent, he would be at an elevated level of longer-term suicide risk.

The introjection process shows how suicidal thinking and behavior can result from within relationships. By imitating each other, people can develop similar thinking patterns about suicide, even to the extent of making a suicide pact. This can also occur when one non-suicidal person will be supportive of a loved one's suicidality because of the same process of introjection, followed by the subsequent amplifying process that can occur in like-minded people.

Chapter 6

Reactions to High Stress

Regression

It is generally acknowledged the more a person is placed under stress, the more he will revert to childhood solutions to problems. This is called regression and means that there is a move from the Parent and Adult ego state into the Child ego state as is shown in the Figure 6.1. In essence, the person regresses to an earlier stage of development and begins to think, feel and behave in the same way he did as a child.

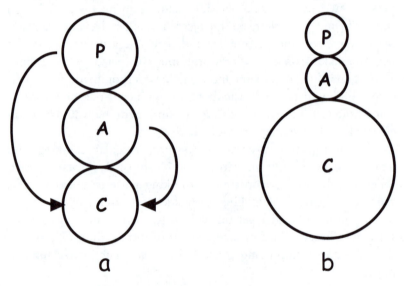

Figure 6.1 The personality structure of the regressed person

Figure 6.1(a) shows that as a person is placed under more and more stress, the more they revert to their early ways of thinking, feeling and behaving. The more childlike they will become in their thinking and behavior, and the more obvious their early decisions will become. They move from their grown-up Adult and Parent ego states into the Child ego state part of self as is shown in Figure 6.1(b). This is supported by research in neuropsychology, as cited by Johnston (2009). When people are placed under stress, they are less able to access the prefrontal cortex of the brain which is associated with the more developed functions such as problem solving, decision making and stress management (Adult ego state). Instead, people tend to access the more primitive part of the brain in the amygdala (Child ego state).

When this happens, the early decisions they made about how to think and feel become more pronounced. These early decisions influence the current decision making more than if the Parent and Adult ego states were fully operational. As a result, one finds such people making decisions that may seem quite out of character for them. Those decisions can seem odd and even bizarre based on the facts at the time because it is the early childlike thinking that is dominating the personality, not the rational Adult ego state.

Three reactions to stress

Generally, there are considered to be three main responses to high stress. In 1915 an American physiologist called Walter Cannon described the fight or flight response. This is a fundamental response to a threat or perceived attack in which the person will either fight the attacker or flee from him. Another response has since been added: the freeze response in which the person does not either fight back or flee but just freezes and ends up doing nothing. This freeze response is seen as the "playing dead" reaction. In the animal kingdom, sometimes an animal will play dead so that its attacker thinks it is dead, becomes bored and then moves away. A good example of this is the mouse caught by a cat. It plays dead in the hope that the cat will tire of it all and become distracted by something else.

Everyone has used all three responses at some time, but we all have one basic response that we use when there is a very high threat or very high level of stress. It is our last bastion, when all other options have been tried. Our most basic response to stress will be the one that we decided upon as a young child and which fits most with our basic temperament. Our temperament affects our decision making and thus will affect whether we choose fight, flight or freeze as our primary solution to problems and stress. Below are some behavioral examples of how a person may respond to threat in each of the three ways.

Fight

This person may physically hit out (as can be the case in domestic violence), verbally hit out, fight for his rights, put in a complaint or sue somebody. In childhood, this person will hit out, shout in his defense, maybe break property or try to hurt the other person in some way. The primary response is to fight the adversary either overtly or covertly. When under great stress, this person will tend to hit out at others physically or verbally. In childhood he may voice disapproval at mother and father or angrily seek to get change in some way in the home. If his mother and father are fighting, the child may actually intervene in some way between them.

Flight

This solution may include using alcohol, drugs or prescription medication. These are a way of getting away from the problem as a means to solving it. The person who quits their job and simply goes elsewhere is engaging in flight. Here he chooses to relocate geographically or move away from the problem, thus solving it in his mind. In childhood the youngster may try to run away from home or hide under the bed as a response to stress in the home. Unlike the fighter, this child does not seek to change the conditions in the home or express his disapproval; instead, he moves away from the problem and waits for it to subside. He wants to slide under the radar. Although this tends to be a more passive response compared to the fight response, it can include some anger. The anger is more self-directed than directed outwards at others.

Freeze

In earlier times this person would have been diagnosed as having a nervous breakdown. This person collapses in on self and goes into a state of incapacitation. He simply falls to the ground or crawls into bed, going into the fetal position. These days, people go on stress leave from work, or they may seek hospitalisation. Some can have panic attacks or agoraphobia, which are both incapacitating conditions that can keep them homebound. In childhood the youngster just stands there and simply does not know how to respond. In the extreme, they can loose bowel or bladder control. Whereas fight is primarily an anger response, freeze is mainly an anxiety response.

Suicide is usually a flight response

One solves the problem by getting away from it and suicide does indeed do that. Interestingly enough, in the histories of suicidal individuals, it is not uncommon for them to report running-away-from-home behavior as a child. Most often, if a child says they are going to run away from home, when asked where they are going to run to, they have no answer. In essence, the child is running away to oblivion.

Suicidal individuals are in a state of considerable distress, often confronted with some very difficult problem, whether a recent event or just an increasing state of malaise, melancholy and distress that has evolved over time. Thus they will regress and act in more childlike ways, as mentioned before. When a client reports flight as a main way of dealing with stress, this is another point to note when making a suicide risk assessment.

However, all people fight suicidal urges to some degree. If they did not, then it would not be long before they did indeed die. If, however, the person has a primary flight response, he will be more willing to give up on the fight and take the flight solution of suicide. If the person has a strong fight response, you know he will be less likely to give up and make a serious suicide attempt. The no-suicide contract can be particularly useful for this type of individual. They can use it as part of their fight response.

The counseling response to stress

Generally speaking, counseling is a fight response. Clients wish to identify the problem, find the cause of the problem and then change it, rather than simply moving away from the problem. One can assume that those with a fight response will be attracted to the counseling type of solution to problems. As mentioned before, all people fight suicidal urges to some degree and thus counseling can play a part at least in such an initial fight.

However, counseling is not always used as a fight response to problems. Some people will use counseling to identify the problem and then seek ways of getting away from it, which is the flight solution. For instance, if the client has a fight response and a problematic relationship with his mother, he will tend to try alter that relationship by changing self or by negotiation. Someone with the flight response will not try to alter the relationship but will tend to take the solution of simply never seeing his mother again. Some people come to counseling to get permission to do precisely that. They seek approval from the counselor and make a decision to terminate the relationship with their mother.

Those with the flight response are more likely to seek a purely medication approach to their problems with suicidal urges. For instance, the medication approach to depression is a example of a flight response. If it is found to be successful, such a person would have little interest in seeking a counseling approach as well. On the other hand, one not uncommonly meets clients who say they do not like taking medication because it does not solve the problem; instead, they will seek to find the cause of the problem and try to remediate it. This is the fight solution.

Sometimes the fight response can be the problem in itself. If the person has a very dysfunctional relationship with his mother that brings him great angst, he can seek to change it. The problem with changing relationships is that it usually requires both parties to change. If the mother refuses to, then there is not much he can do about that. However, the person with the fight response will tend to continue to try to change the relationship. There are some things we cannot change; the person with the fight response will have trouble identifying those things and will get stuck trying to change the unchangeable. The therapeutic goal in these circumstances is for the person to give up their fight, which some can find very hard to do.

Conclusion

The combination of our basic temperament and the illogical decision making of the Little Professor ego state results in each of us taking the fight, flight or freeze reactions to life. Once chosen, these reactions stay with us for the rest of our days. In times of great stress in adulthood, we all will regress to some degree. Our Parent and Adult ego states become less influential in our decision making and we are left with the Child ego state as the decision maker. This leaves us more vulnerable to making poor decisions about how to cope, such as a suicide attempt.

Those who have chosen flight as their response will tend to be more susceptible to viewing suicide as a solution to a problem. It is the "getting away from" solution to life's difficulties. Those who have chosen either fight or freeze may also suicide at some point, but it is less likely because it is less congruent with their primary reaction to stress. This can be another point to note when making a suicide risk assessment.

Chapter 7

Suicide and Self-Harm

There is considerable misunderstanding about the relationship between suicide and self-harm. Self-harm is usually defined as the deliberate infliction of physical damage to the body by oneself without suicidal intent. Common forms of self-harm are cutting self, burning self, wound tampering, punching self, picking at self, sticking needles in self and so forth. Not uncommonly, people who are confronted with a person who has self-harmed will tend to conclude that the person is also suicidal. On the surface, this is an understandable conclusion, but, as one looks closer, it is not the case at all.

Self-harm and suicide are separate

Self-harm and suicide are two quite separate psychological conditions. In the main, the psychological motives for doing them are different. Thus, we have two behaviors, suicide and self-harm, that have different motives and involve alternative psychological processes. This leaves us with three groups of people in relation to suicide and self-harm:

- those who self-harm and have no suicidal urges
- those who have suicidal urges and no urge to self-harm
- those who have suicidal urges and urges to self-harm.

In working with a person who self-mutilates or expresses suicidal urges, it is advisable to define which group the individual belongs to. Sometimes the lines between them are clear and sometimes they are less clear. Often parents can be convinced their son or daughter is suicidal because he or she has cut self, an understandable conclusion to come to for a distraught parent, but sometimes it is simply not the case. Indeed, the same confusion can exist in the mind of the self-harmer, which will only make matters worse. In working with self-harmers, they can feel significant relief when told that because they self-harm does not mean they are suicidal. Case study 7.1 is an example of self-harmer who knows clearly they are not suicidal. Suicide is about ending one's life. Self-harm is not about that, as is described in the eight motives below.

CASE STUDY 7.1: *THE NON-SUICIDAL SELF-HARMER*

A self-harmer reported: "I have recently started slicing my arm and I need to stop, but when I let the blood run it just makes everything go away. It feels like there is no one out there who could comprehend this. I know it makes me bad and I feel like I am bad. I can't tell anyone. I have everything I want and my life should be perfect, so I don't know why I do it. I just keep thinking about all the bad things and they just keep coming into my mind. I'm afraid I might hurt myself badly. I'm not suicidal at all and I know that I would never do that."

Bodily mutilation in context

In understanding self-harm, it is instructive to see it in a wider context. Bodily mutilation is not an unusual activity for humans; they have been physically mutilating themselves since time began. Circumcision is a clear example of genital mutilation. Some Australian aborigines also practice penile subincision. A cut is made along the urethra on the underside of the penis. In some cases, the cut goes from the head of the penis up to the scrotum. Customary unilateral castration (monorchy) is known in central Algeria, Egypt, Ethiopia, southern Africa, and among some aborigines. Bilateral castration was common to produce eunuchs for Muslim harem attendants and for several centuries to produce male sopranos or contraltos called castrati for ecclesiastical chants in the Roman Catholic Church. For females, there has been a long history of culturally sanctioned genital mutilation. Female modifications, including excision of part or all of the clitoris and sometimes also the labia, mons, or both, are evident in much of Africa, ancient Egypt, India, Malaysia and Australia.

In this context, there is nothing odd about the actual act of mutilating the human body; in this sense, it is normal. In addition to these are many other examples of tattooing and scarification, removal of teeth, teeth sharpening, neck lengthening, binding the hands and feet to make them smaller, not forgetting cosmetic surgery which is now almost endemic in many countries. Most of these bodily mutilations, which are usually voluntary, have been around in many cultures since humans first evolved. Most people when confronted with a person who self-harms will, however, be perplexed with the "abnormality" of the act. The point being made here is that mutilating the human body, by others or by oneself, is not an abnormal act at all.

The eight motives for self-harming

However, when one examines the motivation for bodily mutilation, differences are identified. A woman has her breasts enlarged because she believes it makes her looks more sexually attractive in her community. An aboriginal man may cut long scars in his chest so he can later expose the scar tissue to others, knowing that it is a sign of increased status in his community. On the other hand, we have the self-harmer who may cut long incisions in his stomach because he feels so numb and it is the only way he can begin to feel something again. The self-harmer acts much more out of desperation than the other two examples given above.

There are eight principal reasons why a person will self-harm. The explanations of these demonstrate how a self-harmer is different to the person who is motivated to suicide due to the suicide decision being made in childhood.

The eight motives are:

1. self-harming as part of gang tattooing behavior

2. self-harming to make self feel real (found in those who dissociate)

3. self-harming to make self feel something

4. self-harming used as a means of tension relief and to release pressure build up

5. self-harming as a physical expression of emotional pain (providing concrete evidence of the pain)

6. self-harming as a means to self-nurture (allowing the person to care for self, as can be found in Munchausen syndrome)

7. self-harming as a means to punish self and an expression of self-hatred

8. self-harming as a means to manipulate others or as a cry for help.

(This list comes from a variety of sources including the American Psychiatric Association 1994; Favazza and Rosenthal 1993; Gratz and Chapman 2009; Miller *et al.* 2005; and my own observations of self-harmers.)

1. Gang behavior and the tattoo-type of self-harm

Teenagers in particular can cut or harm self because it is what the gang or peer group do. The scar becomes a symbol of belonging to the group, and the harming is a secret ritual that separates them from others, particularly their parents. It is a kind of an exciting and dangerous thing to do that they have read about on the internet. This is similar to members of a motorcycle club who get a tattoo which signifies them as a member. This type of self-mutilation usually does not indicate significant emotional distress in the teenager. The mutilation is often minor and often transitory because they find it hurts too much.

CASE STUDY 7.2: *SELF-HARM IN THE PEER GROUP*

A mother presents with a 15-year-old daughter who has been discovered cutting herself high up her inner legs. Upon further discussion, it becomes apparent that a number of other girls in her peer group at school are doing the same. Sometimes they cut themselves while together. It is a subject of much importance to the peer group and they display their scars to each other. In this instance, the girl sees it as a dangerous and exciting thing that is special to her group of friends and the subject of great secrecy from their parents.

---

2. Self-harming to make self feel real

In this instance, the person could be dissociating, suffering depersonalization or derealization, and thus there are underlying emotional problems, which is not the case in the self-harming described above in Case study 7.2. The individual feels there is a sort of gap between him and reality or even between him and his perception of self. He feels detached from it. The act of cutting or burning, and the resultant pain and seeing the blood flow, allows that "gap" to disappear for a period of time and thus the self-harmer gains a sense of normality again. This most often happens because the Free Child ego state has split off from the rest of the personality as is shown in Figure 7.1. The person feels a sense of disconnection with that aspect of the personality.

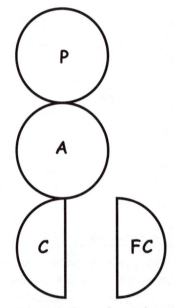

**Figure 7.1 Dissociation where the Free Child is
split off from the rest of the personality**

This person solves the bad experiences from childhood by splitting off the sensitive aspects of self, as is found in the Free Child aspect of the personality. It is in essence a severe form of desensitization in which the child solves his trauma in the short term by splitting off his sensitive responses so they can no longer be assaulted. Although this is a good short-term solution, it cannot work in the longer term. To maintain normal psychological functioning, an individual needs to have access to the sensitive aspects of the personality. If he does not, then other symptoms such as depersonalization will develop which he finds more and more distressing, and thus he experience more urgency to "make self feel real". This is not uncommonly found in bulimics as well. While purging, they can report a sense of standing back and looking at this stranger who happens to be vomiting in the toilet bowl. They experience being separate from their body. Hence, one finds some bulimics can be self-harmers as well.

The dissociated person as shown in Figure 7.1 has no sense of "Who am I?" He finds this question hard to answer in the experiential sense. From his Adult ego state, he will be able describe who he is in terms of age, sex and so forth, but the feeling or experience of who he is cannot be found. The self-harming allows the Free Child to be reconnected for a brief period of time and thus the person feels better in himself and feels more of a sense of realness. From a treatment point of view, this individual needs to close the gap and again re-experience the Free Child aspect of his personality. Once this happens, the need for self-mutilation will diminish.

3. Self-harming to make self feel something

This is similar to number 2, but in this case it is not a sense of disconnection from reality but a sense of having little feeling at all. This person is emotionally anesthestized and may report being numb with little feeling. Indeed, this is one reason why he can cut and burn himself because the experience of the pain is much less than normal. However, he does feel some pain and thus the sense of numbness and no feeling is temporarily relieved. In such cases, it is quite likely that the Child ego state is shut off, which is known as the excluded Child ego state, as shown in Figure 7.2.

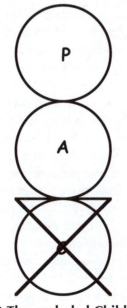

Figure 7.2 The excluded Child ego state

In Figure 7.1, the person solves emotional trauma by splitting off a part of self so that it is protected from any future assaults and distanced from the emotional pain. In Figure 7.2, the feelings of the Child ego state are repressed and thus the pain is not felt as the person becomes numb and any future traumas have much less impact.

In reasons 2 and 3 the Child ego state has been shut off for some good reason, and when one begins to open it up again, those reasons start to become obvious. Often the person has suffered some form of abuse or trauma, often repeated trauma, in their life, and the feelings about that abuse will resurface when the Child ego state is again accessed. With this comes a great deal of emotional pain, which is why the person ends up self-harming as a way to cope. In addition, reasons 2 and 3 illustrate why some self-harmers report the harming has an addictive quality to it and find it hard to stop. If they do not achieve the psychological gains that the self-harming provides— achieving some feeling and a reduction in the dissociation—they would eventually psychologically collapse in on self. Basically, they would become incapacitated and end up hospitalized with someone looking after them because they cannot do it themselves.

4. Self-harming for the relief of tension or stress

When this individual is stressed, he does not have a mature or effective way of dealing with it. He does not have the usual stress coping strategies that most people have. For instance, when most people feel stressed, they can talk to someone about it and "get it off their chest", feel the support of others, engage in some sort of relaxation technique and so on. Such procedures allow the person to reduce their stress levels, thus solving the problem. Some people do not have such skills, which can lead to self-harming as they discover that cutting self can result in a reduction of tension and stress. They discover a way to release the pressure they feel inside and that is by self-harming. Once done, there is a temporary reduction in their stress levels. Tracy Alderman (1997) states that the relief gained from the emotions in this way is usually quite rapid but temporary. In this instance, self-harming becomes a rapid, effective way of dealing with intense feelings, but it is only temporary.

The person has not learned to identify, express or release his emotions in an adult-like way. He has never developed a way to feel and express his emotions so he ends up with intense unexpressed feelings. He finds that self-harming can allow some sense of temporary relief, which again explains the addictive quality to self-harming that some report. It solves an emotional problem temporarily. For example, Green (2009) states: "When I cut myself I feel so much better, all the little things that might have been annoying me suddenly seem so trivial because I'm concentrating on the pain. I'm not a person who can scream and shout so this is my only outlet. It's all done very logically" (paragraph 17).

The counseling plan for this type of self-harm is clear. The individual learns the ABCs of stress, relaxation, emotions and their expression. He learns non self-harming ways to reduce stress and deal with his emotions. This, of course, is easier said than done. There will be some good reason why he has not already employed such methods of stress reduction instead of resorting to self-harm. It is rarely just a lack of information, and there is often some other "deeper" reason why the usual methods of stress reduction are not employed. Obviously, one needs to first ascertain what those reasons are.

For example, the individual may also have a sense of self-loathing as will be described later. Thus, the self-harming serves two purposes: to reduce stress and as a way of behaviorally demonstrating the self-hatred. If he was to use non-hurtful stress reduction methods, this will not feel right because this also says that he is worthwhile, which he does not feel or believe at that time.

5. Self-harming as a physical expression of emotional pain

These individuals suffer considerable emotional pain such as shame, anxiety, depression and despair. Emotional and psychological pain is an intangible thing that cannot be seen or touched. As a result, some tend to minimize or doubt their own internal experience of pain and may feel as if they are making it up or just exaggerating their distress. Cutting self can be a physical expression of the emotional pain that allows the individual to have concrete evidence of the pain. Sometimes self-harmers talk of their wounds and scars as being a way to see the pain they feel inside; by causing their injuries, they are bringing their pain out to be seen and perhaps healed.

6. Self-harming as self-nurturing

Self-injury can have a self-nurturing component. It can allow the person to self-care after they have injured themself. It can give a sense that there is a real injury that needs to be taken care of. Or it may be that the person who drives himself relentlessly can then feel OK about taking time off work or slowing down for a while if he is injured in some way. The self-harming allows the person to be nice to self for a period of time.

Munchausen syndrome, also known as factitious disorder in the DSM-IV (American Psychiatric Association 1994), is an interesting derivation of this type of self-harm. In this instance, the person self-harms with the goal of assuming the sick role. One motivation for taking the sick role is so that he can be cared for by others, often in a hospital setting. He gets lots of attention and caring though the various tests and nursing he receives. This individual can crave such caring and attention as he rarely gets it in his everyday life, and thus self-harming can facilitate obtaining it. This is distinguished from the self-harmer who is malingering or where the individual has some other goal, whether it be financial gain, avoiding responsibility in some way, getting out of work and so forth. In Munchausen syndrome, the goal is to be seen as sick and then to be cared for by others.

7. Self-harm as an expression of self-punishment or self-hatred

Some people self-harm because of feelings of self-hatred or as a form of self-punishment. As a result of childhood experiences, some end up with a self-hatred or self-loathing. This may be because they were told they were useless, worthless, not wanted, hated and loathed by the parent figures. In other circumstances, the child may have been physically and sexually abused. When this happens, sometimes the child, with the magical thinking of his Little Professor ego state, believes that he was abused because there is something wrong with him. It was because of his inherent badness that the parents physically abused them. The child thinks it is his fault and thus a sense of self-loathing and hatred can evolve. If a person has a basic sense of self-hatred, that does not mean he is going to be suicidal. A person will be suicidal if he has made the suicide decision and thus see suicide as a viable solution to his problems. There are plenty of people who have a basic self-dislike who do not see suicide as such a solution.

Those who do have a low self-perception will self-harm in some form but maybe not in the usual sense of the word. They may not self-harm by cutting, burning or stabbing self, but may self-harm by the lifestyle they live. For instance, a woman may prostitute herself at least partly because she hates self. This could be seen as a type of self-harm in terms of the lifestyle she lives. Any person who has a sense of self-loathing will somehow live a lifestyle in which he treats self badly physically and/or psychologically. For instance, addicted drug users can take drugs in a way that amounts to physical self-harm. An example would be intravenous drug use with dirty needles shared with high-risk others and drug use to the extent that the user's veins eventually become mutilated. Most drug addicts also hate themselves for being addicts. They know society views a junkie as being at the lowest level of society. They are seen at least by some as the useless rubbish at the bottom of the pile and often view themselves in a similar light. This can amount to psychological self-harm. Thus the drug addict may hate self and that is expressed by self-harming physically and psychologically.

There is, however, a group of self-harmers who use the more usual methods of cutting or burning as an expression of their self-hatred and self-loathing. They cut self as an expression of these thoughts and feelings. Some self-harmers will talk of bloodletting as a way of getting rid of their badness. As the blood flows out, they see their inherent badness also flowing out.

CASE STUDY 7.3: *SELF-HARM AND SELF-LOATHING*

A 22-year-old female first suffered from acne on her face at the age of 14. She found this very distressing, felt ugly and did not want others to see her face like that. She would use make up to try and hide it. At this time a compulsive "picking" of her face commenced, mainly with her fingers, and has continued until this day. She spends time each day in front of the mirror picking at the marks, pimples and blemishes on her face. She states that she feels good while doing the picking, but then feels very bad afterwards as her face looks worse. In adolescence, this resulted in her having to hide away in her room so that no one could see her. In adulthood, sometimes she will not go to work or venture outside and hides in her home because she perceives herself to be so ugly.

At about age 16 and 17 the picking of her face became particularly bad and she would hide in her room most days, and on occasion would play truant and stay away from school. Around this time there also was a two-year period of trichotillomania, particularly on her legs. The compulsive pulling out of hair on her legs also left unsightly marks which she would have to cover up in some way.

The psychological consequence of this was a strong sense of self-dislike and hatred, a feeling of being unsightly and ugly, and hence having to hide away. It allowed her forced isolation, which she craved and seems quite important for her. She reports an addictive quality to her self-harming. She has tried a number of things such as changing the time of day when she plucks her eyebrows and removing mirrors from the house, but she remains addicted and this has continued for ten years.

This case study is an example of a person who self-harms due to a sense of self-loathing. However, it also shows how people can self-harm for more than one reason. The woman in Case study 7.3 also allows herself time out after she has self-harmed—time to be alone, time away from school, work and the world in general. This is self-harming in order to obtain self-nurturing.

8. Self-harming as a form of manipulation or attention seeking

There is a shock value in self-mutilation. Most people will be shocked when they see the scars of a person who has cut self. It is dramatic and attention-grabbing in most cases. If someone wants to go to hospital or be put into the healthcare system, all he has to do is show the results of his self-mutilation to the appropriate person. Self-mutilation receives a great deal of attention and often there is a group of self-harmers who become well known to the local hospital emergency wards. Indeed, they will often be diagnosed with Munchausen syndrome as described above.

In some circles, this is a politically incorrect thing to say and many self-harmer support groups will actively deny that people self-harm to gain attention or manipulate. They will argue that, for most, self-harming is a highly secret activity with self-harmers going to extensive lengths to conceal their wounds. Unfortunately, this is simply not so. There are certainly those who do keep their harming a secret, but there are many others who do not. I have spoken with many self-harmers who openly admit they cut self to get attention or some other ulterior gain.

Furthermore, with the advent of the internet, self-harmers can now display their self-harming for the world to see and many do precisely that. It took me three minutes to find examples. One only has to go to a photograph sharing website, such as www.flickr.com, do a search for "self-harm" and one has access to over a million photographs. The second photograph clicked showed a woman clearly displaying self-harm scars on her foreman and face.

Even excluding the fakes, one can assume that thousands of self-harmers are quite willing to place their faces, biographical information and photographs of their self-harming on public display so that they can be easily accessed. Clearly, it is not a secret activity for many people. In working with self-harmers, one needs to ascertain if the person does keep his harming secret or if it is being used for some kind of secondary gain. Once done, one has a much better idea of how to deal with the problem.

This type of self-harming does highlight a prejudice that can exist against self-harmers. If they are considered to be attention-seeking and manipulative, there is a view that such people are in some way pathetic and amoral, but mostly wasters of important medical and hospital resources. This results in many of the support groups for self-harmers being quite vigourous in downplaying those who self-harm to manipulate or seek attention. Understandably, they are wanting the public to view self-harmers in a better light, not in a worse light. Some groups deny there are any who self-harm for attention seeking or grossly play down the numbers.

This can, however, have a deleterious side effect for this already fragile group of people. There are people who self-harm to obtain attention. If the support groups say there are not, these people are being told that their perceptions are false. They are being told "What you perceive to be true and real isn't true or real", when in fact it is. Thus they are left more confused and insecure about their self-perceptions by the very groups that are supposed to be helping them.

In the final analysis, they are no different from other types of self-harmers. All people self-harm for some psychological gain— some to feel real, some to reduce stress and tension, and some to obtain attention. One needs to identify what is the psychological gain, then assist the person to obtain that gain in others ways than by harming himself. This is no different for the attention seeker than for the self-harmer who seeks to reduce stress.

Self-harming with multiple motives

Described above are eight alternative motivations for self-harming. Sometimes it is easy to distinguish between the motives and sometimes not. On other occasions, a person may self-harm for a number of reasons as shown in Case study 7.3. The reasons for self-harming are not necessarily mutually exclusive, with another example described here in Case study 7.4.

CASE STUDY 7.4: *MULTIPLE MOTIVES FOR SELF-HARMING*

Stone (2009) states, "I started to deliberately injure myself when I was in my mid teens... When it came to my last year of Uni it really reared it's ugly head as an addiction, one that came with an almost unbearable amount of emotion. I was so stressed out because of the pressure of my studies that I was thinking up ways to harm myself, but I couldn't face the thought of someone else finding out that I had actually done this to myself" (paragraphs 11–12).

A follow-up interview of the individual was placed on the internet (Stone 2010). "T" is myself and "S" is part of the response from the interviewee.

T: Can you describe the type of self-harming that you did? Was there a ritual involved and so forth?

S: No, there wasn't a ritual that I followed, they were all separate events with sometimes weeks or a couple of months in between them as the stress built up. I felt in a very particular kind of mindset each time, though, and one which I came to recognize over the years. I didn't self-harm in the stereotypical way that one hears about these days. As I've said in my original post, I'd never heard of the term or knew that anyone else did anything at all similar. I certainly considered hurting myself with blades etc. but always wussed out! Now that I think about it, punching or inflicting pain with a blunt tool such as a hair brush or edge or a piece of furniture was by far my preference. This created bruising rather than cuts as I felt it easier to do to myself. Twice I created a scene that appeared as though I'd passed out and made sure that I was found by someone. This had a similarly good feeling as it caused people to be really concerned for myself and give me some attention. Other times I created bruising and lied about how I had got them, pretending that I'd been beaten up or similar.

T: How the actual relief came, was it before, during or after the actual act of self-harming? And was there thinking about the self-harming going on in your head at that time of self-harming, and if so, what was it?

S: When I was inflicting the bruising, at first it hurt but after a few minutes it almost became easy as I guess I became used to the pain and managed to block it out. This allowed me to continue inflicting this injury on myself long after I otherwise could have beared, I think. It felt good to actually hurt myself like that, in doing it I felt some form of relief, but with it came a huge chunk of guilt knowing that what I was doing wasn't good, but the "need" to do it was far stronger than any feelings that tried to make me feel bad about doing it. Having created the injury, I then liked telling people about it, lying all the time obviously, but their compassion made me feel good so the more people I told, the better I felt about it. I certainly don't go by "the end justifies the means" ideas at all on the whole, but in this case that went out the window! It was a completely cold, calculated decision that I made each time. I didn't consider the long-term effects of what all the deception was doing to me or others, or whether this was a long-term solution, it just went round and round my own head as I didn't let anyone in on any of it. (paragraphs 10–13)

T: I assume you don't self-harm now, so what changed?

S: So I have no need to hurt myself any more. When I'm stressed about something I talk it through with my husband, mum, sister or close friend before it becomes a big issue. I look at the issue as objectively as I can, ask their opinions about it, weigh them up, ask God for His opinion on it and act from there. If it's something that needs resolving that can be, then I act in the way that I consider best, but if it's just one of those things that you've got to just grin and bear it, knowing that there's an end in sight, then I just get on with it. If I find that I'm still getting stressed, I talk more about it, eat some chocolate, have a long bath, do some exercise—in fact anything rather than just sit and stew about it! (paragraphs 15 and 17)

This case study has some interesting clinical features. The most common methods of self-harm tend to be cutting, burning and wound interference. In this instance, we have an example of hitting self to the extent of causing bruising. As with other types of self-harm, an addictive quality is reported, indicating that her Child ego state is obtaining a significant psychological benefit from the activity. She reports the benefit as a sense of relief, thus indicating reason 4 cited above: she is using self-harm mainly as a means of tension relief.

Also reported is a particular kind of mindset prior to the self-harm. From a counseling point of view, this is important as it indicates the build-up period prior to self-harm and one would enquire as to its nature. Once defined, it can be used as an alarm system so that the individual can develop a plan B with the hope of avoiding the self-harm, plan B being alternative ways to relieve tension and stress. The individual also reports blocking out the pain which means she is capable of significant exclusion of the Child ego state as is shown in Figure 7.2. Treatment would need to include opening up the Child ego state feelings again. However, they have been repressed for some time for some good psychological reason and, in opening up the feelings again, one may come across some emotions that may be quite painful.

This case study demonstrates how the different motives for self-harming are not mutually exclusive. As indicated, the woman self-harms as a means to reduce tension and also mentions that she self-harms as a way to get attention from others. In addition, she reports self-harming as a means to get nurturing, in this instance from others. She reports liking the concern and compassion shown by others and reports regularly seeking these responses.

This shows the possible development of a condition like Munchausen syndrome. By self-harming, she can adopt the sick or injured role with others, and then receives nurturing and compassion. As she matured, she subsequently developed other means of seeking compassion and nurturing from others. If that had not happened, she may have developed fully fledged Munchausen syndrome symptoms. In the last paragraph, she explains how she now deals with stress in ways other than self-harming. She seeks out family and friends to talk to and get support from, which is the psychologically healthy way to deal with stress, and thus any Munchausen syndrome symptoms have no need to develop.

Harm minimization for the self-harmer

As with drug use, we have a group of people who are engaging in activity that may be physically damaging. This raises the question of harm minimization for those who self-harm. What information can the self-harmer use to reduce the physical damage sustained by their self-harming actions? How such information could be useful depends on the motivation for self-harming. The first type of self-harming describes the teenage girl who cuts her arm because of peer pressure and because it allows her belong to the group. In such instances, harm minimization information could be useful because her goal is to belong to the group and not so much to actually damage self.

The same may apply to those who self-harm to make self feel real, to make self feel something, to relieve tension or stress (reasons 2, 3 and 4 described above). For the person who harms as an expression of Munchausen syndrome, as a means to express self-hatred or as a means to obtain attention, such information could be used negatively. They may seek to maximize damage and could use such information in that way. However, such information is freely available in any library and on the internet. It can be found very easily. As a result, it seems worthwhile to articulate harm minimization information here because it could help some self-harmers from damaging themselves unnecessarily.

For the purposes of harm minimization for self-harming, one requires knowledge of surface anatomy—that is, knowledge of the locations of arteries, veins, nerves, muscles and ligaments. Knowledge of this information would give a range of outcomes, depending on the intention. Cigarette or lighter burns mainly cause cosmetic changes to the skin; the disability is minimal compared to a nerve injury inflicted by cutting. If a person wants minimum effect, then cutting an artery or vein and partially severing the muscle would inflict minimal damage. If the person wants moderate, long-term results, then severing a sensory nerve and the partial cutting of a ligament would be required. For severe long-term damage, an incision into a motor nerve and/or a ligament would be required. Most of the damage can generally be repaired.

Langer's lines are of particular importance as many people self-harm by making superficial cuts into the skin. These were described by Carl Langer, an anatomist. Langer's lines are the structural orientation of the fibrous tissue of the skin, forming the natural cleavage lines that, though present in all body areas, are visible only in certain sites such as the creases of the palm. These lines are of particular importance in surgery. Incisions made parallel to them, rather than at right angles, make for a smaller scaring upon healing. See Figure 7.3.

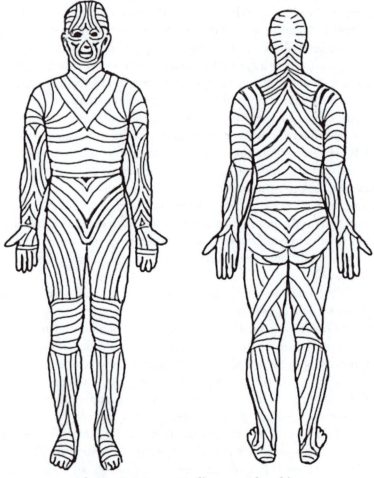

Figure 7.3 Langer's lines on the skin

An exception to this can be cuts on places such as the knees and elbows, where there is a lot of natural bending and thus stretching of the skin. In these places it may be better to make vertical cuts, which should mend more effectively as the natural stretching of the skin during recovery will have fewer negative results.

Conclusion

It seems important to include a chapter on self-harming in a book about suicide, even though the two are different and involve different psychological processes. The eight psychological motivations for self-harm are cited above, and it should be noted that not one of them includes the motivation to die. A person who engages in suicidal actions has the motivation to die at least to some degree, and this articulates the difference between the two: in suicide the goal is to die, whereas in self-harm there is no goal to die.

However, in the layperson's mind the two are often seen as similar, and thus one needs to describe why this is not so. In addition, self-harm can be a concomitant problem along with suicidal urges and thoughts. Some suicidal people do self-harm; others do not. Some self-harm and are not suicidal at all. In working with the suicidal, one needs to diagnose which group the individual falls into and then apply the necessary treatment and management strategies as required.

Self-harm is a vexatious topic in itself. Some view it as the work of weak-minded attention seekers, and indeed this attitude exists in some areas of the helping professions where self-harmers are treated with disdain. This has resulted in the evolution of self-harm support groups to protect the rights of these misunderstood individuals. We end up with a political argument which can help but can also hinder the effective treatment of some self-harmers. Finally, there is the issue of educating such individuals about harming the body physically with harm minimization techniques—another thorny issue that has arguments on both sides.

Part 2

Assessing Suicide Risk

Quantitative Measures of Assessing Suicide Risk

Alternative methods of assessing suicide risk

In the words of Cooper and Kapur (2004), "Suicide risk assessment is an inexact science" (p.20). At the same time it is an area of obvious importance and a large amount has been written on the topic. Unfortunately, the area of risk assessment historically has tended to be rather one-dimensional in its approach, using in essence the mathematical approach. One identifies the higher-risk groups, then has a checklist to see how many groups the individual falls into and finally adds up the number of relevant groups. The more groups the individual is in, the higher the risk. This is the quantitative approach and is discussed in depth in this chapter. Chapter 9 then provides a qualitative approach to suicide risk assessment that does not simply add up the risk factors but provides a method of assessing for the suicide decision, which is seen as the definitive factor of the suicidal.

The problem with the quantitative type of assessment is that it is based on statistical analyses of high-risk groups, but it cannot actually tell you about the individual sitting in front of you. It can tell you about suicide rates of the groups that the individual may belong to, but it cannot tell you if the individual sitting in front of you is suicidal. This approach is typified by Beautrais (2001), who in discussing risk factors amongst young people concludes:

> Current research evidence suggests that the strongest risk factors for youth suicide are mental disorders (in particular, affective disorders, substance use disorders and antisocial behaviors) and a history of psychopathology, indicating that priorities for intervening to reduce youth suicidal behaviors lie with interventions focused upon the improved recognition, treatment and management of young people with mental disorders. (paragraph 5)

The problem with this statement is that there are plenty of young people with substance use disorders and affective disorders who are not suicidal at all.

In addition, the Australian Psychological Society (2010) makes the following comment:

> Suicidal behavior results from a complex range of personal, social and situational issues affecting an individual. Often it may appear that a particular incident has "caused" the suicide, but in fact it is usually due to a combination of issues or a pattern of earlier difficulties. Listed below are situations and events that typically have a negative impact.
>
> Situations:
>
> • A history of depression or other mental illness in an individual, or in their parents or carers
>
> • Domestic violence or abuse—physical, emotional or sexual
>
> • Conflict over sexual identity or other sexual issues
>
> • Misuse of alcohol or other drugs
>
> • Patterns of poor communication and isolation
>
> Events:
>
> Events include any major anticipated or actual loss, disappointment or humiliation:
>
> • Loss through death, divorce or moving
>
> • Relationship break-up
>
> • Perceived academic or work failure
>
> • Unwanted unemployment
>
> • Being in trouble with authorities
>
> • Sudden disability or serious illness
>
> • Feared pregnancy. (paragraph 4)

These situations and events are based on the same assumption as mentioned above. Some people in these identified groups are at a higher risk of suicide. However, there are many who have relationship break-ups, fail academically and have a history of depression who never consider suicide in any serious way. These factors cannot tell you if one particular individual is suicidal or not. It can make predictive statements about the group that the individual may belong to (such as those with a history of depression). One can say that the quantitative factors in suicide risk assessment do help, but they are limited in their predictive ability and therefore one needs to use them in conjunction with the qualitative assessments.

Suicidal thoughts

In the literature, one often comes upon the term "suicidal ideation". It is therefore necessary to distinguish between suicidal ideation and suicidal thoughts. In the technical sense, the term suicidal ideation usually refers to the person who is thinking about suicide with some degree of intent. It does not mean the person is at imminent risk, but his thinking is becoming a bit more serious compared to the person who has suicidal thoughts. Almost everyone has suicidal thoughts at some point. They have thought about what it would be like, questioned whether they could actually do it, or if they felt particularly bad one day, they might have thought about jumping off a cliff.

Thus one needs to keep the concept of suicidal thoughts in context, as suggested by Steele and McLennan (1995) who have researched suicidal thinking. They found that 66 percent of the general population in Australia have at some time had thoughts of committing suicide. Thirty-two percent of the general population have had significant thoughts of committing suicide. An analysis of a number of studies by Steele and McLennan (1995) concludes that 6 percent of the general population actually attempt suicide.

Sixty-six percent of people have considered suicide at some point, thus making it a statistically normal event. Fortunately, for the great majority it only ever remains a thought, with the vast majority never turning those thoughts into action. Obviously, if a client reports suicidal thoughts, one needs to assess whether those suicidal thoughts have in fact become suicidal ideation and whether further risk assessment is therefore required. However, the point is that if a person reports some suicidal thoughts, one needs to keep that in context and not panic or become anxious about it.

The quantitative approach

This chapter and Chapter 9 will describe in detail the quantitative and qualitative methods of suicide risk assessment. First is the quantitative method which, as mentioned before, adopts a kind of mathematical approach to assessing risk, in which the higher risk groups are matched to the individual and then added up. Much less common is the qualitative method of assessing suicide risk, in which one seeks to identify the presence of the suicide decision in the individual. A combination of both methods would seem to provide a robust and multidimensional approach to suicide risk assessment.

As already mentioned, one way to assess suicide risk is to look at the risk factors which show up in the research. These are called the quantitative measures of suicide risk. Through research over the years, the higher risk groups for suicide have been identified. For instance, the Australian Psychological Society (1999) states: "According to Moscicki (1995), a history of substance abuse, often multiple substance abuse, is associated with a majority of suicides. Intoxication at the time of death, most frequently with alcohol, has been found in approximately half of youthful suicides" (p.12). We therefore know that if a person has a history of substance abuse, they are in a higher risk group and thus they have one of the indicators of increased suicide risk. The assumption is that the more high-risk groups a person belongs to, the more their potential for suicide increases.

Accuracy of client information in reporting suicidal thoughts and behaviors

These measures focus on the practical things one can look for in assessing suicide risk, rather than the psychological component of suicide risk, in which one estimates the presence of the suicide decision. When asking questions of people who may be suicidal, one must never assume that they are giving the truth or the whole truth. This is not because suicidal people are pathological liars; instead, they are very unhappy people who make bad decisions as a result. Cooper and Kapur (2004) state: "For example, risk assessment is influenced by gender; men tend to downplay risk compared to women" (p.29). Some will downplay their risk of suicide because they are embarrassed by it or because they think it may cost them their job, which indeed it may. Some may overstate their suicidality because they know it forces the helping professional into a course of action which they have to take due to their "duty of care". That may include hospitalization or further investigations that the assessor must take in accordance with the laws of the land or the ethical guidelines of professional organizations.

Those who downplay risk may say they have a bit of medication in their possession, when in fact they have stockpiled a large quantity, or that they have some fleeting thoughts about killing self, when in fact they think about it most days. When one gets the information from the areas discussed below, it needs to be taken in this context. Due to the state of mind of the suicidal person and the fact that one is discussing the topic of suicide, the possibility of being given misleading information is very real.

There are some who will actively not tell the truth to mislead the suicide risk assessor. This is particularly so of those who do not tell others of their suicide secret, such as the individual known as the deliberate suicide risk (DSR), discussed in detail in Chapter 10. I met a number of inmates in prison who stated openly to me they knew which words to say and which words to not say in order to stay off suicide watch. If a person has made a decision to suicide, then it is easier to complete it if there are not others closely watching. Between 20 and 30 percent of people who suicide do precisely this; if they are asked of their suicidal intent, they will deny there is any.

However, probably more common are those who are lying to themselves. Humans are very good at this. They do it in a whole variety of ways, such as repression, denial, minimization and intellectualization. In each instance, the person is feeling or thinking something that he finds quite frightening or repugnant. To cope with this, he uses some form of defense mechanism to avoid having to see it, at least in full. For instance, if a person is feeling suicidal, which he finds frightening, he can minimize it to himself. He can convince himself that it is only a passing thing, that everyone feels this from time to time or that it's really not too bad. Alternatively, he may use sublimation, in which he blocks the unacceptable suicidal impulses and becomes a counselor who works with the despairing and suicidal. Thus, the individual can focus on others suicidality and not his own.

We all use such defense mechanisms every day, and in most instances they are not that important. In some cases, however, they are, as with suicidal impulses that are defended against so that the person is either unaware of them or significantly underestimates them. Obviously, if the person is unaware of them, when asked about them, he will state that such thoughts are either not present or only present in a minimal form. One must always, therefore, be alert to the lack of reliability of self-reporting by the suicidal person and never assume the information obtained is fully accurate.

Quantitative measures

1. The tendency and degree of regression

The psychological process of regression involves a person reverting to an earlier state or mode of functioning. The person stops thinking, feeling and behaving like an adult and begins to think, feel and behave in more of a childlike way. As discussed in Chapter 6, when an individual regresses, not only do they behave in a more childlike way, but they also begin to think in a more childlike way. In the brain, the regressed person is less able to access the prefrontal cortex of the brain which is associated with the more developed functions such as problem solving, decision making and stress management (the Adult ego state). Instead, people tend to access the more primitive part of the brain in the amygdala (the Child ego state). This is shown in Figure 8.1 (a and b) in which the Parent and Adult become much less influential in the personality.

This has two main effects in terms of suicide risk assessment. First, the person stops thinking in the grown-up Adult ego state and starts to think like a child in prelogical ways. It is not until the age of eight that a child begins to comprehend that death is irreversible; before that age, a child can have all sorts of mistaken beliefs about death and what it means. As a result, if a person has significantly regressed, he can begin to think about death in such a childlike way. With his Adult ego state poorly functioning, he can have magical thinking about death—for example, that death is reversible, that when you die you can still somehow see others and how they are reacting, or that you go to heaven where you can meet and see others.

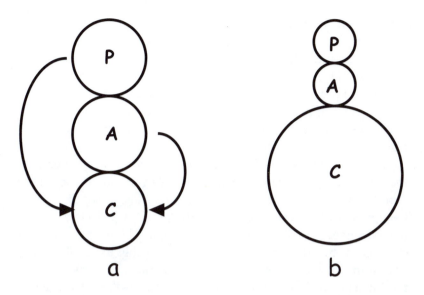

Figure 8.1 The personality structure of the regressed person

Such beliefs or thoughts about death would make it easier for the individual to suicide, and thus the risk level could be seen to go up for the regressed person.

REDUCTION OF PROTECTIVE FACTORS

The other feature of the regressed person is that the protective factors become less influential. Protective factors are those things that can be seen to protect people from suicide. For example, Cooper and Kapur (2004) cite the following four:

- hopefulness
- receiving mental health care and support
- being responsible for children
- strong social and family supports. (p.44)

For instance, the suicidal individual may think "If I kill myself, then my children will be very hurt and damaged by that" or "If I kill myself, my mother will feel guilty about what more she could have done to save me". This type of thinking and the protective factors listed above are functions of the Parent and Adult ego states. In regression, those two ego states are much less influential in the person's decision making, which is dominated by the Child ego state. Thus, the protective factors become less protective as they are considered less or not given as much weight by the suicidal person. In this sense, one can see suicide as quite a selfish act which hurts many others besides the suicidal person; indeed, it leaves the bereaved with many months or even years of psychological distress. The regressed individual has much less concern for the welfare of others compared to the non-regressed person.

Some people can simply spontaneously regress as they employ the defense mechanism of regression. This is more commonly found in the hysteric, dependent and borderline personality types. Compared to the average citizen, these people will have a greater natural tendency to regress as a means of coping. However, regression can happen by other means as well, most notably in people with a significant mental illness such a schizophrenia and in those under the influence of drugs and alcohol. These two will be discussed in much more detail later. The point at hand, however, is that a person who does regress significantly may be at higher risk of suicide than the non-regressive individual, and thus we have one of the factors to be considered in suicide risk assessment.

An examination of the regressive qualities of a person can be particularly useful in the assessment of suicide risk for the reasons cited above. One would want to make an assessment of the person's thoughts about death when regressed or of his childlike magical thoughts about death (for example, its reversibility). This can be done by questioning the person and finding out what his Child ego state thoughts and beliefs are about death and dying.

The theory behind regression is that the individual has arrested psychological development. He did not successfully complete a particular developmental stage in his childhood. Thus he becomes fixated at that developmental stage. There are many child development theories, ranging from Freud's psychosexual stages of development, to Erik Erikson's eight ages of man, to John Bowlby's theory of the development of attachment between mother and child.

In each of these, the child has to complete a set of developmental tasks at each stage; if he doesn't, he cannot psychologically move on and thus becomes fixated at that early stage. In adulthood, when the person regresses, he will regress to the fixation point, or stuck point, in his emotional development. The earlier the point, the more childlike the person will be in his thinking, feeling and behaving when he regresses. The more childlike he is, the more magical thinking he can have about death and dying, and the less influential the protective factors are.

INCREASE IN PRELOGICAL AND MAGICAL THINKING

When a person is regressed, if asked, he can often state what age he feels he is. From a suicide risk assessment point of view, the younger he reports he is, the more at risk he is, especially if he reports being younger than age eight. As Piaget and Inhelder (1969) note, up to the age of eight the child is egocentric with prelogical magical thinking. This means he can have some very faulty non-logical beliefs about death that can include the belief that death is reversible, thus making the act of suicide much easier to do.

It should be noted that when a person regresses, he is not playing the role of a young child; he is actually re-experiencing being that age again, which includes all the thoughts and feelings of that age. This is what the Child ego state is. The person in the Child ego state is not remembering and role-playing himself as a six-year-old child. He is re-experiencing and reliving first-hand being as he was when he was six years old. Many people at the point of the suicidal act are significantly regressed and thus in that childlike psychological state of mind.

2. History of high-risk behavior

People who repeatedly place themselves in high-risk situations can be displaying a form of suicidal intent. This is the point at which the line between accidents and suicide can be unclear, as discussed in the Chapter 2. In this measure, the main suicide decisions are "I will kill myself by accident" or "I will get you to kill me". Although some with these decisions will acknowledge that they do feel suicidal, many will strenuously state they do not feel suicidal and say they feel fine and have everything to live for. Thus this aspect of suicide risk assessment is somewhat unique. One could conclude some level of suicide risk, even when the person reports feeling happy and state they have everything to live for.

CASE STUDY 8.1: *HIGH-RISK BEHAVIOR*

A thirty-year-old man states he has had thoughts of suicide but says he could never actually do it. He has never made a suicide attempt. Instead, he describes his reckless behavior: "It's in the bad times when all the controls I have on myself I just let go of and it's 'I will just do what I want'. This is when my drug taking becomes reckless. Also it's in those times when I can get full of drink, get in the car and go driving recklessly." When he is in this frame of mind, the intravenous amphetamine use becomes reckless and there have been a number of hospitalizations due to overdose.

This man reports that he simply can never imagine himself taking his own life. He cannot imagine it in his behavioral repertoire. However, he has made the suicide decision and sees suicide as a viable solution to problems. Thus, the suicide decision is to set things up so that others will kill him, or to behave in high-risk ways so that a lethal "accident" eventually occurs.

ASSESSING THE LEVEL OF RISK IN BEHAVIOR

To assist with a risk assessment using this category, two researchers from the Centre for Applied Psychology at Liverpool John Moores University, Newcombe and Woods (2010), have developed a risk assessment model. This uses an analysis of the annual mortality risks of different types of drug use and other activities in the United Kingdom in the 1990s. Using the official causes of death, they have been able to establish a list of activities and the risk involved in doing them. A summary of their risk assessment model is shown below:

- very high risk—tobacco, methadone, injecting drug use, BASE jumping, grand prix racing, cancer, heart disease, space travel

- quite high risk—heroin, morphine, barbiturates, alcohol, hang-gliding, parachuting, motorbike racing, sudden infant death, working in mining, asbestos poisoning, strokes, prostrate cancer, shaking of babies, off-shore oil work

- medium risk—solvents, benzodiazepines, motor sports, water sports, canoeing, diabetes, skin cancer, influenza, suicide, giving birth, helicopter travel, liposuction, working in farming, being in police custody, working in construction

- quite low risk—ecstasy, MDMA, speed, cocaine, contraception pill, GBH, fighting sports, snow sports, soccer and rugby, asthma, AIDS, meningitis, cervical cancer, food poisoning, air travel, being murdered, choking on food, electrocution, drowning, passive smoking, factory work

- very low risk—LSD, magic mushrooms, Viagra, fairground rides, swimming, riding sports, food allergies, syphilis, malaria, appendicitis, pedestrian crossings, clothes catching fire, falling out of bed, vaccination, abortion, storms, terrorism

- extremely low risk—marijuana, cannabis resin, indoor sports, playgrounds, peanut allergy, measles, insect stings, copulation, starvation, dogs, lightning, nuclear radiation, police shootings

- negligible risk—caffeine, nitrous oxide, ketamine, computer games, masturbation, smallpox, leprosy, sharks, cats, meteorites, executions, volcanoes.

FAILURE TO ACCURATELY ASSESS BEHAVIORAL RISK

In this measure, although one is looking for those who repeatedly engage in high-risk activities, one is also looking for those who do not assess risk accurately. The most obvious example of this is the adolescent. Adolescents are sometimes inaccurately described as being a group of risk takers. This is seen as a common attribute of the adolescent personality, whereas this is not actually so. Adolescents are not risk takers but are poor risk assessors. It's not that they take risks, but rather that they do not see what they are doing as involving significant risk. Someone cannot be a risk taker if they do not see the task they are doing as risky in the first place.

An example of this is provided by Collins (1991) who discusses research about adolescent attitudes to HIV and AIDS. Although the vast majority of adolescents are knowledgeable about AIDS and its transmission, 68 percent of females and 63 percent of males had not changed their sexual behavior since learning of its possible effects. This was explained as demonstrating that adolescents believed AIDS was not their concern and instead was a problem for other people.

They assumed they had a very low possibility of contracting AIDS, and this was seen to reflect their attitude of egocentric uniqueness.

Teenagers are often described as having the attributes of egocentricity, feeling omnipotent and indestructible, of being narcissistic and having special abilities. When the teenager drives a car at high speed, he believes he has special driving abilities: should he get into difficulty, he has the driving ability to get himself out of trouble. He has not accurately assessed the risks involved, and so, in his mind, he is not taking a high level of risk, even though he actually is.

In this category, this is what the suicide risk assessor is looking for. Does the person think like a teenager in the ways just described? Does he have a sense of indestructibility, of omnipotence—that it is only others who get hurt? Is he accurately assessing the risks in what he is doing? At times this can be hard to ascertain. I have never been a BASE jumper and I can safely say that I will never be one, so it is difficult for me to make a judgement if the person is doing BASE jumping in a safe fashion or not. In these circumstances, one would suggest the person talk with other BASE jumpers to get their views of the risks taken and report them back. Other than that, one is looking to see if the person thinks like a teenager as described above. If he does, then one knows that at some point the person will take unrealistically high risks that could put his life at significant risk. If he has made the suicide decision "I will kill myself by accident", then one would assess the person at an elevated risk of suicide.

3. History of substance use

This area is very often encountered in suicide risk assessment schedules, and, in my view, tends to be done poorly. For instance, the At Risk Management System used to assess inmates in prison suggests that the assessor should look for those who have a history of substance use. What does this mean? An inmate may have been a heavy marijuana user for five years and thus has a history of heavy substance use. However, he has not used marijuana for the last four years, which could significantly alter the risk assessment. One needs to get much more detailed information about the substance use, rather than just a *history* of substance use. Drugs can take so many different forms, can be ingested in many different ways, vary considerably in their lethality and be used for many different reasons.

One needs to consider these factors of the drug use in making a suicide risk assessment, not simply discover if drugs have been used in the past.

RECENCY OF DRUG USE

One needs to establish the pattern of person's drug taking. First, are they still taking the drugs, and, if not, how long ago did they stop? If someone has used heroin, then they have a history of potentially lethal substance use. However, if they stopped using ten years ago, this is much less of an indicator of suicide risk than if they are currently using. It seems reasonable to conclude that the longer the time period between now and when the person stopped using, the less this quantitative measure of suicide risk can be used in a risk assessment. If a person has not engaged in any significant substance abuse in the last ten years, one could say they do not meet this criteria to be counted in the suicide risk assessment. Indeed, a five-year gap would probably be considered quite a considerable period of time of non-use, similar to the person who has never used.

LETHALITY OF DRUG USED

The risk assessment model developed by Newcombe and Woods (2010) described above provides insight into the different risks levels of a variety of different drugs. For instance, in terms of lethality, marijuana is a very safe drug which is virtually impossible to overdose on when used on its own, whereas heroin and barbiturates can be quite lethal drugs. As was described above, this equates to high-risk behavior of the individual, especially if the person has made the suicide decision of "I will kill myself by accident". This behavior is articulated by the Australian Psychological Society (1999) which states: "There is evidence that heroin addiction is associated with elevated suicide rates, although it can be difficult to distinguish suicide from accidental overdose" (p.12).

Lethal drugs are a convenient and relatively easy way to make a suicide attempt. If the person is currently using quite lethal drugs, as shown by Newcombe and Woods (2010), this can be quite a significant suicide risk indicator. One also needs to assess how close to death the person is prepared to go. If the individual reports having survived a number of overdoses and is still using, then one could take this as an indicator of elevated suicide risk.

METHOD OF DRUG INGESTION

How the person takes the drug relates to the lethality of the drug use. Ingesting heroin intravenously is potentially more lethal than smoking it. The model developed by Newcombe and Woods (2010) indicates that injecting drug use is considered very high risk. If the individual is injecting heroin or amphetamines, he is involved in a higher risk method of ingestion than taking the amphetamines orally or smoking heroin.

Drinking games played by young adult males and females can also be a more risky method of consuming alcohol when compared to normal social drinking. For instance, sculling alcohol involves drinking a large glass of alcohol faster than others in order to "win" the game. Having alcohol poured into one's mouth using a funnel is another common type of drinking game. This leads to high levels of intoxication, very rapidly, by inexperienced drinkers, and often the individual lapses into unconsciousness. Thus the individual is at increased risk of subsequently vomiting and choking to death on his own vomit. There have been many high-profile examples of this type of death, including Jimi Hendrix and the original lead singer of AC/DC, Bon Scott.

WHY THE DRUG IS USED

It is not the actual fact of drug use that is under consideration in suicide risk assessment; it is the how and why of the drug use that is important. It's not about an individual taking drugs, but rather about the people who are attracted to engaging in some form of substance use. People take drugs for many reasons, and the Commonwealth Department of Human Services and Health (1994) cites four common ones:

- Experimental use: trying out the drug to experience its effects and to decide whether or not to adopt an ongoing pattern of use.

- Social and recreational use: using the drug as a means of enhancing social interaction or the enjoyment of some leisure activity.

- Symptomatic use: using the drug as a means of reducing unpleasant sensations or experiences or to avoid challenging situations or responsibilities.

- Dependent use: using the drug with a sense of compulsion, so that other responsibilities are neglected and harm may result. (p.7)

Recreational users form the largest group by far, and these are those who are at least risk of suicide in terms of the reasons for substance use. Recreational use does not indicate a higher potential for suicide. The drug is used simply for enjoyment and to enhance social interaction. This is quite different from the symptomatic user. This person is in considerable emotional pain and is using a drug to reduce that pain. In this way, there is no difference between a person who uses heroin to reduce their mind-numbing depression or severe anxiety and an individual who takes antidepressants and anti-anxiety prescribed medication. Both parties are medicating themselves, one legally and one illegally, to reduce their level of emotional pain.

The point here is that these people are in pain, sometimes quite considerable emotional pain, and often they come from backgrounds where abuse and trauma were present. Those who have made the suicide decision view suicide as a viable solution to a problem. After attempting to medicate the pain away for many years, they find that life is still not good and can choose suicide as a solution to their ongoing emotional pain. Those who are using drugs, either prescribed or illicit, to medicate away some emotionally distressing symptoms are at higher risk of suicide than the average individual.

Finally, there are the dependent drug users, who are the true drug addicts in the usual sense of the word. These people who find it very, very difficult to give up their drug of choice for any great length of time. These people live tragic lives that involve a lot of emotional pain, soul-searching and great personal struggles with self and their desire to keep using. Their lives tend to be chaotic and have numerous legal, health, financial, family and social difficulties that are ongoing and substantial. Dependent drug users can be at increased risk of a suicide attempt because at times they will get very desperate about life and how they live. They are living a self-destructive lifestyle anyway and often have a low self-image, and thus it is not such a great leap to the next step of a suicide attempt. Combine this with the person who has made the suicide decision and there is a very real risk of a suicide attempt at some point in time.

DRUG USE AND REGRESSION

Many mood-altering substances allow the individual to psychologically regress. In transactional analysis terms, such drugs decommission the Parent ego state first, then the Adult ego state, leaving just the Child ego state functioning. This progression over time is particularly noticeable with alcohol, whereas drugs such as marijuana and heroin tend to decommission the Parent and Adult much more rapidly. Figure 8.2 shows the effect of alcohol on the personality over time.

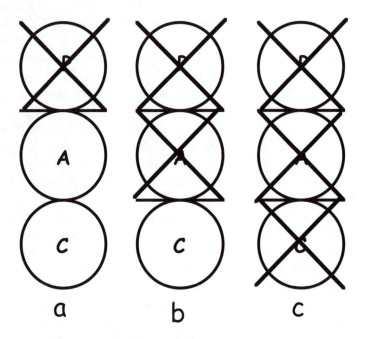

Figure 8.2 The process of regression over time when drinking alcohol

When the individual begins drinking, the first effect is to decommission the Parent ego state; thus the person becomes disinhibited, as shown in Figure 8.2(a). The Parent ego state controls and inhibits the wants and feelings of the Child ego state, and therefore the person tends to "loosen up" as he is less restricted by his internal Critical Parent telling him how he should be, what he is not doing right and so on. Hence he will tend to socialize more easily as his internal critic is silenced and he becomes more uninhibited.

Any hostess at a dinner party will want the guests to do this because it will make the party more of a success as the guests will be less inhibited and have more fun.

If the individual keeps drinking, eventually the Adult ego state is decommissioned and thus the person starts to make ill-informed decisions, which he would not usually make, as shown in Figure 8.2(b). The individual is now disinhibited and making poor Adult decisions; and thus he can begin to behave in sexual or aggressive ways, which he would not normally do. As a consequence, males tend to get into fights and females can engage in sexual behavior, which they would not normally do. If the individual keeps drinking, eventually the Child ego state is decommissioned and he passes out or loses consciousness, as shown in Figure 8.2(c).

As Figure 8.2(b) shows, the individual is only left with a functioning Child ego state, and thus the wants and feelings of the Child are left to roam free and unrestrained. This person is also in a regression or a regressed state as he begins to function in a more childlike way. Hence we hear people referred to as a happy drunk, angry drunk, sad drunk and so forth. This means that, underneath, the person is basically happy, angry or sad. When all Parent and Adult ego state censoring and inhibitions are taken away, the individual is left with the true feelings underneath to come out and be expressed. This can also relate to those who are suicidal.

When one takes away the usual thinking, sometimes the protective factors become less effective. For instance, a person may not act on his suicidal urges as he knows his death would leave his children feeling very bad. This is seen as a protective factor. When he is regressed by the drug, this will be less important as the protective factor is a Parent and Adult ego state function. Although alcohol disinhibits aggressive acts against others, it also does the same for aggressive acts against self. As a consequence, in a regression, people are more likely to act on their suicidal thoughts due to the disinhibition of aggression impulses against self.

CASE STUDY 8.2: THE EFFECTS OF ALCOHOL

A 33-year-old man lived most of his childhood and teenage years on farms. He reports many instances of his father threatening suicide. He can recall these happening when he was as young as six or seven years old and persisting until he was about 14 years old when his family left farming and moved to the city. Typically, his father would begin drinking in the late afternoon and would continue until late into the night. When he had been drinking for some time, he would get very morose, and on some occasions would state that he did not want to live anymore. He would then get a rifle from the gun cabinet, load it, place it next to the chair he was sitting in and continue to drink.

His wife would be crying and trying to convince her husband not to do anything and to put the gun away. He repeatedly threatened to shoot himself in the head and kept the loaded gun next to him as he got more and more intoxicated. He never carried out his threat.

Case study 8.2 shows the disinhibiting effect of alcohol so that the father's Child ego state urges to kill self became more pronounced as he continued to drink. As his Parent and Adult ego states became less influential, he became more regressed, and out came the suicidal statements and behavior. The Australian Psychological Society (1999) states: "Intoxication at the time of death, most frequently with alcohol, has been found in approximately half of youthful suicides... Intoxication may disrupt the protective factors which would otherwise enable the person to resist suicidal thoughts and impulses" (p.12).

In assessing suicide risk, one needs to make an assessment of magical thinking when the person is under the influence of some drug. One needs to enquire how this person has reacted in the past when they have regressed due to drug consumption. In particular, how do they react when their Adult and Parent ego states are not functioning well? Indeed, as mentioned before, in counseling one can use regressive techniques to regress the person. This enables the assessor to get a much better understanding of how this person thinks, feels and behaves in a regressed state, and thus be better informed as to the level of suicide risk when this person regresses through substance use. As can be seen, there is much more to suicide risk assessment in this area than just a history of substance use.

4. History of mental illness

One must look at mental illness in more detail than just a "history of mental illness" to use it realistically as a measure of suicide risk. This measure mainly relates to those who have a psychiatric history of psychotic or pre-psychotic symptoms most notably found in schizophrenia, bipolar disorder and the borderline personality.

EGO STATES AND PSYCHOSIS

From an ego state point of view, one would diagram a psychosis, particularly schizophrenia, as is shown in Figure 8.3.

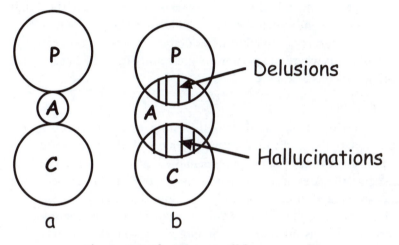

Figure 8.3 The two possible personality structures of the psychotic individual

The essential feature of any psychosis is a very poorly functioning Adult ego state. The Treatment Protocol Project (2004) states: "Schizophrenia is a serious mental illness characterized by distortions of thinking and perception, a disorganization of thought and behavior, cognitive impairment, disturbances of interpersonal communication and social and functional impairment" (p.287). For a psychosis to be diagnosed, the Adult ego state functions of the perception of reality, thinking ability, organization of thought and cognitive ability must be severely disrupted.

In Figure 8.3(a), for some reason the Adult ego state is poorly functioning, and thus psychotic type symptoms such as disorganized thought or cognitive impairment can evolve. Alternatively, in Figure 8.3(b), we have what is called a contamination of the Adult ego state; this can be either delusions or hallucinations. If a person has the belief that the water is being poisoned by the government and assumes that to be factually true, then he is mistaking a personal view for a fact. The Parent ego state opinion is mistaken as an Adult fact. Thus the Parent ego state has contaminated the boundary of the Adult ego state.

If a person has the Child ego state sensation of a peculiar smell and takes that to be an actual smell, then the Child ego state has been mistaken for Adult ego state fact. What is a personal sensory event is assumed to be an actual event that all others would experience as well, and thus the Child ego state is seen to contaminate the Adult ego state. As these delusions and hallucinations get more severe, the Adult ego state function deteriorates and eventually reaches a certain point where the person is significantly disturbed as to merit a diagnosis of schizophrenia.

REGRESSION

The main point here is that as the Adult ego state becomes less functional, the individual regresses more and more. Indeed, a diagnostic feature of schizophrenia in the DSM-IV is regression. For instance, the American Psychiatric Association (1994), in discussing the social and occupational dysfunction that can be present in schizophrenia, states: "For a significant portion of the time since the onset of the disturbance, one or more major areas of functioning such as work, interpersonal relations, or self-care are markedly below the level achieved prior to the onset" (p.285). In other words, the person has regressed from a higher previous level of functioning in their day-to-day life.

As was mentioned before, with regression can come childlike thinking about death and a reduction in the influence of the protective factors. In a suicide risk assessment, if one is dealing with a person who is displaying psychotic or pre-psychotic symptoms then one needs to assess the level of regression apparent. If there is significant regression shown, one seeks information on what this means in terms of Child ego state magical thinking about death and how the protective factors may be compromised. If both are present, then the possibility of a significant suicidal gesture increases.

TIMING OF SUICIDE

The timing of the mental illness can give more information for a suicide risk assessment. The American Psychiatric Association (1994) and Treatment Protocol Project (2004) both state that about 10 percent of those who suffer from schizophrenia will suicide, with the initial five or ten years being the highest time of risk. Most suicides occur in the non-florrid stages, in which the person is relatively free from acute symptoms. This is because, for a completed suicide, one needs some level of planning, and in the florrid phase of a psychosis the Adult ego state planning functions are virtually non-existent.

Although I am unaware of any research, it has been my experience that those with a chronic psychosis such as schizophrenia are also susceptible later in their lives. As one listens to them talk, there are those who just generally tire of life and living. A psychosis can be a very unpleasant thing to live with, particularly if it is chronic. The medications can have quite adverse side effects, and the hallucinations and delusions just make life painful and unpleasant day after day. Over time this takes its toll, and thus suicide may become a solution to the pain that some chronically suffer. In these cases, a sense of hopelessness grows and grows over time. Unfortunately, I have personally heard after time of a number of chronic schizophrenic sufferers who have suicided, probably due to the circumstances just described. From a risk assessment point of view, when one is working with such a chronic sufferer, one needs to focus particularly on the sense of hopelessness and how the person is dealing with that.

COMMAND HALLUCINATIONS

In assessing risk, one can look for command hallucinations—that is, hallucinations that command the individual to suicide. The Treatment Protocol Project (2004) states: "Suicidal ideas are especially likely if the individual is hearing voices that command suicide. The strength of these thoughts and the person's ability to act on them must be assessed" (p.291). Case study 8.3 is an instance of a man whom I got to know well after his suicide attempt.

CASE STUDY 8.3: SUICIDE AND COMMAND HALLUCINATIONS

A 35-year-old man attempted to end his life by cutting an artery in his neck. He used a razor blade and very nearly died, but was found at the last moment and was revived. Subsequent discussion with him showed that he suffered from chronic schizophrenia and was on regular antipsychotic medication. One month prior to the attempt to end his life, he stopped taking his medication as he felt that he was well and did not need it anymore. Having stopped the medication, over time he developed hallucinations and strong delusions. One of his hallucinations was that he was talking with God. God started to tell him that he wanted

> him to come and be with him, and to do that he had to go to heaven. To get to heaven, the man attempted to kill himself as described above.

When such auditory hallucinations are present, one needs to find out what the voices are saying. Obviously, one is searching to see if any of the voices are instructing the person to kill self, to be with God and so forth. One also wants to know how active the voices are at this point in time, as this is good information for ongoing monitoring, particularly if the person has a history of taking himself off his medication without telling anyone. If the auditory hallucinations are increasing, that may be because the person is not taking his medication correctly or not taking it at all. When this happens, the risk of suicide can increase rapidly as a result of the rapid rise in command hallucinations.

BORDERLINE PERSONALITY

In the literature on mental illness and suicide, one sees statistics cited about the rates of suicide related to personality disorders, particularly the borderline personality (Moscicki 1995). Unfortunately, this area can be quite unclear about what is suicidal behavior and what is not. For instance, consider Case study 8.4.

CASE STUDY 8.4: SUICIDE AND THE BORDERLINE PERSONALITY

A 25-year-old man with a diagnosis of borderline personality is brought to me for counseling after a serious suicide attempt. He has a long history of very unstable and volatile relationships with female partners. On this particular day, he was speaking with his girlfriend on a public telephone in the city, which meant that there were quite a few people around. During the call she stated that she was ending the relationship and hung up on him. He became enraged at what he perceived as abandonment by yet another woman in his life, later stating that he was consumed with anger.

He was an avid fisherman and had his fishing tackle with him. After the call ended, he pulled a fishing knife out of his bag and stabbed himself two or three times in the neck, severing a major artery in the process. He then punched and broke a small pane of glass in a shop window which resulted in non-lethal cuts to his hand and forearm. He then sat down because he was losing a large amount of blood from his neck wound. All this happened in the space of about 45 seconds.

By this time, he was being noticed by a number of people around him who came to see what was going on. He was deteriorating quickly due to the massive blood loss. By pure chance, someone who came to help him knew how to stem the flow of blood from his neck and he survived. If no one had helped, it is very likely he would have died in quite a short space of time.

Was this a suicide attempt? Probably not. If he had died, would it have been recorded as a suicide? Probably yes. Technically, it is an accident because it was never his intention to kill himself. As was mentioned in Chapter 2, for behavior to be considered suicidal, the individual must have the intention of killing self. He never had the thought "I am going to kill myself"; instead, he became enraged at the abandonment and simply lashed out angrily in a spontaneous way. He angrily attacked property (the glass window) and angrily attacked himself by cutting his neck. It is quite possible that if the girlfriend had been there, he would have angrily attacked her. This was simply an unsophisticated display of anger expression and not a suicide attempt in the usual sense of the word.

As a consequence, the statistics about suicide on the borderline personality and other impulsive, acting-out type of individual need to be considered in this context. The Treatment Protocol Project (2004), in describing the characteristics of such individuals, states: "A tendency to act impulsively without consideration of the consequences of those actions. In many cases the impulsive behavior will cause potential harm to the individual" (p.558). If a death occurs, it is more of an accidental death rather than a suicide. In Case study 8.4, if the man had wanted to kill himself, he should have removed self to some isolated place, then cut the artery in his neck and he would have died quite quickly. This, of course, requires some planning, which the impulsive suicide attempt does not have.

Regardless of whether it is an accident or a suicide, the individual still ends up deceased, and thus, from a practical point of view, a risk assessment still needs to be done. This is not an easy thing to do with such individuals because the time it takes to move from few suicidal urges to strong suicidal urges and action can be very short indeed, as in Case study 8.4. Instead, one is looking for triggers and then assessing the likelihood of such a trigger occurring. In this case, a trigger for suicidal actions is the perceived abandonment or relationship breakdown with his partner. In subsequent discussions with him, one would be enquiring as to the status of his current relationships. If they seem to be going well with little disharmony, then the suicide risk would be assessed as lower. If there is increasing instability in his primary relationships, then the risk of a spontaneous suicide attempt increases.

With such impulsive individuals, one is seeking to identify the triggers that can lead to a suicide attempt and then monitor the likelihood of such a trigger occurring. From a counseling point of view, one would also want the individual to be aware of these himself, so that he can take his own preventative action. He can notify someone if he feels the likelihood of a trigger is increasing.

5. Lack of any secondary gain

This is presented now because some personalities, such as the borderline personality, can at times be manipulative. If a suicide attempt or suicidal statements lack any secondary gain, then there is a higher risk of subsequent suicidal actions, particularly well-planned actions. Some people attempt suicide because they want to die, whereas others attempt but do not want to die. They are said to be seeking secondary gains from making suicidal statements— for example, manipulation or making a "cry for help". The fewer secondary gains, the more the person has made the decision that suicide is a viable option to solve a problem, and thus the likelihood of a completed suicide attempt increases. Case study 8.5 provides an example of a borderline woman who used suicide attempts as a means to get her boyfriend to show his love for her.

CASE STUDY 8.5: *SUICIDE AND SECONDARY GAIN*

A 23-year-old woman articulated suicidal thoughts on many occasions. Her common pattern was to take medication and then contact her boyfriend who would come and save her by getting medical assistance. The most common means of her contacting him was by email, which she had done on a number of occasions before. In the final instance, she contacted him by sending an email that she knew he was very likely

to get. There was a one-in-a-hundred chance he would not get it. As it
turned out, he never got the email and she died from the overdose.

This case study clearly shows the secondary gains obtained from
making suicidal statements and gestures. This means she is at less
risk of a completed suicide; however, on occasion, as in this case,
the individual does die because the attempt is completed even
when the person did not want it to be. Again, technically, this is
an accidental death, not a suicide. In assessing the risk of death in
these circumstances, one is in particular seeking information on
the lethality of the suicidal gestures. If they are clearly non-lethal
gestures, then the risk is lower. In Case study 8.5, the woman was
obviously making lethal gestures, and thus the risk of death increases
and the line between accident and suicide is once again unclear.

While working in the prison system, I came across suicidal
gestures for secondary gains on many occasions. At times the
inmates were quite open about it because they knew procedure had
to be followed and it was too risky for any staff member to "call their
bluff". By making suicidal statements or cutting self superficially,
they would be moved to other sections of the prison, and thus it
became one way they could get moved around the prison.

With this risk assessment measure, the information from the
individual is notoriously unreliable if secondary gains are evident.
One tends to get overstated suicide risk and one tends to make false
positive risk assessments. Of course, one must err on the side of
caution as it is better to make false *positive* risk assessments than
false *negative* risk assessments. When one is dealing with a person
who has made many false suicidal statements and made a number
of clearly non-lethal suicide attempts, it is easy to get complacent,
even irritated or tired of them. This, of course, tests the suicide risk
assessor's resolve as Case study 8.5 indicates. Accidental deaths do
occur, and amid the many implausible suicidal statements there may
be one that is serious.

6. The prison population as a high-risk group

In the literature, one finds many statistics indicating that people
who are incarcerated are at higher risk of suicide than the general
population. For instance, McArthur, Camilleri and Webb (1999)

note that suicide is the leading cause of death in Australian prisons, accounting for around 50 percent of all deaths. Temby (1990) states that the rate of suicide in prisons is between 2.5 and 15 times more than in the general population. In addition, Dalton (1999) states that the rate of suicide in Australian prisons is about ten times that of the general population. The statistics are clear and compelling, but, in my view, unfortunately misleading.

Having worked in the prison system, in a adult male prison of about 750 inmates, one finds a very diverse group of individuals. For example, in terms of their crimes, they can range from simple fine defaulters and credit card fraudsters to those who committed the most heinous of crimes against other humans. Or they may be people with poor impulse control and low IQ, so they are easy to catch. To my mind, if one is going to use this quantitative measure in a suicide risk assessment, one needs to look at the person in more detail, given the great diversity of personalities one finds in a prison.

THREE SUBGROUPS OF PRISONERS

For example, three discernible groups of people are often found in the prison system. First, there is the antisocial personality or the criminal personality who lives the lifestyle of the criminal. This person has little problem in breaking the law, and shows a pattern of personality traits which include a lack of conscience, inability to empathize, rejection of authority, lack of anxiety and high-risk behavior, drug use, promiscuity and an inability to form attachments to others (modified from Midgley 1993).

Thus, we have some indication of where to begin our risk assessment with the prison population. With this group, there can be a history of substance use which is described above in quantitative measure 3. This includes assessing such things as the recency of drug use, lethality of drugs used, method of ingestion, drug use and regression, and why the drug is being used.

This personality type can include those who take great risks both in their in everyday lives and indeed in their crimes—for example, armed robberies or driving cars in highly dangerous ways. Personality research has shown some similarities between the personality of the teenager and the criminal personality. As mentioned before, teenagers are often mistakenly viewed as a group of high risk takers when they are more accurately seen as a group of poor risk assessors due to their sense of indestructibility and omnipotence. The criminal personality can be the same. This person does not assess risk accurately and therefore tends to underestimate the risk of what he is doing. The risk assessment categories as described above by Newcombe and Woods (2010) can help with assessing the suicide risk of such a prisoner.

In the second group of prisoners is the drug user. This person is not the antisocial personality in the same way as described above. This person breaks the law because he needs money for his drug use. If he is currently clean and thus not needing money urgently, he will tend to remain crime-free. He does not lead the criminal lifestyle, at least not to the extent of repeatedly breaking laws that carry a prison sentence. In essence, he is not a "criminal" but a drug-dependent user. Thus a suicide risk assessment would include the factors just mentioned—recency of drug use, reason for using drugs, method of ingestion, for example.

The third group of prisoners are those with a significant mental illness, usually with psychotic symptoms of some kind. In the 1960s and 1970s western governments started to empty their psychiatric hospitals as new medications allowed more patients to reside in the general community with varying degrees of assistance. Unfortunately, some do not get the assistance they require; they fall through the cracks of the system and end up in very low-cost housing or on the streets. Once there, they stop using their medication properly and develop delusional belief systems or hallucinations. For various reasons, this results in them committing crimes so that they end up being cared for in a prison rather than in a hospital. These individuals, like the drug user, are not the criminal personality, and when properly cared for, most are reasonable people who would not habitually break the law.

In this category, one assesses this prisoner's suicide risk with the same criteria as one assesses any person with a mental illness. These criteria include command hallucinations, the level of regression caused by the psychosis and so on. The suggestion here is that the criterion of simply being in prison is far too ill defined for a reasonable suicide risk assessment. However, the statistics quoted previously use this wide-ranging definition. For instance, the rate of suicide in prisons is between 2.5 and 15 times more than in the general population. In my view, these are largely meaningless statistics and one must look at the subgroups of prisoners within the prison system and their rates of suicide to gain useful statistics.

HIGH-RISK SUBGROUPS OF PRISONERS

To assist in assessing high-risk prisoner subgroups, one finds various lists circulating in prison systems around the world. I am not sure of the research behind these; they may have been compiled by prisoner suicide risk assessors over the years of observing prisoner behavior. However, it does seem useful information to have in order to make better risk assessments with prisoners. These lists suggest four high-risk times or situations.

1. *Out-of-prison issues involving family and loved ones.* Suicide risk can increase when there is a family crisis of some kind involving close family members such as a spouse or children. This can include the death or serious illness of that family member, anniversaries of the death of a loved one, and, in particular, relationship breakdowns where the inmate is told that a relationship has ended.

2. *When the prisoner is involved in a significant incident inside the prison.* This can include an attempted escape, riot, cell extraction, hunger strike, going "out of bounds" (for example, climbing on to a roof) and resisting arrest. The period of time after an assault or fight, when disciplinary action is taken against the prisoner resulting in a loss of privileges or solitary confinement, would also be considered a high-risk time, as would the period after an attempted or completed suicide by another prisoner.

3. *When there is a significant change to the prisoner's life in jail.* Suicide risk can increase when a prisoner is told of a transfer to another prison, especially if he does not want to go. This is particularly so at the beginning of a prisoner's sentence or period on remand, especially if it is the first imprisonment. Another example would be when a prisoner is upgraded from minimum security to medium security or from medium security to maximum security, or when the prisoner's term of imprisonment is increased, especially when the sentence was much longer than expected.

4. *Prison transfers or movement of the prisoner so that he has the access to means of suicide out of the usual prison environment.* Most modern prisons are designed to be "suicide difficult" environments—for example, by the removal of "hanging points" where a length of rope or some sort of cord can be tied. Increased access to the means of suicide can increase the risk of a suicide attempt occurring. This can be particularly so when a prisoner is being transferred in a vehicle, being held in interim incarceration in a transition cell or waiting in transit centers.

OTHER ASSESSMENT CONSIDERATIONS FOR THE PRISON POPULATION

As was mentioned before, a prisoner may be at higher risk when first incarcerated. In this instance, one is assessing the prisoner's attitude in relation to being future-focussed. The newly imprisoned person can sometimes see his life as having come to an end. He feels he has hit rock bottom and can go no lower, and as a result suicidal thoughts can increase quite rapidly. Over time that tends to dissipate as the person gets used to prison life and accepts his lot for the next *x* years.

It has been said by those involved with suicidal prisoners that there is a critical period with very long-term prisoners—those who are imprisoned for life and will never be released, or those who will definitely be in prison for the next two, three or four decades. As they reach years 5–7 of their sentence, this can be a time of considerable reflection. It seems that around this period the prisoner truly starts to understand what their life will be like for a very long time into the future and this can result in an increase in suicidal urges. I am not aware of any research on this, but this has been reported to me by some who have worked in the prison system for many years. In my counseling of such long-term prisoners, I found some truth to these ad hoc observations, so they could be helpful in making a suicide risk assessment with the longer-term prisoner.

Although I have suggested that to make conclusions about prisoners as one whole group is a doubtful pursuit, there is one feature that does apply to a large section of the prison population. Eyland, Corben and Barton (1997) note that when a person is placed into custody, they experience a significant loss of outside relationships, as well as a physical and emotional breakdown. Although this does not apply so much for the habitual criminal who views prison time as an occupational hazard, it does make the point that the vast majority who do end up in prison are living a tragic lifestyle. These people are willing to live a lifestyle outside what most others are prepared to, and that includes breaking significant rules of society.

As a consequence, their lives are more dramatic and extreme than most. They are living what transactional analysis refers to as a third-degree lifestyle whereas the average member of society lives a first- or second-degree lifestyle. The third-degree individual will do things and get involved in situations that are more extreme and often more dangerous than most. The vast majority of people never do any prison time; to end up in a prison means one is prepared to live a third-degree lifestyle. Not uncommonly, a third-degree lifestyle involves some kind of tissue damage so that the person ends up in hospital or perhaps dead. Therefore, killing, being killed or killing self is more likely, indeed much more likely, to happen to someone who lives a tragic or third-degree lifestyle. From this one could say that, as an overall group, prisoners are at greater risk of suicide because of their willingness to behave in ways that are more dramatic and tragic than the average citizen. Having said this, one simply has to go into a prison to see that it includes a huge array of individuals; drawing conclusions about the group as a whole can only be done with great caution and with the considerable risk of over-generalizing.

7. Depression as an indicator of suicidal thoughts and actions

A great deal has been written about suicide and depression and one sees all sorts of statistics quoted. For instance, George (2008) states: "A retrospective study of 132 young people who completed suicide in Western Australia found that nearly three quarters had shown definite signs of depression in the weeks prior to their death" (p.25). Or: "Depression increases the risk of suicide by 15 to 20 times, and about 4% of people with depression die by suicide." (Hawton and van Heeringen 2009, p.1373). Based on this research, that means that 96 percent of people with depression do not die by suicide. On this point, the research presents varying figures. Clark and Fawcett (1992) estimate that 15 percent of those with a diagnosis of major depression will complete a suicide. The statistics tend to waver around the 10 percent mark, meaning that the vast majority of those with depression will not complete a suicide attempt. There are many depressed people who are not suicidal at all. Of course, this does not mean that one forgets about making an assessment of suicide risk with the person reporting depression, but one needs to be realistic about its occurrence, which is not often stated in the literature.

KEY SYMPTOMS OF DEPRESSION RELATED TO A RISK ASSESSMENT

In real terms, depression is merely a collection of symptoms. It's not so much that depression is linked to suicide; it just happens that people who are suicidal have symptoms which are not uncommon in depressed people. In using this measure of suicide risk, one does not enquire about depression per se; one enquires about some of the symptoms found in the depression that the person is displaying.

The DSM-IV provides a list of symptoms which define depression:

1. depressed mood most of the day which can include a sense of hopelessness

2. loss of interest or pleasure (in all or most activities, most of the day)

3. large increases or decreases in appetite (significant weight gain or loss)

4. insomnia or excessive sleeping (hypersomnia)

5. restlessness as evident by hand-wringing and similar other activities (psychomotor agitation) or slowness of movement (psychomotor retardation)

6. fatigue or loss of energy

7. feelings of worthlessness, or excessive or inappropriate guilt

8. diminished ability to concentrate or indecisiveness

9. recurrent thoughts of death or suicide.

(American Psychiatric Association 1994)

In this diagnostic system, one needs to have five or more of these symptoms to be diagnosed as depressed. Every suicidal person automatically has one symptom of depression already as shown in symptom number 9. The best clinical predictors of suicide in depressed people include previous self-harm, hopelessness and suicidal tendencies (Hawton and van Heeringen 2009). Beck *et al.* (1985) and Beck, Brown and Steer (1989) also found hopelessness to be one of the best indicators of suicide risk. If the depressed person reports a loss of appetite, psychomotor agitation, excessive guilt, hypersomnia and increased indecisiveness, he meets the criteria of depression but shows none of the best clinical indicators just described. Indeed, unless the depressed individual reports the last symptom—recurrent thoughts of death and suicide—it seems safe to say that the person is not a suicide risk at this time. He is not even thinking about suicide at this point, even if he has all eight other symptoms of depression. If a person presents as depressed, one firstly asks if he has thoughts of suicide (symptom 9), and if he does, one also enquires about a sense of hopelessness and any previous self-harm. If he presents with all three, one is getting a much more accurate assessment of the current level of risk.

In the literature, one finds very little research on the estimates of those who are depressed with suicidal thoughts and those who are depressed with no suicidal thoughts. There are three such studies. The first, from many years ago, was made by the "father" of depression, Aaron Beck (1967). Beck presented research results which examined the presence of suicidal wishes in the depressed person. He makes the distinction between neurotic depression or the milder forms of depression and psychotic depression or the more severe forms of depression. (This distinction will be discussed later in this chapter.) The results were:

Mild or moderate level of suicidal wishes present:

Neurotic depression—58 percent

Psychotic depression—76 percent

Severe level of suicidal wishes present:

Neurotic depression—14 percent

Psychotic depression—40 percent

More recent research by Akechi *et al.* (2000) reports that 53 percent of patients with major depression had suicidal ideation. Wada *et al.* (1998) report a similar finding of around 50 percent of those with major depression also having suicidal urges. This allows the conclusion that about 50 percent of those with some form of depression do not report any recurrent suicidal thoughts. Thus it seems safe to say that 50 percent of depressed people are not at risk of suicide because they are not even thinking about suicide, let alone planning it.

TIMING AND STRUCTURE OF THE DEPRESSIVE EPISODES

If the individual does present as depressed and does show the principal signs of recurrent suicidal thoughts—a sense of hopelessness and previous self-harm—then this definitely requires more investigation. One of the more important aspects to investigate is the course and stage of the depression. As stated by the Treatment Protocol Project (2004), depressive episodes can be single, recurrent or chronic, and this has significant implications for the assessment and management of the suicidal individual.

For about 5–10 percent of depression sufferers, the depression is chronic. If an individual with chronic depression also has recurrent thoughts of suicide, then the level of risk increases, and over time it could be seen as continuing to increase. In the longer term, this person could be at quite a significant risk of suicide. One would want to question the individual as to his feelings about tiring of life and particularly a sense of hopelessness. This individual has a poor quality of life with spirit-crushing depression and often quite unpleasant side effects from the medication such as obesity or lack of energy. If he has tried just about every type of medical and psychological treatment with little improvement, one would be assessing a definite increase in the risk of suicide.

To make matters worse, there is not much one can do in this person's management. A no-suicide contract is of less use because there is no end in sight for the depression. As the suicide risk increases over time, one can place the individual in hospital or on some kind of suicide watch, but what does that achieve? It simply relocates him geographically, and how long does one keep such a person in hospital when he will still be depressed upon release?

However, most depression is cyclical as shown in Figure 8.4, with the mood changing over time from a normal level to a depressed level and back.

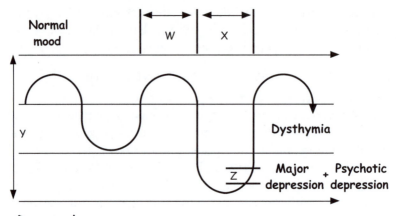

Key: W = length of non-depressed period

X = length of depressive episode

Y = depth of depressed mood

Z = high risk period of the depressive cycle

Figure 8.4 The cycles of depression

As stated in the Treatment Protocol Project (2004), the rate of recurrence of depressive episodes is quite high: "50% of people who have had one episode of depression will relapse, 70% of people who have had 2 episodes will relapse, and 90% of people who have had 3 episodes will relapse" (p.159). The average duration of an untreated episode is about 20–26 weeks, but many can have much briefer episodes of around 4–6 weeks. If treatment is obtained early, then the duration and severity of the episode may be significantly reduced.

TYPES OF DEPRESSION

In using depression as a measure to assess suicide risk, one needs to distinguish between a number of different types of depression. As shown in Figure 8.4, one can move from a normal mood range down into the range of dysthymia. In this phase, the depressive symptoms are at a moderate degree. Historically, this has also been known as neurotic depression, and I use the terms interchangeably. This is seen as less severe than the next level down, which is called a major depression. In this phase, the depression symptoms are at a severe degree. Sometimes this is called "clinical depression", in which the individual is significantly incapacitated and very depressed. Also at this level, one can have a condition known as psychotic depression. This is where the individual has the symptoms of major depression plus some psychotic symptoms. This terminology has been around for many years, and psychotic depression is well summarized by Beck (1967) who says it is "characterized as including patients who are severely depressed and who give evidence of gross misinterpretation of reality, including at times delusions and hallucinations" (p.82).

In summary, in this model we have:

- normal mood
- dysthymia or neurotic depression
- major depression and psychotic depression.

In Figure 8.4, we have an individual who begins with a period of normal mood and then moves into a phase of depression that is consistent with the diagnosis of dysthymia. Eventually, that depressive episode ends and he recovers again for a period of normal mood. Unfortunately, at a later time he again moves into a more severe episode of major depression, from which he eventually recovers and moves back to a state of normal mood. To assist with making a suicide risk assessment, one can create a graph like this for the person who complains of depressive episodes.

In assessing the depressed person, one needs to look at four aspects of the depressive cycle: W, X, Y and Z. First, one is wanting to assess the length of the non-depressed periods (W) and the lengths of the depressive episodes (X). Of course, this relies on the person having had previous episodes and one simply takes a history of the person in this way. How many episodes have there been and how long were they? Also, were there any precipitating factors such as marital problems or financial difficulties that led to the depressive episode? These can then be charted on a graph as is shown in Figure 8.4. People tend to behave in patterns, and one is obtaining this information to assist in predicting future episodes and thus future times when suicidal urges may increase in conjunction with the depression. Of course, future episodes may be different to past ones, but this does give some guidance to assist the suicide risk assessor.

For example, if there is a pattern in the timing of the episodes, one then knows when to approach the person for a risk assessment in the future. A good example of this is with what has become known as

Seasonal Affective Disorder or SAD. Typically, the depressive episode begins in autumn/fall or winter and remits in spring. Alternatively, previous depressive episodes may be related to particular events, such as examination time at college or when a loved one has to travel away for work. Plotting the W and X of the depressive cycle will allow the risk assessor to improve the timing of assessments.

DEGREE OF DEPRESSION AND SUICIDALITY

One also needs to assess the quality of the depressive episodes by making an assessment of the Y component. Here one assesses how depressed the person becomes and how the person has felt in past episodes, particularly in relation to suicidal thoughts. As mentioned before, the system being presented here distinguishes between normal mood, dysthymia or neurotic depression, major depression and psychotic depression.

This is an important component to distinguish in a suicide risk assessment as there is some research which concludes that those who are more depressed are more prone to suicidal thoughts. In their research on depression and suicidal thoughts, Garlow *et al.* (2007) report: "These results suggest that there is a strong relationship between severity of depressive symptoms and suicidal ideation in college students..." (paragraph 1). In addition, Perroud *et al.* (2009) state: "Increases in suicidal ideation were associated with depression severity..." (p.2). Finally, Beck (1967) cites research which shows that a severe level of suicidal thoughts were present in 14 percent of those with neurotic depression and in 40 percent of those with psychotic depression. In conclusion, the more depressed a person is, the higher the risk level of suicidal thoughts. Thus one can see the importance of making the Y component assessment of the reported depressive episodes.

As just noted, the person with major depression or psychotic depression is at more risk of suicidal thoughts than the person with dysthymia. However, it seems reasonable to conclude that the person with psychotic depression is at even more risk than the person with major depression because a psychotic depression involves a major depression *plus* the presence of psychotic symptoms. The person experiences severe depression as well as psychotic delusions and hallucinations, and thus the features discussed above in point 4 (History of mental illness) become apparent as well. There is sort of doubling effect of suicide risk factors in this instance. For example, the person with psychotic depression is likely to be more regressed than someone with major depression because the psychotic features result from very poor Adult ego state functioning, and thus there is increased regression. In addition, the psychotic is more prone to command hallucinations. As a result, of all the types of depression, a psychotic depression is probably the one of highest risk value when making a suicide risk assessment.

Finally, in Figure 8.4 one needs to make an assessment of Z in the depressive cycle. Suicide risk may increase as the person improves, particularly in a major depression or a psychotic depression. In these depressive states, the person is so depressed they can become incapacitated; they literally do not have the energy to think seriously of suicide or certainly to make any definite planning. As the depressed state lifts, there is an increase in energy, which may bring about an increased ability to act on any self-destructive wishes; as the person improves, one may need to be more vigilant as he reaches that part of the depressive cycle.

In addition, for the individual with psychotic depression, as the depression lifts, the psychotic symptoms may begin to subside as well. Their Adult ego state becomes more functional and thus planning a suicide attempt becomes more of a possibility. Most suicides occur in the non-florrid stages of a psychotic episode when the person is relatively free from acute symptoms. Of particular note in a suicide risk assessment, if the person is at one of the lower points in the depressive cycle, such as at stage Z, and all of a sudden shows significant improvement, that may be ominous sign. He may have made the decision to kill self and is just getting organized and waiting for the right time.

8. Single people are more likely to suicide than those who are married

HUMAN ATTACHMENT

This is a somewhat misleading statement because it more accurately refers to the "psychologically" single person and the "psychologically" married person. This measure considers psychological attachments in the individual's life, and thus the assessor is looking to see if the person has any significant psychological attachments to others around him. This comes from the original work by John Bowlby (1971) on human attachment. Since that work and the massive subsequent work on human attachment, the importance of human attachment to psychological health has been well documented. For a person to remain psychologically healthy, it is essential to have at least one significant attachment. It is indeed psychologically better to have one attachment that is unhealthy in quality than to have no attachments at all. Wilkinson and Marmot (1998) note that it has been convincingly demonstrated that social support and good social relations are an important contributor to psychological health and that connectedness appears to provide some protection against suicide.

In a suicide risk assessment, this works in two ways: in providing psychological stability and health and in adding to the protective factors.

PSYCHOLOGICAL STABILITY AND HEALTH

With attachment comes more psychological stability and health. With no attachment, there is quite a rapid psychological deterioration resulting in depression and eventually marasmus. With no attachment or bond to another person, a human being will basically waste away psychologically, like a young child does in an orphanage where there is little emotional care. As the person psychologically deteriorates, the risk of a suicide attempt will increase if he views suicide as a solution to his problems.

Thus the assessment needs to investigate the individual's current attachments. First, are there any? One is making an assessment of how psychologically isolated the person is in terms of attachment, and not necessarily at a practical level. For example, some people can be married but may remain quite emotionally isolated. Some can be "in a relationship" but have a weak attachment with the other, which is typified by the schizoid personality. Thus a risk assessment on this measure does not look to see if the person is married or has friends; instead it is an assessment of the person's psychological attachments.

ASSESSING THE DEPTH OF ATTACHMENT

Fortunately, this is not too hard to do as has been articulated by White (1986). He reports that the more robust an attachment one has to another, the more severe will be the grief and loss reaction should the other person suddenly die. If there is a very strong attachment, then the pain and grief at the loss will be quite severe. With less of an attachment, the pain of the loss will be less intense. One can produce a list of those whose loss would cause the strongest grief reactions. The suicide risk assessor can gain some insight into the current state of the individual's most intimate relationships and attachments. If the list includes two or more significant attachments, one knows this does not indicate a higher level of suicide risk. If there are only one or two and the grief reactions would not be all that strong, this could indicate an increase in risk level.

The other thing about attachment that Bowlby identified early on was the notion of the need to maintain proximity. He found that the stronger an attachment from one person to another, the more that person had a need to geographically seek the other out. They have a need to maintain geographical proximity to the other. If, in questioning a person, he reports that, after not seeing someone for some time, he still does not have much of an urge to "catch up with" or seek out the other, then you know the attachment to that person is not all that strong. Thus, on this measure, the suicide risk increases. These days, with the advent of the internet and easy telecommunications, one can maintain a sort of proximity without actual geographical relocation. However, if one is not in communication with the other and there is little increase in the level of discomfort, then the attachment is of a weak nature.

It takes time for a psychological attachment to develop to any significant degree. As a history between two people develops, so can their psychological attachment. This is a problem if one's primary attachment figure should die or suddenly have to move away so that the contact is greatly reduced. Some people structure their relationships so that they have one strong singular attachment and very few others. This person is more vulnerable than the person who has three or four quite strong primary attachments to family and friends. One can assess a higher level of risk to that person who has only one primary attachment figure, or at least predict that the level of suicide risk would increase should that attachment figure be removed from the individual's life. If this should happen, then the risk may increase significantly because not only does the individual find himself emotionally isolated, but the grief and depression from the loss will also be drawing on his psychological reserves.

ATTACHMENT AS A PROTECTIVE FACTOR

The second point about human attachment is that it adds to the protective factors of suicide—those circumstances that make it more difficult for the person to choose suicide as a solution. Earlier in this chapter, I noted a number of those factors, such as strong social and family supports, which I am addressing here in terms of human attachment. With attachment to others comes more compassion, empathy and caring of the others. A suicidal husband knows that his children, wife and mother are also attached to him. He knows that if he should suddenly suicide, they will suffer much pain and grief; they may also experience terrible guilt at feeling that they should have seen more or done more. This is a protective factor because his compassion and caring for his loved ones makes it harder for him to choose suicide as a solution. The fewer primary attachments he has, the less this will be a protective factor, and thus the level of suicide risk goes up.

However, as I mentioned before, the biggest enemy of protective factors is the psychological mechanism of regression. The more regressed a person is, the less compassion and caring he has for his loved ones. He can quickly rationalize away these factors with thoughts such as "I am such a downer and so depressed that in the long run they will be much better off without me anyway". If a person is capable of significant regression, this can cancel out the protective factors provided by strong attachment.

If one has ongoing contact with the person, whether that be in a counseling situation, in a prison or in some other healthcare role, then the relationship between the individual and the counselor can develop an attachment as well. This can then also develop as a protective factor, as well as provide the person with a sense of belonging and the psychological stability that can come from such psychological attachments. Although this can be helpful, it can also be a significant problem because it involves all the dynamics of a transference relationship between client and counselor.

ATTACHMENT IN THE THERAPEUTIC RELATIONSHIP

Many years ago I counseled a woman on and off for about three years. She presented with significant chronic depression. She would feel very depressed day in and day out, and there seemed to be little relief, no matter what she tried, medical or psychological. Along with this, she reported regular and significant suicidal urges over a number of years and saw suicide as a viable solution to her difficulties. There were times when I truly wondered if she would make it.

Case study 8.6 gives her description of her depression which would probably be diagnosed as a major depression.

CASE STUDY 8.6: DEPRESSION

Depression is difficult to live with, because most people don't understand it, so you're reluctant to talk to anyone about it. It's also difficult to explain, because when you're depressed, everything in your world looks different. Situations and events that once were very meaningful and important look meaningless. You feel indifferent to things going on around you. You don't feel anything, you just don't care, you just want to die—anything, to escape the horrible way you feel inside.

Depression also affects the way you think. It's hard to think clearly. It's difficult to remember things or to think through a situation or problem to a logical conclusion. You become confused easily. Nothing looks exciting or interesting anymore. It's hard to think at all! You just want to sleep.

It's a state in which you're totally incapable of "getting out of it" by yourself, and you can't see how. Most people can't comprehend how someone could become so depressed that suicide looks wonderful. Life may be going relatively OK on the outside, but the feeling of depression can still envelop you, until you reach a state of hopelessness.

As one can see from her comment, she sees suicide as a possible solution to her very distressing state of mind. At one point, she attended a weekend therapeutic group in the country which I conducted. After that finished I saw her individually about a week later. At that time she reported to me that when she left the weekend group in her car, she had seriously considered suicide on some quiet country road on the way home. She had the items in her car necessary to gas herself. She reported to me that one of the reasons she did not kill herself was because she knew it would be bad for me, both personally and professionally, being so close to the therapy group. Due to her attachment to me in the therapeutic relationship, I had become a protective factor for her and had played some role in her avoiding the potential suicide attempt.

However, the therapeutic relationship is a potentially problematic relationship. I never used it or encouraged her to see me as a protective factor in her suicidal thinking as that can be too dangerous. Much more will be said about this in Chapter 14 on the no-suicide contract, but the counselor, doctor or mental healthcare professional must never attempt to use himself as a source of guilt or motivation as a protective factor for the suicidal individual. This is highlighted in the brief exchange described in Case study 8.7.

CASE STUDY 8.7: *THE COUNSELOR AS PROTECTIVE FACTOR*

A 30-year-old male, who reports suicidal thoughts, states that he has attempted suicide a few times in the past and indicates that at least some of them were quite serious attempts.

Counselor: Are you willing to make a no-suicide contract?

Client: No.

Counselor: Why is that?

Client: Well, it depends who I am making it with. If I am making it as a promise to you, then if I get angry at you, I know I might try and kill myself as a way of getting back at you.

Counselor: Actually, a no-suicide contract is not a promise to me but something that you make with yourself. It is an agreement that you have with yourself.

Client: I feel like it would lock me in too much. The word contract sounds like a legally binding sort of word and I don't want to feel locked in like that.

In those circumstances, where there is an ongoing relationship between the patient and the counselor or doctor, then a transference relationship will develop from the client to the counselor. Sooner or later, the therapeutic relationship will evolve to the stage of negative transference, in which the patient will develop angry and hostile feelings towards the counselor. If the attachment to the counselor or doctor has become a protective factor, when the client enters the negative transference, as is shown in Case study 8.7, the client can express his anger by attempting suicide as a means of hitting out at the counselor or doctor. The therapeutic attachment and its effect on the client's suicidality is a problematic situation that is discussed in much more detail in Chapter 14 on the no-suicide contract.

MARRIAGE AND ATTACHMENT AS AN ADDITION TO SUICIDE RISK

Pursuant to the above, although some correctly argue that relationship and attachment can be a protective factor, in other circumstances it can significantly add to increased suicide risk. This draws on the material presented in Chapter 5 on modeling and the suicide pact. Marriage will only be a protective factor if the spouse is of a certain view about suicide. This can work in three ways.

First, some people are of the view that suicide is everyone's right. Each person has the right to choose when and how to die, for whatever reason he may have. Some view this as an inalienable human right, and indeed there is cogent argument to back it up. If a woman is suicidal and her husband is of this view, it seems that the marriage may in fact contribute to the level of suicide risk, not reduce it. One needs not only to assess for the presence of an attachment but to consider the views of the attachment partner in relation to suicide.

Second, Chapter 5 looked at modeling, imitation and introjection, and how these can relate to views about suicide in a relationship. In a marriage, one party can be of the view that suicide is a reasonable solution to psychological problems. Over time the other party can introject these views into his or her own personality structure, and one ends up with two like-minded individuals convincing each other of what they already believe in. This can result in a suicide pact or in one party supporting the suicidal individual in the suicide currently being contemplated.

Third, living with a person who is suicidal over an extended period of time is very emotionally draining and taxing on the psyche. If a loved one repeatedly makes suicidal statements and suicide attempts, that can take a large toll on the relationship. Eventually, the non-suicidal partner will, in part, want it all just to end. If he sees the suicidal gestures as potentially going on for a long time to come, he can start to feel that a completed suicide by his spouse would end it all. It would finally allow him to get some relief from the ongoing significant stress, and indeed let him get on with his life again. Such loved ones can at times become supportive of the suicide attempt at least unconsciously.

In conclusion, being married or having an attachment can be a protective factor against suicide. In a suicide risk assessment, one needs to look deeper and ascertain the views on suicide of the marital partner. Sometimes the partner's views may in fact support the suicidal thoughts and actions. If this is found to be the case, the risk of suicide significantly increases in the risk assessment.

9. Previous history of suicide attempts as an indicator of suicide risk

Allen and Allen (1978) report that "50% to 80% of those who ultimately commit suicide have a history of previous attempts" (p.166). The person who makes a suicide attempt has shown he is prepared to cross that line of putting suicidal thoughts into action. However, as with most of the measures listed here, one needs to look in more detail at this area so as to get any meaningful information in a suicide risk assessment. Suicide attempts come in all shapes and sizes, and vary greatly in their potential lethality, spontaneity and amount of secondary gain.

LETHALITY OF ATTEMPT

If possible, one needs to get as much detailed information as one can on why any previous suicide attempts were not completed. This can provide invaluable information about the likelihood of subsequent attempts and about the nature of the person's overall suicidality. First, one needs to find out how serious the suicide attempt was and why it was not completed. If it was serious and not completed, that was due to good luck rather than its incompletion being planned to some degree, consciously or unconsciously. If it was luck that kept the person alive, then his level of suicide risk could be seen to be elevated.

Some attempts are obviously non-lethal, but this can be due to a lack of information. One would ask the suicidal individual about his knowledge of the physical consequences of what he did. If it is not due to a lack of information, then the individual is making the attempt(s) for some sort of secondary gain. One needs to ascertain what that gain is and then deal with the issue at hand. For example, it may be an attempt to stop someone leaving a relationship, or it may be because the person is in great psychological pain and does not know how to deal with that. In this case, the level of suicide risk is not high because it is not the goal of the person to kill self even though he can still die in a suicide attempt that is accidently completed.

SECONDARY GAINS

Cutting the wrists across the forearm is very unlikely to be lethal, especially if the cuts are relatively superficial. If secondary gains are apparent, there is always the possibility that, in recounting the facts of the suicide attempt, the individual will exaggerate the lethality of the method employed. This is particularly likely if no one saw the suicide attempt being performed or saw the individual soon after the attempt was made.

If the method used was potentially very lethal and the person did not die due to some lucky circumstances, the risk of future serious suicide attempts increases significantly. Secondary gains are less likely to be influencing in the behavior. One is looking for patterns of behavior because people tend to repeat what they do over and over, such as with triggers. What events or set of circumstances resulted in the person making a suicide attempt in the past? Once identified, one knows that a similar set of circumstances could cause the same behavior and thus the suicide risk increases as the same set of circumstances arises. Of course, the more recent the attempt was, the more significant that is.

In the final analysis, a person who has made a serious suicide attempt has shown he is willing to cross that line that most others won't. In any area of psychology, there is a very big difference between thinking something and acting on those thoughts. Many people—indeed, over half the population have thought about suicide. There is also a sizable group of people who have had serious thoughts about suicide that may have involved some significant planning. However, there is only a relatively small number of people who have acted on those thoughts and planning in a serious way. If a person made a serious suicide attempt in the recent past, with no identifiable secondary gains, which they survived due to luck, then the risk of suicide in the future increases significantly.

10. The suicide note as a measure of assessing suicide risk

There is some research which indicates that about 20–30 percent of those who complete a suicide will leave a note of some kind (Shioiri *et al*. 2005). Suicide notes can provide considerable information about the risk of suicide, about the state of mind of the suicidal individual and about future treatment and management strategies with them.

OBTAINING THE NOTE

This is an important aspect to consider. How was the suicide note obtained? How much did the suicidal person want the note to be found before the attempt, or was it only meant to be read after a completed suicide? If it had been well hidden, indicating that it was not meant to be found before an attempt or only found after an uncompleted serious attempt, then the information in it can provide much insight into the person's state of mind around the time of the attempt. If the note was so located that it was likely to be found before an attempt or if it is provided unsolicited, then the likelihood of some form of secondary gains increases. For instance, the suicide note may be written as a threat, in the hope that a partner won't leave the relationship. It can be a cry for help or a statement that the person is in considerable emotional distress and does not know to deal with it, or it could be an acting-out piece of behavior that seeks attention. As stated before, the more significant the secondary gains, the less risk there is of a completed suicide, which also means that if there are no secondary gains, then the suicide risk increases. If a note is clearly saying goodbye and was not meant to be found, that would indicate a significant level of suicide risk.

TIMING OF THE NOTE

How recently was the note written? Sometimes notes written many months before are found well hidden with a person's intimate possessions. Other times the note may be written just prior to the attempt. There may be a number of different notes written at different times, so that they form kind of a diary. The more recent the note, the more current the state of mind of the individual being shown, and thus the more important to a current assessment of suicide risk. However, notes written long ago are also valuable as they indicate the state of mind of the person when he was suicidal. One then has indicators to look for when making a suicide risk assessment to see if the previous state of mind is being replicated.

CONTENT OF THE NOTE

What does the note actually say and what does it imply? Case study 8.8 is a suicide note provided by a 23-year-old woman of her 50-year-old father who had been widowed a number of years earlier. In this case, the suicide attempt had been completed so the note was of little use in terms of risk assessment. However, for demonstration purposes, if the suicide had not been completed, one could have gleaned certain information from it for future dealings with the suicidal man.

CASE STUDY 8.8: SUICIDE NOTE

I am sorry for what I have done and hope you do not feel too hurt.

My will and insurance papers are in the safety deposit box at the bank. I have included a list of how I want my things split up between you and your sister and the few others.

[Then followed a long list of two pages with various items such as paintings, pictures, stamp collection, trinkets and so forth being assigned to half a dozen different people known to him. Nothing of great financial value but obviously of great sentimental value. There had been many changes made as the list was being compiled with the crossing-out of items to one person then being assigned to others.]

Love you

Daddy

This suicide note is, in essence, a business letter indicating he was in a state of regression so that his Parent ego state had been significantly weakened but his Adult ego state was fairly well intact as shown in Figure 8.5.

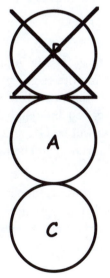

Figure 8.5 A regression involving only the Parent ego state

This is the worst combination of all in terms of suicide risk. The note shows a well-functioning Adult ego state because it is coherent and no confusion is indicated; it is a well-planned and well-structured letter. This means that if he is planning a suicide attempt (as he was), that is also going to be well planned and well structured (as it was). Thus, there is a much greater chance of a completed suicide, which is indeed what happened.

To make matters worse, the Parent ego state was poorly functioning, which is not so common. As a person regresses, usually both the Adult and the Parent ego state functions deteriorate simultaneously, at least to some degree. As mentioned before in the discussion on regression, as the Parent ego state decreases, the protective factor of family and loved ones also decreases. In this instance, the Parent decreased but the Adult remained well-functioning. An examination of the letter shows that 95 percent of it relates to the Adult ego state business about who gets what possessions. Only the first short sentence gives any indication about recognizing the pain that the suicide will cause to his loved ones, which is the protective factor. In this way, it shows a man who, at that point, is in a quite self-centered and narcissistic state of mind.

When a suicidal individual has regressed so that he has high Adult functioning and low Parent ego state functioning, then the level of suicide risk increases, with the potential for a significant increase. Compare this to the suicide note from a man aged 40:

> To my dear son Axel,
>
> It is time for me to go as life is just too hard. With your mother gone my life seems to have no meaning anymore. I love her so much. You must be good with your sister. She loves you and will help you get through this. Over time you will be OK and live your life. One day we will meet in heaven and be together again. Take care my son.

The full content of this short note is about the well-being of his son, which indicates that his Parent ego state still has its functions of empathy and compassion. He is not in a regressed state like the man shown in Figure 8.5. This is a suicide note from a man who died at this attempt, and thus the protective factor of his attachment to his son was not enough to stop him in this case.

As was shown in Chapter 4 about the different types of suicide decisions, sometimes a suicide can be done from an angry or hurtful position. This is found in the suicide decisions "If you don't change, I will kill myself" and "I will kill myself to hurt you".

An example of this in a suicide note is provided below:

> To Merle,
>
> You know what you have done to me. You have ruined me. You get those lawyers to kill me and take every thing I have ever worked for in my life. You have the house, shares and all the money. You have taken it all, you won it all and have beaten me at last. You were only ever interested in the money as I now can see. With me gone now you don't even have to pay the lawyers anymore.
>
> I have a few possessions left. I want them to go to my brother. Can you do that at least for me? They are not worth much if you sold them and he would like that. Can you do that one last thing for me without the hate you have for me?
>
> You always said how much I hurt you, but I was the one that was hurt by you. You were so cruel and unloving to me and I just tried to make it all good. Well now you have another death you have made. First your mother and now me. I hope that makes you happy.

This note shows that part of the motivation to suicide was the result of a relationship problem and a desire to hurt the other party. The other required component is the presence of a suicide decision; there are many ways to hurt someone other than to suicide and blame the other person. In such hurtful and angry suicides, the key ingredient is relationships. They are connected to relationship problems, whereas other suicides may not be at all. If the content of a suicide note is about hurting another, then, to make a risk assessment, one needs to access information about the individual's current intimate relationships. In essence, one keeps tabs on the status of his current relationships. If they are deteriorating and the person is feeling angry and hurtful, then the level of suicide risk at that time increases.

11. Way of talking about suicide

The way a person talks about suicide or the type of language they use can give an indication of the level of suicide risk. Below are some examples of how people talk about death. These are single statements, and, of course, one would not make a judgement based on one sentence alone. These are meant to reflect the theme of what the person is saying. They can indicate the level of suicidal thinking or lack of it. These were originally presented in White (1991).

Such statements can reflect the psychological basis of suicidal thinking. The most forthright statement one can get about suicide is "I want to kill myself". This is a Child ego state statement that is action-oriented and would indicate a level of greater risk than most other statements. Compare this to a statement such as "I want to die". This is also Child ego state, but it is less action-oriented. "I want to die" is more passive than "I want to kill myself". However, they are both clear Child ego state statements and thus represent greater risk because the Child is that part of the personality that is most influential in the long run.

Sometimes one hears other statements such as "I have to kill myself (die)". The "have to" comment shows this is a Parent ego state statement and thus less psychologically potent. In this case, the person feels he has to complete some task that has been placed on him or given to him. In this sense, it is coming less from the heart, which is the Child ego state. It is not a direct want but more of a "I have to do it".

Some statements about suicide show faulty belief systems (delusions). One can hear statements such as "I have to kill myself (die) to keep someone else alive". Clearly, this represents magical thinking. Alternatively, there can be fatalistic statements such as "It is inevitable that I will kill myself (die)" or "By the time I'm 30, I will be dead". The degree of suicide risk in such instances depends on how strong and resilient the delusion or faulty belief system is. If the delusion begins to crumble when Adult information is given, then the risk is reduced. In other cases, the faulty belief will persist, no matter how much clear factual information is given, and thus the risk is increased.

On the other hand, there can be Rebellious Child ego state statements such as "I want to cheat death" or "I will show them by killing myself". This type of suicidal urge varies in risk depending on what is currently happening in the person's life. Is he currently in a situation that will promote the Rebellious Child ego state? Is he currently in contact with a parental or authoritative type of person, with the most usual being the individual's parents? The more a parent is being parental and authoritative to such a person, the more likely that person will respond in a rebellious way. If he has suicidal urges that have a rebellious origin, this increases the possibility of the person acting on those urges.

Finally, one gets the more passive statements about suicide such as "What's the point of living?" or "I want to go to sleep and stay asleep" or "I want to disappear and never come back". These statements indicate a lesser degree of risk because they are not action-oriented. As with any such comments, however, they require further investigation.

12. Planning suicide

The amount of detail a person has put into planning a suicide attempt can give insight into how committed the person is to carrying out such a plan. As a general rule, the more specific the planning, the greater the risk of a suicide attempt. This tends to be one of the better indicators of suicide risk.

How much planning has gone into the when, where and how of the suicide attempt? For instance, has the person started to collect and store medication? If so, how much does he have? With answers to questions like these, one has to be especially aware that the person may not be fully candid, and thus the answers must be taken in that context. For a hanging, has the person obtained a rope, has he surveyed a place to tie it up, does he know how to tie the noose and so forth? If he is going to jump off a building or throw himself under a train; has he been to an area to survey it? Has he considered coordinating times for the suicide with the movement of friends and relatives, in order to be found by the "right" person or not be rescued or saved?

Has he researched the topic at all? Has he purchased books such as *Final Exit* (Humphry 1991) which is subtitled "The practicalities of self-deliverance and assisted suicide for the dying"? This book goes into detail about a wide variety of ways by which a person can kill himself and the advantages and disadvantages and the risks involved in each approach. If a suicidal individual has acquired such specific information, it would seem that they have seriously contemplated suicide at some point.

This measure is of less use for those who are more prone to spontaneous suicide attempts, as mentioned in Case study 8.4 above, concerning the 25-year-old man who was told by his partner on the phone that the relationship had ended. He flew into a rage and within a minute had slashed his throat so badly that he almost died from loss of blood. Obviously, here there is virtually no planning at all. If one is dealing with a person who has a history of spontaneous suicidal acts, then a lack of planning does not necessarily reduce their current level of suicide risk.

13. Those with a flight response to stress

As was discussed in Chapter 6, it was noted there are three responses to high stress—flight, fight or freeze. Suicide is primarily a flight response which can also include behaviors such as alcohol or drug abuse, prescription medication or simply a pattern of dealing with stress by geographically moving away from it—for example, by leaving a job or relationship. Gaining a history of the person in this way will indicate if he has flight as a primary response to stress. Furthermore, enquiry into his childhood reactions to stress can also provide useful information. If he tends toward a flight response, then one has another indicator of a potentially suicidal individual.

Conclusion

Described above are the most common measures used in a traditional suicide risk assessment. Other suicide risk schedules include different measures, but this list constitutes the most common, plus a few more that I have developed over the years. A summary is presented below:

Summary of the quantitative measures of suicide risk
1. The tendency and degree of regression

- reduction of protective factors
- increase in prelogical and magical thinking.

2. History of high-risk behavior

- assessing the level of risk in behavior
- failure to accurately assess behavioral risk.

3. History of substance use

- recency of drug use
- lethality of drug used
- method of drug ingestion
- why the drug is used
- drug use and regression.

4. History of mental illness

- ego states and psychosis
- regression
- timing of suicide
- command hallucinations
- borderline personality.

5. Lack of any secondary gain

6. The prison population as a high-risk group

- three subgroups of prisoners
- high-risk subgroups of prisoners
- other assessment considerations for the prison population.

7. Depression as an indicator of suicidal thoughts and actions

- key symptoms of depression related to a risk assessment
- timing and structure of the depressive episodes
- types of depression
- degree of depression and suicidality.

8. Single people are more likely to suicide than those who are married

- human attachment
- assessing the depth of attachment
- attachment as a protective factor
- attachment in the therapeutic relationship
- marriage and attachment as an addition to suicide risk.

9. Previous history of suicide attempts as an indicator of suicide risk

- lethality of attempt
- secondary gains.

10. The suicide note as a measure of assessing suicide risk

- obtaining the note
- timing of note
- content of the note.

11. Way of talking about suicide

12. Planning suicide

13. Those with a flight response to stress

One of the difficulties with these measures is that they are dependent on client reporting. The accuracy of client information in reporting suicidal thoughts and behaviors must be taken in context. One can never assume that one is being told the truth or the whole truth. As a group, the suicidal are very distressed, often with poor Adult ego state thinking, regressed to varying degrees and probably using all sort of defense mechanisms and thus telling falsehoods to themselves as well.

Despite this, one can get quite a good assessment of the status of the person using these measures in the ways described above. However, it is clearly better to use these together with the qualitative measures of suicide risk assessment considered in Chapter 9. This makes an assessment of the suicide decision, which is often made by the suicidal individual in childhood. If one can ascertain the presence of such a decision (or not), then one is much better placed to make a more informed suicide risk assessment.

Chapter 9
Qualitative Measures of Assessing Suicide Risk

In this chapter the qualitative measures of suicide risk are described. These measures detail the definitive feature of the suicidal individual in the psychological sense: that person who has made a suicide decision or "don't exist" decision in childhood. In Chapter 4, seven such decisions were described:

- "If you don't change, I will kill myself."
- "If things get too bad, I will kill myself."
- "I will show you even if it kills me."
- "I will get you to kill me."
- "I will kill myself by accident."
- "I will almost die (over and over) to get you to love me."
- "I will kill myself to hurt you."

When a person makes such a decision the suicidality literally becomes one aspect of his personality. It forms part of his personality structure. The quantitative measures described in Chapter 8 are things that happen to the person or things that may be part of the person's current life; they do not form part of who the person is psychologically. For example, a person may become depressed due to marital breakdown. As we know, 50 percent of depressed people have no thoughts of suicide and 50 percent do. The concept of the suicide decision can explain this. Those depressed people in marital difficulty who have suicidal thoughts have also made the suicide decision in early life. Those depressed individuals who have no suicidal thoughts or urges have not made such a decision.

Assessing long-term suicide risk

This concept adds an extra dimension to the assessment of suicide risk. The quantitative measures listed in Chapter 8 mainly assess the level of *current* suicide risk. If an individual is diagnosed as having made the suicide decision, that certainly can add to the level of imminent risk and can do so significantly. However, if the person is not at any imminent or current suicide risk, having made the suicide decision identifies him at an increased level of longer-term suicide risk. This person has made the decision that suicide is a viable solution to a problem and this is in his personality structure. It can vary as to the "depth" or importance to that personality structure, but it is a bit like a time bomb waiting to go off. When life is good, it is of no concern. When life circumstances take a downward turn, it can assume considerable importance indeed, and the level of current suicide risk increases.

The suicide decision is not something that comes or goes; it is always there. When it is identified, one knows the longer-term risks and one puts in place strategies to monitor that risk. First one would identify which of the seven suicide decisions is made and articulate what kind of circumstances would need to happen for the decision to become "operational". Then one would have a predetermined plan ready for the person to adopt as his risk of imminent suicide increases. As the suicide decision forms part of the individual's personality, Chapter 15 describes a form of treatment which is designed to alter the early decisions made. This, of course, is the best long-term solution as it can significantly alter the suicide decision so that it becomes far less prominent in the person's personality structure.

Identifying the suicide decision

All children have to make sense of the world, themselves and others. They have to come to conclusions (decisions) about their own worth, the worth of others and about life in general. Most theories of child development propose this in one form or another. Children make many such conclusions and decisions. Some are very basic and important to them, and others are more "surface" decisions and less pivotal to a sense of who they are. Some children come to the conclusion that they, or their parents, would be better off if they were dead, and this can form the basis of the suicide decision. For some reason, the child comes to the conclusion that his own death is a viable solution to a problem.

This chapter is about identifying if a child made such a decision and provides various means by which that can be achieved. Most often this is not a particularly difficult endeavor. Even though most people generally remain unaware of their early decisions, including the suicide decision, usually it is not too hard to determine them. Once done, it is relatively easy to see how the early decisions influence current behavior, including suicidal behavior.

1. The Stopper Analysis questionnaire

There have been various questionnaires developed over the years to ascertain a person's early decisions, including the suicide decision. One that has been widely used is by Bob Avary (1976) and called the Stopper Analysis questionnaire. Appendix A includes a copy of the questionnaire and the scoring mechanism. As with all questionnaires, one needs to treat it with caution, especially on an important topic such as suicidality. There is always the potential for false positive and false negative results. One must only use these test results in conjunction with the other ways of assessing for the suicide decision. However, it is useful in providing one part of the puzzle in making an assessment of suicide risk. If one scores a positive result in either of the two ways on the Stopper Analysis, one must then seek confirmation of these with other measures. Of course, the same applies if one obtains a negative result on the questionnaire.

2. The "don't exist" interview

What are known as life script questionnaires have been around for many years, such as the one by McCormick (1971). In such questionnaires one finds a list of questions that can be asked of the person in order to determine what his early decisions were. Some of these questions refer to the suicide early decision. In the normal clinical interview, one would not usually ask all these questions straight off the mark in a row, but rather one would weave them into the general questioning and history taking of the person. In asking such questions, one is wanting to ascertain if the person came to the conclusion as a young child that to kill self was a realistic solution to a problem. These questions, it is deemed, are particularly potent in assisting with that task. Thus one can be seen to be conducting an interview to ascertain the presence of the suicide or "don't exist" decision in what could be called the "don't exist" interview.

There are two approaches or lines of questioning in the interview. The first is what the child perceived the primary parent figures to be saying about his worth and life in general. Such things can be "said" by the parents either by verbalizing such displeasure or by some action such as a hitting or neglect. Indeed, one could say that physical actions "say" a lot more to a child about his worth than any verbal statements. In the questioning one is looking for the verbal statements made by the parents and the "verbal" content that the child deduces from the parents' physical actions towards the child.

For example, Cutajar *et al.* (2010) note: "Studies of community samples have consistently shown a substantial association between reports of CSA (child sexual abuse) and suicide attempts and other self-destructive behavior in young people and adults" (p.184). In such circumstances, it is not so much what the parents said to the child but the meaning the child deduces from their behavior, which in this case included sexual abuse. It seems that when a child is sexually abused, he not uncommonly deduces that things would be somehow better if he was not here or dead; hence, we have the suicide decision and thus an increase in completed suicides, as the research indicates. The child decides the parents are saying that he should be dead, is of little worth and so on. This is what the interviewer is wanting to ascertain in the "don't exist" interview.

Example of "don't exist" interview questions

Determining the event that may have resulted in an early decision:

- What did mother (father or primary parenting figure) say or do when she(he) criticized you or told you off?

- What did mother (father) say or do when she (he) was really angry with you or others?

- What was the worst thing she (he) ever said or did to you?

Determining the cognitive conclusions the child came to in response to those events described above:

- What sense did that young child think when he heard (saw) that?

- What decisions did he make about it?

- What conclusions did he come to and what did it mean about him and others?

CASE STUDY 9.1: *PARENTAL CRITICISM AND THE SUICIDE DECISION*

Question: What did mother (father or primary parenting figure) say or do when she(he) criticized you or told you off?

A 40-year-old man reports early childhood experiences with his father who criticized him severely. He was told repeatedly that he was useless and would never amount to anything as the father developed a competitive relationship with him. At age ten, his mother and father were having marital problems. The father stated to him on a few occasions that they were trying to get romance back into their marriage and that he was *in the way*. He told him a number of times that he was *not wanted and just got in the way*.

In italics are the key phrases in his statement that may indicate the presence of a suicide decision. In this case, the father made direct statements to him, and the interviewer would be seeking to find out how the child made sense of these. What cognitive conclusions did the child come to about such statements? What do these italicized statements mean for the person? Thus, one would proceed with follow-up questioning such as:

- What does "in the way" mean for you?

- What sense or conclusion did the Child part of you make of the statements, "in the way" and "not wanted?"

By ascertaining the cognitive conclusions the child came to, one will then find if a suicide decision was made or not. Sometimes there is no such decision and the person may report that he felt hurt, concluded that he was worthless, and from that day on he would keep seeking father's approval. Thus he has not concluded that such statements mean things would be better if he was dead, which would be the suicide decision. As it happens, in this instance he did make a suicide decision. He reported that "in the way" meant that he was hated by his parents and they thought it would be better if he was out of the way, which meant being dead. His subsequent history included a number of near-fatal motorbike and car accidents, which means one could diagnose him as having made the suicide decision, "I will kill myself by accident".

CASE STUDY 9.2: PARENTAL ANGER AND THE SUICIDE DECISION

Question: What did mother (father) say or do when she (he) was really angry with you or others?

A 28-year-old woman reports an episode in her house when her father became very angry. He was reportedly quite a passive man who would rarely speak an angry word until it had built up over many months, and then he would explode. In this instance, she was in the dining room with her mother when her father became very angry, picked up a stack of plates, threw them to the floor, creating a very loud noise and breaking them all into pieces. She says that in that room there was a wooden floor and the plates left small dents in the wood. She reports noticing those dents in the floor for years afterwards. In reaction to her father being very angry and the smashing of the plates, she felt that she had *to leave and get away from it all.*

The italicized words are the kind of thing the interviewer is looking for and would investigate further. As with Case study 9.1, the interviewer is wanting to find out what "leave and get away from it all" means. She is giving the kind of statement that indicates that things would be better if she was not there, or that the problem can be solved by her not being around. In terms of fight, flight and freeze, she is describing the flight response that can be associated with the suicidal individual.

However, one needs to discover what her Child ego state means when it does not want to be around. It could simply mean to relocate geographically and have no suicidal content. Or it could indicate a more significant form of getting away which includes some form of suicide decision. In contrast to Case study 9.1, the child was not being told something by the parent; instead, the child was observing the parental behavior, making her cognitive conclusions based on that behavior and her feelings about the anger. With further questioning, it was determined that the young girl simply did wish to relocate geographically and used to hide under the house to get away from these angry events. She had not made any kind of suicidal decision.

Interestingly, she did have a long history of trichotillomania from the age of 15 until the present. Although she did not make any suicidal decisions, she did use this kind of self-harm primarily as a way of reducing tension. She stated that she found it soothing and she could camouflage the bald patches well so they were never detected. This illustrates the differences between self-harm and suicide. She had made no suicide decisions, thus the psychological forces behind the suicidal person were not present and she had never contemplated suicide in any serious way. However, she discovered that she could reduce psychological tension by self-harming with the trichotillomania. Thus she developed the psychological basis of the self-harming individual as the more mature ways of reducing tension were never developed. Suicide and self-harm are based on two quite different psychological foundations.

CASE STUDY 9.3: THE FIGHT RESPONSE AND THE SUICIDE DECISION

Question: What was the worst thing she (he) ever said or did to you?

A 28-year-old woman reports episodes where her parents had loud arguments that at times became physical to the extent that on a few occasions the police were called to quell the domestic disturbance. At these times she was about eight and nine years old. When the arguments began, she would usually approach her parents and respond in an angry way by shouting at them and telling them to stop. She would enter into the argument to try and distract their attention from each other in the hope that the conflict would diminish. This did not happen and usually mother would tell father how he was upsetting his daughter. He would then angrily tell her to go away and get out of his sight. Eventually, she would leave and usually go to her bedroom. She could then spend hours in there ruminating, angry at her parents and thinking of *ways she could get them back.*

As with the other case examples, one needs to ascertain what her Child ego state meant when it wanted to extract its angry revenge as is indicated in the italicized section of her statement. In this instance, she had a fight rather than a flight response which can form the basis of the following suicide decisions:

- "If you don't change, I will kill myself."
- "I will show you even if it kills me."
- "I will kill myself to hurt you."

Subsequent questioning sought to find out the cognitive conclusions the young child came to in relation to her suicidality. During her bedroom ruminations, what conclusions did she come to, what sense did she make of it all, and what did it mean about her? As it turned out, she did make such a decision and saw dying as a way of obtaining revenge and hurting her parents. She would have fantasies of being at her own funeral and seeing her parents crying by the grave site, as she had seen her mother cry when their dog died a year earlier.

CASE STUDY 9.4: *THE PASSIVE SUICIDE DECISION*

Question: What did mother (father) say or do when she (he) was really angry with you or others?

A 37-year-old man reports that during most of his childhood he had a very dominant mother who decided for him what he would do and how he would do it in his schooling, social life and so forth. She was also prone to angry outbursts most days, he says. These were most often in relation to her husband who was a passive man and would just listen to her angry raving, which could go on for hours, it seemed to the young boy. When this happened, he would usually retreat to his sanctuary, which was to climb under the table in the next room so that nobody knew he was there. He felt safe and protected there. When there, he reports that *he felt like nothing, a kind of numb despair and he used to wish that he was not here.* He also reports *prolonged emotional neglect* in that he was never shown any positive love or affection.

Further questioning about the numb despair and the wish not to be here could show up some level of suicide decision. As was mentioned in Chapter 8, under point 11 of the quantitative measures of suicide risk, people can talk about suicide in different ways. Sometimes they are passive statements such as "What's the point of living?" or "I want to go to sleep and stay asleep" or "I want to disappear and never come back". This man had made such a passive suicide decision, thus indicating some level of suicide risk but at the lower levels in the shorter term. He reports that he did not actively think of suicide but had a definite sense of not wanting to be here or alive.

If he was prone to angry outbursts himself, then it could be a suicide decision such as "I will get you to kill me" because he could get involved in some violent exchange in which he was killed. He did not tend to do this and usually was quite passive in relationships, so one could also look for a decisions such as "I will kill myself by accident", which can be a more passive means of suicide, or even perhaps "I will almost die (over and over) to get you to love me". He had no history of suicide attempts but was living a life in which he was becoming more and more isolated, thus indicating the possibility of a longer-term suicide risk assessment. He could end up living a life with few relationships and little sense of meaning and start to wonder what is the point of it all. At such a time, his level of suicidality could increase significantly.

It should also be noted that any time a person reports significant emotional neglect, the possibility of making a suicide decision increases. The child is being told he is not wanted by inaction on the parents' behalf. Thus, at least some of the time, the child will take that on and decide that things would be better if he was dead and make the suicide decision.

CASE STUDY 9.5: THE SUICIDE DAYDREAM

Question: What did mother (father or primary parenting figure) say or do when she (he) criticized you or told you off?

A 38-year-old woman reports a childhood of persistent and intense criticism by mother who was very controlling. She felt that she could do nothing correctly and each time she did something as simple as walking or eating food she would be criticized for not doing it the right way. This ended up being intolerable and she reports *wishing she was not alive* some of the time. She even created a small rhyme for herself that she used to sing when on her own: *"I wish I was dead, I wish I was dead, I wish I was dead…" sung as a little melody.*

These answers would indicate the possibility of a person who has made the suicide decision. However, upon closer examination it was found that she never actually decided that she wanted to kill herself. She stated that as a child she wanted to be dead at times, but never that she wanted to kill herself or be killed. In essence, the wish to be dead was a comforting daydream that she created to ease some of the distress she felt in her everyday life. She never made the suicide decision and was not at a higher level of suicide risk in this way.

The point at hand is to highlight the kind of statements the interviewer is looking for in the answers during the "don't exist" interview. An examination of the responses to the questions merits further investigation.

In Case study 9.1, the person is told directly that he was not wanted, and thus it is possible the child would conclude that suicide is a way of fulfilling the parental directive. What the child does conclude is entirely up to him, but parental pressure is being applied for that type of decision to be made.

In Case study 9.2, the child was not told anything directly but observed frightening parental behavior. Her reaction to want to get away from it all indicates the *possibility* she made a suicide decision, which was finally determined not to be the case.

In Case study 9.3, the child involved herself in an angry exchange with the parents and left with the desire to extract revenge on them. Such an approach can lead to a suicide decision being made from an angry position.

Case study 9.4 shows a child who adopted a passive role in his relationship with mother, leading him to a state of numbness and despair and the cognitive conclusion that he did not want to be alive. This, combined with neglect by the parents, resulted in a passive suicide decision being made.

Finally, in Case study 9.5, one finds an example where the suicide decision was not made, even though the child created a comforting daydream about being dead to get away from her day-to-day emotional pain.

So far the "don't exist" interview has focussed on how the parents and the child relate. The second line of investigation in the "don't exist" interview seeks information on where the person sees himself heading with his life. It is often surprising how clear some people can be about how they will be at the time of their death and how it will occur. Sometimes these will include indications of a suicide with comments such as "I'll be dead before I'm 30".

The following "don't exist" interview questions are designed to elicit how the person sees himself ending up in life:

- What happens to people like you?

- If you keep going the same way you are now, where will you be in five, ten or fifteen years?

- How do you think you may die, and at what age?

- What will it say on your tombstone?

- You are watching your funeral: who is there and what are they saying?

CASE STUDY 9.6: *RESPONSES TO THE "DON'T EXIST" INTERVIEW*

From Annalynn:

What happens to people like you?
They suffer every day until the day that they find the strength to kill themselves once and for all. Then and only then will they be set free from all the pain and misery in this world.

If other people are suffering the same emotional pain or worse than I currently am, this world is a very cruel place and is not worthy of my presence. I can't live in a world where people do violence to one another. It's not right.

And I can only hope that my friends and family would understand this.

It is devastating to think that my death would probably cause them unbearable pain. But, I think that's a sacrifice that I may be willing to make.

If you keep going the same way you are now where will you be in five, ten or fifteen years?
Dead. But one can only hope.

How do you think you may die and at what age?
Suicide, within the next few years. They say that the brain is fully developed after you reach 25. I'm 22 now. I'll do my best to live it out until 25, but no promises.

I'm reminded of a quote by Doug Stanhope, "Life is like a movie, if you've sat through more than half of it and it's sucked every second so far, it probably isn't gonna get great right at the end and make it all worthwhile. None should blame you for walking out early."

What will it say on your tombstone?

I don't want my tombstone to say anything. I am no different from the people that die each day and are buried in unmarked graves because no one knows who they are. I am no better than they might have been.

You are watching your funeral: who is there and what are they saying?

I have thought about this on many occasions. I would not want a funeral. But that is really not my choice to make. A funeral is for the living, not for the dead. I want the people who know me to have the opportunity to mourn in a healthy way and find closure. My mother and father, a few friends would probably attend. I don't know what they would say. (Comment 8, cited in White 2010)

Although this example of responses to the "don't exist" interview carries much pain and angst, it does provide a very good clinical example because it is so candid. This is a person who is at obvious imminent suicide risk as she is making clear statements about her suicidality. Her answer to the first question—"What happens to people like you?"—shows up a suicide decision of "If things get too bad, I will kill myself". The badness is her pain and suffering, which is at such a level that it may override the protective factor of the pain caused to family and friends by her suicide. Her level of emotional pain and suffering is a key to the suicide risk assessment in this case. The more it goes up, the more the level of suicide risk goes up.

The second feature is her statement about the timing of her death. As mentioned before, some people can be quite specific about the age by which they will be dead. From a suicide risk assessment point of view, this is obviously of great importance as the person begins to near that age. She is quite specific, and her metaphor of the movie indicates a raised level of suicide risk at this time: she may choose to "leave the movie at any time if it does not get better". From a treatment point of view, it is interesting that she chose 25 years of age because that is when the brain is fully developed. Why is having a fully developed brain significant? If a person passes that age without suicide, another age can be set, and one ends up in the same circumstances all over again as the suicide decision is still quite functional in the mind.

Finally, there are the comments about her funeral. Her comment "I have thought about this on many occasions" shows her potential to have magical thinking about death. The fact that she has thought many times about her funeral can indicate a sense that, after her death, she will be somehow capable of magically watching her funeral take place. Her answer may indicate this, and it is definitely a line of questioning that would take place subsequent to her answering these questions.

3. The "Bad Day at Black Rock" exercise

This is an extension of the previous method of risk assessment or a more elaborate type of "don't exist" interview. It was originally presented by John McNeel (1980) and allows the person to demonstrate a more experiential and Child ego state view of a possible suicide decision. The individual is invited to recall a scene from his early life in childhood. This can be done simply by questioning the person or by getting him to regress, usually with some form of guided imagery. He adopts a relaxed posture, closes his eyes and is taken on a guided imagery to his childhood where he can recall an unpleasant scene that usually involves family members.

He is requested to recall a time when something very bad happened and he became quite upset, usually within the first ten years of life. If it is too hard to remember that early, a later scene will suffice. Once such a scene has been found, the individual is requested to recall such things as what was happening, who was there, what they were saying, doing and feeling, and what he was doing, saying and feeling.

As this is for the assessment of suicide risk, it has to be an unpleasant scene because it is in those circumstances that the child will make significant decisions about his lack of worth, how he is meant to be, the worth of others and, in particular, suicide decisions. One is looking for the cognitive conclusions the child came to when he was highly distressed and under considerable emotional pressure. The young child will have made some conclusions about how he needed to be in the future and what it all meant to him. The decisions will vary from child to child. However, some children will decide such things as "If things get too bad, I will kill myself", "I will get you to kill me" or "I will kill myself to hurt you". One is looking for some kind of decision by the client that, for him, death was a solution; or a decision where to kill self was a logical consequence of what that early scene meant to him. This is one of the best ways to ascertain if a person has made a "don't exist" decision.

CASE STUDY 9.7: "BAD DAY AT BLACK ROCK"

Figure 9.1 is an example of a "Bad Day at Black Rock" drawing by a 33-year-old woman who was about six or seven years old at the time these events occurred.

Figure 9.1 A case example of a "Bad Day at Black Rock" drawing (White 2010a)

Once the drawing has been done, the person is invited to describe what is happening in the unpleasant scene. The following description was given.

> At this point, my dad is a big marijuana smoker. He keeps some frozen in the freezer outside, he grows some outside, and has marijuana dealers over nearly every day. He also drinks.

My mother doesn't mind that he smokes or drinks, as long as he keeps it out in the garage. She doesn't want me exposed to his lifestyle. But, of course, I am. She can't protect me when she is at work. I even liked the drug dealers 'cause every time they would come over they would bring me candy. During the holidays they would even give me money.

This day my mother came home from work. Occasionally she gets home later than usual; meaning that she didn't drive straight home from work. I think the reason she gets home late is that she does not want to see me.

She gets home. I don't remember the conversation between my father and my mother. I don't think I understand completely what they are saying. Mom is saying that she doesn't want those drug dealers coming over anymore after one of them was shot. My dad has been drinking. They argue. And then my dad starts yelling. And my mom is screaming. And my dad is hitting my mother. I want them to stop fighting. They don't. Please stop fighting. I'm crying and screaming now too. I grab on to my dad's leg and try to stop him from hitting my mom. I start hitting him too. He pushes me away. But I come back. He's yelling at me and pulling my hair. And then he stops hitting my mother. I did it. I stopped their fighting. But wait, why can't I breathe anymore? He picks me up and throws me to the wall. He goes outside to the garage.

At some point my mother has run up the stairs to her bedroom. I want to see my mother. I want to see that she is OK. I go upstairs and turn the door knob. Locked. I knock and tell her it's just me. It's OK. He's outside. She won't let me in. She doesn't want to see me.

I go to my room and lock myself in. (paragraphs 2–7, White 2010a)

As the individual recounts the story, often he will begin to cry or get emotional. If this happens, he is regressing into his Child ego state, and when asked questions about the cognitive conclusions, he is more likely to be accurate. Of course, each of us has many unpleasant scenes that we can recall, given the appropriate prompting. If the scene elicits a suicide decision made by the child, then one knows such a decision is part of this person's personality. If it does not elicit such a suicide decision, that does not mean such a decision has not been made. It simply means that this person did not make such a decision in that particular scene. We all have about half a dozen primary decisions that form the basic structure of the personality. If one has ongoing contact with the person, this same exercise can be repeated a number of times and one is afforded a much more comprehensive understanding of the individual and his potential suicidality. If one does not come across a suicide decision being made after this exercise has been repeated a number of times, one can be more confident that such a decision does not exist for the person.

The next part of the process is to find out what decisions the young girl came to in that scene. There may be a number of them or there may just be one. The following questions can be asked:

- What did she conclude about herself and life and others?
- What sense did she make out of all this?
- What cognitive conclusions did she come to?

The following was reported:

CASE STUDY 9.7 *CONTINUED*

If I hadn't been born my parents would not be currently fighting. I am a burden.

My own mother, who I care about more than anything, doesn't even want to see me. I am unlovable.

I have to handle my physical and emotional pain on my own. I can't depend on others.

There must be something wrong with me. (paragraph 9, White 2010a)

These are beginning to given some hint of a suicide decision being made, with such comments as:

- "If I hadn't been born…"
- "I am a burden."
- "…doesn't even want to see me."
- "I am unlovable."
- "…something wrong with me."

If a child is thinking like this, it does not take all that much to take the next step and decide that "Life, my parents, and/or I would be better off if I was dead". At this point, one can conclude there is a real possibility of a suicide decision being present, based on the recall of this early scene. One can follow up with other questioning such as:

- Look again at the drawings of the little girl there. What do you see when you look at that little girl?

- Do you like her?

- What is she feeling and what is she wanting?

- Imagine what she is feeling and begin to feel again some of the emotions that she was feeling at that age.

- Allow yourself to re-experience that situation and the feelings that went along with it.

- Look at that little girl and, as you experience her, what sense did she make of it all? What conclusions did she come to and what decisions did she make?

- Did she make any decisions about not being there, being dead, dying or being killed?

The goal is to invite the drawer to go back into the Child ego state and re-experience the early scene, which people are generally willing to do in varying degrees. Some will regress right back and others will not go there at all either because they are highly defended about the event or because it is simply too painful to go back there. Whatever the response, the goal is to get to the cognitive conclusions the child came to in that early scene and in particular, for the purposes of this exercise, any decisions about not existing, being dead or dying.

CASE STUDY 9.7 *CONTINUED*

She responded with:

1. How old is she?

She is around eight years old, I guess. The earliest memories I can recall are about third grade, where I would have been eight. And this is one of them.

2. What do you see when you look at that little girl?

I see that she does look little. She is little. She looks like an innocent, helpless human being who shouldn't have been put in that situation.

3. Do you like her?

I don't know if I like her or not. I feel as if I don't even know her. She is there. But I don't know her.

4. What is she feeling and what is she wanting?

I can imagine what she would be feeling, but I don't know what she is actually feeling. As an adult I can say that she must have been sad and afraid. I do know that she had to be stronger than who she was and that she just wanted her parents to love her. (Comment 1, White 2010a)

These answers would seem to confirm the possibility of a "don't exist" decision being made. This woman is at risk of suicide in the longer term, even if she is not currently experiencing any suicidal thoughts.

CASE STUDY 9.8: ANOTHER "BAD DAY AT BLACK ROCK"

Figure 9.2 is another "Bad Day at Black Rock" scene produced by a 29-year-old male who has a significant history of suicidal thoughts.

**Figure 9.2 One man's distressing scene at
home with his family (White 2010b)**

> I was about ten years old and was in the washroom doing some laundry with my sister. My mom was sitting at the table next to the kitchen. I heard this loud noise and lots of swearing and shouting. It was my dad in the garage. He came into the house from the garage and walked by my mom saying "F..." and "S..." to her. I looked up from the laundry as the door was open and I could see my dad walk into the door way. He saw me there and he picked up a telephone book and threw it at me. It hit my right shoulder so that it turned me around a bit. It hurt real bad. He then just walked off, he didn't say anything or do anything more. I thought "That's weird". It was always so confusing. No one ever said what was going on. My sister said nothing, but I felt sorry for her, and my mom said nothing. It was treated like it never even happened.
>
> But I knew my dad hated me. He said many times that I looked like his father and he always hated his father. He was always so angry and he hated me so much. I knew he didn't want me. He told me that. I was unwanted and unlovable, so I wanted to die. (paragraphs 2–3, White 2010b)

A clear statement is made about the conclusions the youngster came to at the end of his reciting of the scene. The father had directly informed the son that he was unwanted and unlovable. In this instance, the child took that on and made the early decision that it would be best if he died. He shows no signs of the fight response to the actions of his father or mother. He adopts a more passive position and goes into confusion rather than an angry rejection of what is being said and done to him. The suicide decision is quite clear in this case. Thus he is a suicide risk and one needs to ascertain what factors he anticipates would cause an increase in his suicidality and therefore make the suicide decision become operational. Alternatively, one may look at his history when the suicidal thoughts become more pronounced and the triggering factors can be identified.

CASE STUDY 9.9: *EARLY DECISION TO SUPPRESS FEELINGS*

See Figure 9.3

Figure 9.3 An incident when the woman respondent was in hospital as a child (White 2010c)

That was me when I was around eight years old. I had fallen from a ladder and broken my arm and elbow badly so I had to go to hospital and have the arm operated on. I had three operations and I could never again fully extend my arm. Because I just slept all day and left it so late (until the pain was unbearable), they said that I nearly died.

I remember for the first few days I was in the children's ward with a bunch of other kids but then they moved me to a ward that only had grown-up women in it. They said that I had been moved to keep me safe from infection and stuff like that. I don't remember feeling bad about the change—I think I was too sick at the time.

My mum would visit me every day and I must have cried when she left because after I was in there a week or more my mum told me that if I cry when she left to go home, the hospital wouldn't let her come and visit me anymore. My mum always looked worried when it was time for her to say goodbye. (Comment 4, White 2010c)

As mentioned before, subsequent questioning on the cognitive conclusions include questions such as:

- What do you see when you look at that little girl?

- Do you like her?

- What is she feeling and what is she wanting?

- Imagine what she is feeling and begin to feel again some of the emotions that she was feeling at that age.

- Allow yourself to again re-experience that situation and the feelings that went along with it.

- Look at that little girl and, as you experience her, what sense did she make of it all? What conclusions did she come to and what decisions did she make?

- Did she make any decisions about not being there, being dead, dying or being killed?

The result for the drawer was to report that she perceived her mother had told her not to cry. Thus, she made the early decision that crying and sad feelings were not OK. In her subsequent life she has always had problems with sad feelings and crying. She has a strong dislike of them and tends to replace them with angry feelings. When she feels sadness, she experiences a significant level of discomfort and tends to get angry instead of crying. She has made the decision "I won't cry or feel sad, but I will get angry instead".

This is what the young child was thinking about and deciding. When asked about being abandoned, being shown a lack of worth because her mother left her time after time, there was nothing from the person. She did not come to any conclusions about being worthless or a burden to mother.

This indicates that a suicide decision was not made in this case and shows how fickle a young child's decision making can be. Another child could quite easily have come to the conclusion that he lacked worth and was causing his mother problems, and thus his continued existence could come into question. This did not happen in Case study 9.9 because the child was almost distracted into deciding about crying and sadness. It's not that the child decided she is worthwhile; instead she simply did not make any decision about such matters. One can conclude from this person's report that she did not make a suicide decision, at least in this instance, and thus the level of long-term risk would be seen to decrease.

This highlights another feature of early decisions, including the suicide decision. In the final analysis, it is the child who decides, as was described in Chapter 4. Parents can say or do what they like to a child, but in the end it is the child's interpretation of what is being said. In adulthood, the recollection of the facts may be quite erroneous, but that does not matter because it is what the person recalls he decided as a child that is important. Sometimes this approach is criticized because it is seen to blame the parents for everything. Of course, blaming parents never achieves anything good for the suicidal person in the long run, and the decision-making process described here actually says it is the child who makes the final choice.

This is why some children can come from quite horrific backgrounds and end up reasonably healthy in emotional terms. Despite all the abuse received, they still managed to come to some OK decisions about themselves and others. It is just the way they interpreted things at the time of making their decisions. On the other hand, some children can come from emotionally healthy backgrounds and still make some unhealthy decisions, including the suicide decision. Again, it is their unsophisticated thinking and decision making that counts in the end and this can be quite erroneous at times.

CASE STUDY 9.10: *VERY EARLY DECISIONS*

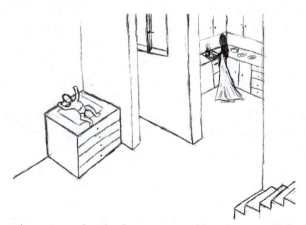

Figure 9.4 A drawing by a 44-year-old woman recalling an event that occurred very early in life (White 2010d)

See Figure 9.4.

Mother is busy in the kitchen. The baby is waiting to be taken care of. It is crying, crying and crying. The baby is noisy and needy but it does not get picked up.

It's not mother's fault because she is simply busy. It's the baby's fault.

Father is working and mother is overloaded. She is just young and has duties that she never had to deal with before. The baby is just one extra duty on a long list. The baby is not one year old yet. It is not an emotional priority.

Why should this baby come first? Mother was overloaded and creates a sense of guilt in the child.

It thought, "I don't deserve to get my needs met. I make mother's life harder, it would be better if I was not here." (paragraphs 1–5, White 2010d)

In terms of the fight, flight or freeze response to stress, there is clearly no fight response in this case. It shows how the suicide decision can result in such circumstances as it did here. The baby does not view mother as treating her unfairly, which would tend to be the fight response: "I am not being treated in the way that I should be, so it's her fault" (anger).

Instead, the response is to see mother as being over-burdened with her domestic duties already, and the baby is simply making mother's life harder. Thus, it's the baby's fault that she is not being picked up. (Consider this in contrast to the child in Case study 9.9 above, who could have easily concluded the same but did not.) Thus it is not hard for the child in this case study to make the decision that things would be better for all concerned if she was not here. One could see this as the flight response, and the feeling reaction is one of sadness and passive acceptance.

In being questioned on this scene, the individual found it hard to say what her thoughts were. She stated that there were very few words and that there were more feelings and noises instead. This indicates that the suicide decision made in this case could be preverbal, which also fits with the child being less than one year old.

If this is the case, then one knows that the decisions made in this scene, including the suicide decision, are going to be very resilient because they were made at such a young age before the child even had language. This implies that this individual will, to some extent, be potentially suicidal all her life. These very early decisions form the foundations of the personality and thus are harder to alter through counseling compared to decisions made at older ages. The impact of the decisions can be changed, but to expect them to be completely altered would be quite unusual and unrealistic. Thus, there will always be a suicide decision there to some extent.

Of course, a person less than one year old cannot recall such events as drawn here. For the purpose at hand, it does not matter if it actually happened or not. These drawings and descriptions are really just visual, cognitive and kinesthetic representations in the person's mind of the structure of her personality. This event describes part of her personality—for instance, in cognitive behavioral therapy terms, the thinking errors she has. It does not matter if the event even occurred as it is the visual, cognitive and kinesthetic representation the person currently holds in her mind that allows her to have consistent personality structures. This is what the person uses to actually have a personality.

I have always been surprised at how easily people will produce these early distressing scenes, as well as convinced of their authenticity. There is never a sense of people making up a story or telling a tale. Instead, they produce a drawing of what they believed happened to them, which can be quite elaborate and detailed. In addition, the feelings and early decisions that were made as a result of the event can also be quite easily articulated. This, of course, is good for the person trying to diagnose the presence of a suicide decision, which is one of the important tasks of the suicide risk assessor.

4. Reaction to the no-suicide statement as a means of assessing suicide risk

This was originally presented by Goulding and Goulding (1978). One sets up a situation in which the person is asked to make a statement and then he is assessed on his reaction to that request. The person is requested to say, "No matter what happens, I will not kill myself, accidentally or on purpose, for x amount of time". He is then asked to report his internal responses to making such a statement. This person is either making a no-suicide contract as part of his treatment or he is making the statement to assess how he would react if he was making such a contract. It should be noted that the purpose of the no-suicide contract here is diagnostic only and is not being used for treatment purposes. Some find it hard to make such a such a statement, whereas others find it not difficult at all.

After the statement has been made, three things are assessed:

1. Does the person make the statement or refuse?

2. What are the feelings he has when he makes the statement? (Relief, increased anxiety, anger, etc.).

3. If he makes the statement, does he qualify it in some way— for example, by changing the words or with incongruent body language.

CASE STUDY 9.11: *REFUSAL TO MAKE A NO-SUICIDE CONTRACT*

A 30-year-old male, who reports suicidal thoughts, states he has attempted suicide a few times in the past and indicates that at least some of the attempts were quite serious.

Counselor: Are you willing to make a no-suicide contract?

Client: No.

Counselor: Why is that?

Client: Well, it depends who I am making it with. If I am making it as a promise to you, then if I get angry at you, I know I might try and kill myself as a way of getting back at you.

Counselor: Actually, a no-suicide contract is not a promise to me but something that you make with yourself. It is an agreement that you have with yourself.

Client: I feel like it would lock me in too much. The word contract sounds like a legally binding sort of a word and I don't want to feel locked in like that.

This response is a sign that he may be at some risk of a suicide attempt in the future, but not necessarily imminently. This is suggested by his complete refusal to make such a contract and the feeling that it would lock him in. This implies that he does not want the option of suicide in the future taken away. However, people can refuse for other reasons besides being currently suicidal, and he may therefore not be at current risk.

Some refuse because the therapeutic relationship does not allow it, and Case study 9.11 may be an example of this. The client saw the counselor in a parental role or a position of authority. He recognizes this may, at a later time, result in him switching to a rebellious position and acting on suicidal urges, just as one does with the suicide decisions "I will show you even if it kills me" and "I will kill myself to hurt you". In this instance, the refusal was a positive move due to his awareness of the internal psychological processes occurring within his psyche. If he had agreed to "lock" himself in, that could have elevated the level of current suicide risk. For others, it is simply an act of defiance or rebellion in which the refusal is a way of fighting a perceived authority. Just as some people will miss appointments on purpose or refuse to comply with treatment such as taking medication, some will refuse to make the no-suicide statement; their refusal is based on the dynamics of the relationship, not because of their suicidality.

Some people refuse because they they view suicide as an escape hatch. For some the thought or fantasy of suicide can be a soothing experience because they see it as an escape from their current pain, and yet there is no way they will make a serious attempt. Case study 9.5 above is an example of this. The young girl developed a suicide fantasy and even created a small rhyme for herself that she used to sing when on her own: "I wish I was dead, I wish I was dead, I wish I was dead…" sung as a little melody. She was not suicidal but used the fantasy to soothe herself. Suicide as an escape hatch will be discussed in much more detail in Chapter 14 on the no-suicide contract.

Others may refuse because they want to fake bad. They know if they refuse to make a no-suicide contract, that increases the likelihood of them being hospitalized or subject to extra investigation. One needs to view the refusal in the context of any secondary gains there may be. The fewer secondary gains apparent, the greater the possibility of a suicide decision being present and an increase in the person's level of suicide risk.

Having said all this, a refusal can be a significant indicator that the person is currently at risk of a suicide attempt. To assist with this assessment, one looks at the feelings that go along with the statement, which is the second kind of assessment made about the statement. This aspect of this diagnostic procedure is to assess the person's emotional reactions to making the statement. The process is relatively easy. The person makes the statement and then is asked what he feels about saying it out aloud. One gets a variety of responses with some of the more common being:

- *A reaction of scare or fear.* This is usually not a good sign and can indicate the person who sees suicide as a solution. That individual sees suicide as a way out of his pain and making the contract results in that solution being removed.

- *A reaction of frustration.* Some people feel that by dying they can "show those others at last" or "Now they will really miss me". If this is the case, the contract maker may feel frustrated because his way of fighting back is thwarted.

- *A reaction of relief.* This may occur when a person feels driven to kill self. It's as though the person has a voice inside his head saying "You must kill yourself", and the individual needs permission not to do so. A no-suicide contract can be such a permission and the person will feel relief: "Now I don't have to do it".

- *A reaction of solidness.* This reaction is a sign of someone who does not want to kill self and occurs more so in the person who feels as if he is just going to fade away into oblivion. This is a kind of passive suicide. In these cases, the contract can give a solid grounding so that the tendency to just fade away is halted.

- *A reaction of derealization, depersonalization or some kind of dissociation.* If this form of disorientation occurs, this is not a good sign. The person may feel he is being asked to say something that is very unpalatable or fearsome. To cope with this, he dissociates, which can indicate that the option of suicide is important to him, or he senses it as a very real option and making the statement scares him. There is little or no emotional reaction. In such cases, the person may have made the statement in a parrot-like or mechanical fashion and it has no meaning for him. Alternatively, the option of suicide is not one he has and he is at no risk of suicide.

Those feelings that are unpleasant reactions, such as fear, frustration or some kind of dissociation, indicate that the act of suicide has some meaning for the person and thus increases the likelihood of a suicide decision being present. When there are more "positive" feelings, such as relief or solidness, suicide may also be a option for him, but the contracting process provides a sense of "I can get out of this". Such a person can be at either short- or longer-term risk, but he is demonstrating he is ready for some treatment and does want to reduce his suicidality and change his suicide decision. Little or no reaction is usually the best sign and shows that the suicide decision has not been made by the person in his early life and hence he is at little risk of acting in a suicidal fashion. No reaction can also happen if the statement has been said in a mechanical fashion. If this is the case, one needs to investigate why the person stated it mechanically. This can indicate some level of suicidality as the person may have tried to avoid the no-suicide contract by intellectualizing or distancing himself from it by being robotic in his statements.

The third aspect of the assessment is to look for any qualifications. If the person agrees to make the statement, he can do a wide range of things to qualify it. Body language becomes important as a way of qualifying the verbal statement. Most often this is done without the person being aware of it, which makes the outside observer useful. He can observe the statement maker and pick up any cons or incongruities being made. These are described below.

1. Behavioral incongruities occur when the person's behavior is incongruous with what he is saying. For example, while making the statement, the individual may be shaking his head as though his body language is saying no. I have seen people cross their fingers while making such a statement, just as children do when making a promise they will not keep. One is looking for any body language that takes away from the potency of the verbalized words. Other examples may be looking down at the floor, closing one's eyes, saying the words very softly, speaking while standing on one's toes and so on. The list is endless. As an observer, it is necessary to ask oneself the question: "Does the body language appear to support what is being said, or does it make the words fragile?" At times it is even advantageous to ask the individual: "If your body language had a mouth now, or could speak, what would

it say?" The answer wanted is one where the body language confirms the verbal language. The less it does, the greater the likelihood of a suicide decision being present.

2. In the statement the person is asked to nominate a time-span during which he will not take his own life. The time chosen can indicate incongruities. Some people will make it a very long time such as 50 years. The goal of the exercise is to choose a relatively brief period of time that is realistic for the person and this may indicate a qualification. Some will say "I will live until I am 99 years old". Why 99 and not 100 years old? A score of 99 in sport is a score that just falls short. This may be another potential indicator of undermining the contract.

Other examples include:

- "The contract I am making is for the rest of my life." It is easy for the observer to assume that the "rest of my life" means many years. However, that is not what the words say and it may mean a very short time. Further clarity is needed on exactly how many weeks this person intends to keep himself alive.

- "The contract is until April 1st." In Australia, this is also known as April Fools' Day, when it is customary to play practical jokes and tricks on each other. This is a risky connotation to have associated with a no-suicide contract. This also highlights the extra care that must be taken when someone from a different culture is making such a contract. Dates such as this and the behavioral incongruities can have different meanings from one's own culture.

- "The contract is until Good Friday." Good Friday is the day Jesus died. For a religious person in particular, this may represent an incongruity.

These examples demonstrate that the observer needs to be vigilant as to what is actually being said. It is easy to make the many assumptions about what is being said as we do in normal everyday conversation. The key point is to listen to what is actually being said by the contract maker, and not just hear what we expect to hear.

3. When making such a contract, some people get technical and start looking for the fine print. Examples may be:

- "Does harming self include having drinks at home after work?"

- "What about real accidents? You can't take them into account."

- "No one can ever predict what is going to happen to himself during the time period contracted for."

Making no-suicide contracts with clients who do this is often quite difficult. If someone is getting technical as indicated, it is necessary not to get caught in all the fine print because one can always find a loophole if motivated to. The aim is to address the motivation for making the contract and look at why he is making it and who benefits from it. If the person remains with technicalities, that indicates an unwillingness to make the statement and indicates the possibility of a suicide decision and increased suicide risk.

4. Sometimes the contract can even be renamed by the contractor. A recent example was: "I sometimes feel quite shaky, and I want to make one of those contracts, that are called...um...a suicide contract." In this instance, the person had renamed the contract from a "no-suicide contract" to a "suicide contract"—clearly an incongruity.

5. Sometimes people make statements about who they are making the contract for. Examples can be:

- "I want to make a no-suicide contract so the children wouldn't have to be in the terrible position of having a mother who killed herself."

- "My wife is very worried that I am going to kill myself so I want to make a no-suicide contract."

Ultimately, one is looking for the individual who wants to live for himself. To be living for someone else, something else or some ideology is a much less safe position to be in. Should the person, thing or ideology disappear or alter, then the individual has a problem. The more the contractor views the contract as being for himself, the more solid it is, and thus the level of suicide risk could be seen to decrease.

There are many ways people can qualify the no-suicide contract statement to make what they are saying incongruent with how they are saying it. The more incongruent, the greater the likelihood of a suicide decision being present, and thus the longer-term risk is increased.

Conclusion

This chapter has considered four qualitative measures of assessing suicide risk. These complement the quantitative measures outlined in the previous chapter. Obviously, by using both, one gets a more comprehensive suicide risk assessment of the person. In addition, the qualitative measures set out to identify the person who has made the suicide decision early in life; if he has, then his long-term suicide risk level is increased. Unfortunately, suicide risk assessment is an inexact science, but the methods outlined above can provide some good signs as to the suicidality of the person.

Part 3

Supporting the Suicidal Individual

The Suicide Secret and the Deliberate Suicide Risk

Disclosing the suicide secret

The literature on suicide often reports that the majority of people who make a suicide attempt have talked about it beforehand. Most suicidal people have told someone of their suicidal thoughts before they make an attempt.

People reassure themselves with the idea that the majority of people who make a serious suicide attempt will tell someone about it prior to the attempt. Obviously, this is a positive thing, and people will tend to think this means we can prevent many suicide attempts because they will disclose the suicidal urges and thus can be helped. Once told, they can then be saved; that is the hope of many. We hope everyone tells of their suicide secret, but unfortunately many do not.

It is true that the majority do make some kind of statement to someone about their intent to harm self prior to the act. The research indicates that 70–80 percent do disclose to someone prior to acting on suicidal thoughts (Clark and Horton-Deutsch 1992; Hayes 1995). Although these seem reassuring figures, they also show that 20–30 percent do not disclose. About one in four people who are seriously suicidal do not let anyone know about their intention to kill self. I think one could argue that 25 percent, or one in four people, is quite a significant number.

Unfortunately, these people are not well considered; in fact, they are not considered at all. In discussing how to recognize suicide risk, Miller *et al.* (2005) make the statement:

> Research suggests that 80% of those who complete suicide communicate through their behavior, thoughts and feelings their intent to kill themselves to someone prior to the suicidal act. One of the difficulties is that we may not be fully aware of what the signs mean or

they may be very subtle so we do not recognize them easily. (p.15)

The writers then go on to list the warning signs for the suicidal person. This is a very common approach that one finds in the literature, but there is just one problem. What about the other 20 percent who do not tell or show signs? Miller *et al.* (2005) ignore them, which is common in the literature. They simply do not get mentioned again. We are talking about 25 percent of suicidal people, or one in four, who do not mention their suicidal thoughts. Perhaps if the figure was only 2 percent, then while not being particularly humane, one could perhaps rationalize simply forgetting about them, but the group is 25 percent, which is a significant number.

Most prisons around the world have a system for managing suicidal inmates called the At-Risk Management System (ARMS). It is a very widely used system that operates by first identifying the at-risk inmate and then categorizing him as either high, medium or low risk. Once done, the appropriate action is taken, depending on the level of risk identified. However, the whole system rests on the same assumption as described above: that the inmate will disclose his suicide secret in some way. As we know, about 75 percent will, which also means 25 percent won't. Those 25 percent are simply disregarded and ignored. They are not mentioned again in the ARMS approach.

When I worked in the prison system, I used to look out my window at the units where the inmates were held, all 750 of them, and I knew there were some out there who were currently feeling suicidal and not saying anything to anyone. They were keeping their suicidal thoughts and urges a secret. In my time working in the prison system, no inmate completed a suicide, but three went very close to killing themselves. They were quite lucky they did not die. Two of those inmates were not known to myself as the coordinator of ARMS or anyone else involved with ARMS in the prison. Two of the three had not disclosed their suicide secret to anyone before making a very serious suicide attempt.

I was caught in a corner because the ARMS approach simply ignored the inmates who kept their suicidal thoughts a secret. I knew they were out there in the prison population because, as Dalton (1999) notes, the suicide rate in prisons is at about ten times greater than in the general population. As a result, I set out to see if I could identify any prisoners with suicidal intentions and I found about half a dozen. I saw many inmates daily for a whole variety of reasons unrelated to any suicidal thoughts. In talking with them, I would eventually start to allude to suicidal thoughts. Some would have a moment of suspiciousness or look furtively around. They would give some kind of behavioral sign that I had touched on something. With these men, the issue of suicide was talked around, just alluded to or only ever implied. Some of them even stated to me they knew the right words to say and not to say so that they would never go on suicide watch. I never thought any were at high risk. What I did do was have regular contact with them and develop a working relationship with them in which we discussed, for example, how they were getting on. In my view, this could have contributed significantly to their psychological well-being. I initiated contact with them and maintained it over time so that they could talk about what was going on inside them. Thus their sense of isolation would have been significantly lessened and any suicidal urges would have been less likely to arise. However, we never discussed suicide in an open and frank way because the system did not allow that to happen.

Why did the suicide watch system in prison ignore them? These inmates were forced into a position where they could not disclose their suicide secret. They knew if they said to me or anyone else that they were feeling suicidal, then they would have been put in the ARMS program and placed on suicide watch to some degree. So they did not disclose because they did not want all the fuss and attention. If they are being watched closely, it makes it harder for them to prepare for a suicide attempt.

The current legislation in Australia and most other western societies makes it legally incumbent on a counselor to break confidentiality and inform the relevant authorities if they believe a client is in significant danger of harming self. This is deemed their duty of care and they are legally bound to break confidentiality in such instances. It is the same in a prison. If a prisoner mentions suicidal thoughts, the person being told is duty-bound to take some action, whether the inmate wants it or not. The law forces these people into a position where they have to keep the suicide secret. Thus they are worse off and more likely to make an attempt due to a sense of isolation. The law has the opposite effect for these individuals; it puts them in more danger, not less.

As noted before, this is a group of people that constitutes 25 percent of suicidal individuals—a group which is sizable enough to warrant more realistic treatment legislatively and not simply be forgotten about. In my view, there needs to be legislation that allows me to identify such non-communicative suicidal people. Once identified, such legislation would specifically forbid me to break confidentiality if they start to talk about suicidal thoughts. Thus they would be more likely to talk with me about their suicidal urges, which means they are less likely to act on them.

CASE STUDY 10.1: *KEEPING THE SUICIDE SECRET*

A 29-year-old male suffered severe social phobia most of his life. When first seen, he was quite worried about his future because of the social phobia and the enormous restrictions that placed on his everyday life. He had a sense of hopelessness about his life then and for the future. He reported no suicidal thoughts and never even alluded to the topic. As we developed more rapport, this sense of no hope changed somewhat as he became more positive about the future. One would expect such a thing to happen as his sense of isolation reduced due to our ongoing contact.

At no point did he mention any suicidal thoughts. After about a month, I again raised the topic, and he smiled and nodded in the affirmative. Then he said, "I can't really say that." I asked if that was because he would then be watched more closely and he indicated that it was. In my view, he clearly understated his suicidal urges, and I felt that if he became more focussed on a suicide attempt, he would give even less indication of any suicidal intent. This was because the law forced him into such a position. At that point I could have placed him on suicide watch, but how long do you keep a person on suicide watch when they are saying they are feeling fine, not feeling depressed and having no suicidal thoughts?

When I was dealing with this man, he had been in trouble with the law and was being assessed for possible deportation to the US. This held a great many fears for him as he had not been in the US since he was a young child. He had never returned and knew of only two cousins there whom he had never met. In essence, he knew no one in the US and was a man with a severe social phobia. If the immigration authorities decided to deport him, then he would be at a very high risk of suicide, and it is likely, even highly likely, that he would never make any mention of his suicidal thoughts to anyone.

The deliberate suicide risk

Obviously, those who do not disclose the suicide secret are not thinking suicidal thoughts for any secondary gain. These are the people who are serious about completing a suicide attempt. In addition to non-disclosure, there are other features that indicate the type of person known as the deliberate suicide risk (DSR). This is the highest risk group of all for a completed suicide.

To kill oneself is not an easy thing to do as the body has many back-up systems to stop the person dying. If someone is going to have a concerted effort at killing self, he is going to have to do some planning and preparation. Below are detailed some personality features a person needs to have to make a very deliberate attempt at suicide.

1. The DSR person will tend to stay unnoticed and quiet, at least about his suicidal urges. If someone wants to complete a suicide, it is best to have those around not watching out for the signs of suicide preparation. Thus we have the first common characteristics of a DSR person. He may be quiet, stay in the background and will not be demonstrative. He tends to do little self-disclosure. When this person suicides, those around him will tend to be shocked and surprised because they did not even suspect something was awry. This person will tend to keep the suicide secret completely or at least prior to a serious suicide attempt.

2. As stated before, to kill oneself is not an easy thing to do. Thus we have the second characteristic of the person who is going to make a significant attempt to kill self: he is capable of effective planning. He must have the ability to think about how he would suicide, to plan how to obtain the necessary items and arrange the necessary time and place so he is not discovered mid-attempt. This means someone who is brain-damaged, of low intelligence, actively psychotic, has poor planning ability, tends to be disorganized or, for whatever reason, has poor thinking ability does not have the intellectual

capability to plan a DSR suicide. The more effective he is at making a plan and keeping to it, the more likely he is to complete a suicide attempt.

3. To complete a suicide, one has be somewhat determined, patient and deliberate. Not only is it a task to kill self; the person also has to make sure he is not found during the attempt. This is less likely to happen if the person is capable of patience and determination to find the right place and time. Indeed, some who suicide want to be found by a particular person in a particular way. In this case, a person not only has to determine his own actions but also has to coordinate that with the movements of others.

4. When asked, the DSR person will tend to understate matters. As mentioned before, if someone is contemplating a serious suicide attempt, he is unlikely to give too much away which would bring him to the attention of others and increase the likelihood of the plans being disrupted. He may be conservative in his statements about self generally. For instance, he may report having had a bit of trouble sleeping and, when asked for the actual details, reports he has been sleeping only two hours per night for the last two weeks. He may report collecting some medication, when in fact he has stockpiled a large quantity. He may also tend to be a bit self-effacing.

5. The DSR person will almost always have made the suicide decision in childhood. As indicated above, such a person approaches the task of making a suicide attempt in a deliberate and well-planned way. This means he has considered the idea of killing self for some time and concluded that suicide is a viable solution to his problems. This is what the suicide decision is. It is a decision made in childhood in which the person decides that, should certain circumstances arise, suicide is a valid solution to the problems at hand. If someone has made that decision, then it is possible for him to seek that solution over an extended period of time with comprehensive planning.

The suicide secret is a central part of the DSR person. The more a person has of these five qualities, the more he will be able to make a very serious attempt at suicide. In summary, one makes an assessment of how the person completes tasks in his life—whether that is building a backyard barbecue, being president of the local tennis club, having a dinner party or repairing a child's push-bike. Does he go about it in a well-planned, systematic manner with little complaint or fuss so that it is successfully and efficiently completed? If he does, then should he give himself the task of completing a suicide attempt, he is likely to go about that task in the same way. Combine this type of person with one who keeps the suicide secret and this is a person at a very high risk of completing a suicide.

CASE STUDY 10.2: *NO WARNING SIGNS*

A 40-year-old man was successful in his catering business for many years. He was devoted to his job and in many respects was a mentor and emotional support to many of his staff over the years, helping them significantly in their struggles with life. As a result, he built up a small army of dedicated employees who gave much to their job and boss. He ran his business well, in an effective and efficient manner, and as a result it was financially successful for many years.

In the months prior to his suicide, he had lost some money in an endeavor to expand his business. The financial losses, although reasonably large, were by no means dire, and he could have easily traded out of the difficulties in a year or two. He had confided these concerns to a close friend but gave no indication of any suicidal feelings or planning. All he mentioned was his distress about the financial problems. A short while later his wife found he had hanged himself from the knob of the bedroom door. All his family, friends and many employees were completely shocked by his suicide.

Conclusion

When a DSR person or someone who keeps the suicide secret completes a suicide, the bereaved loved ones often say how shocked and surprised they are. The DSR individual gave little or no indication that he was even feeling suicidal in the first place, let alone planning an attempt. The bereaved will also tend to do some soul-searching and question themselves about how attentive or observant they were;

they will chastise themselves for not recognizing the signs that, upon reflection, they think were given.

The person who keeps the suicide secret does not give out the usual signs, so those left behind have not missed anything or been negligent in their care of the other. As Case study 10.2 shows, the suicidal person may have mentioned that he was not feeling good or had been a bit depressed of late, but these signs will be in the "normal" range that everyone says at some point in life. These factors do, however, give some retrospective insight into the personality of the DSR individual at the time of their death, which can provide some solace to the bereaved loved ones. They did not miss anything because the person deliberately set out to give no pre-suicide warning signs.

This whole area is a contentious one. Most people want to do something to help the person who is feeling suicidal. Most want to assist the person to stay alive. In that desire, as a society, we have rushed in and made laws that compel people to break confidentiality in these circumstances. Undoubtedly, this would have helped in some cases, but it also forces many—possibly one in four—suicidal people not to talk about their inner thoughts and feelings. This forces their sense of isolation to increase significantly. This is most undesirable as the one thing such individuals need is an opportunity to express their inner thoughts and turmoil and to feel a sense of support and human contact. These laws and professional practice guidelines put the highest risk groups at even greater risk of a completed suicide.

Chapter 11

Pseudo-Suicide, Suicide and Teenage Suicide

People make suicidal statements or gestures for many different reasons. As with all human behavior, there is often a myriad of motivations which is particularly so when one distinguishes between the suicidal and the pseudo-suicidal. This chapter endeavors to highlight some of these alternate motivations, leaving one in a better position to manage and treat such people. In addition, there is also a distinction between the adult suicidal person and the teenage suicidal individual. The younger suicidal individual is a special case again because his ability to think and reason is not yet fully formed and thus he can make suicidal gestures for another set of motives.

The following groups of people are considered:

- non suicidal
- suicidal

  suicide decision

  command hallucinations

  impulsive acts

- pseudo-suicidal
- teenage suicide.

The non-suicidal

First is that group of people who are not suicidal. They have never made the suicide decision and do not see that killing self a valid option to solve problems. They have no significant suicidal thoughts and they do not display suicidal behaviors.

The suicidal
The suicide decision

The suicidal group includes those who do make suicidal statements and gestures. There are a number of reasons why they may do so. First, there are those who are seen as being truly suicidal in the psychological sense of the word. They have made the suicide decision or "don't exist" decision in early life. As a consequence, when certain circumstances arise, they will start to feel the urge to kill self. They see self as confronted with difficult problems and begin to view suicide as the only realistic solution to such difficulties.

About 75 percent of this group quite often end up in some form of counseling or come to the attention of some kind of support service. For the rest who keep the suicide secret, obviously they do not come to the attention of any support service. Many in this overall group will at some point in life have strong suicidal urges, and some may even make a concerted effort to end their life by their own hand. It is primarily this group of adults who will complete a suicide attempt or are at the most risk of doing so.

Command hallucinations

Others who display suicidal behavior do so due to command hallucinations. These people are not suicidal in the psychological sense of the word as they may not have made the suicide decision. They attempt suicide because they are psychotic, most often with schizophrenia or bipolar psychosis. They do not suicide in order to solve some intolerable problem; instead they suicide because they are being commanded to do so by some kind of hallucination—for example, to be with God or because they are evil. The goal is not to solve a problem but to achieve some kind of status. The management of these individuals revolves around managing the psychosis and the hallucinations.

Impulsive acts

Those who are prone to impulsive acts and explosive behavior can also make suicidal gestures and some will complete a suicide attempt. In the DSM-IV, the American Psychiatric Association (1994) refers to a condition know as the Intermittent Explosive Disorder. This is where a person fails to resist aggressive impulses and this results in some kind of assault on others or property. This can also extend to assaults on self and thus the potential for a completed suicide.

CASE STUDY 11.1: THE IMPULSIVE SUICIDAL

A 25-year-old man with a diagnosis of borderline personality is brought to me for counseling after a serious suicide attempt. He has a long history of very unstable and volatile relationships with female partners. On this particular day, he was speaking with his girlfriend on a public telephone in the city which meant that there were quite a few people around. During the call she stated that she was ending the relationship and hung up on him. He became enraged at what he perceived as abandonment by yet another woman in his life, later stating that he was consumed with anger.

He was an avid fisherman and had his fishing tackle with him. After the call ended, he pulled his fishing knife out of his bag and stabbed himself two or three times in the neck, severing a major artery in the process. He then punched and broke a small pane of glass in a shop window which resulted in non-lethal cuts to his hand and forearm. He then sat down because he was losing a large amount of blood from his neck wound. All this happened in the space of about 45 seconds.

By this time, he was noticed by a number of people around him who came to see what was going on. He was deteriorating quickly due to the massive blood loss. By pure chance, someone who came to help him knew how to stem the flow of blood from his neck and he survived. If no one had helped, it is very likely he would have died in quite a short space of time.

This man became very angry very quickly and did not have the Adult or Parent ego states available to control the Child ego state rage. Thus he exploded. One never knows how that explosion is going to be expressed. It can go in any direction—against others, property or self. It may, to a large degree, simply depend on who or what is within reach at the time of the explosion. These explosions are quite similar in quality to a small child's temper tantrum.

As reported in the DSM-IV, this is most common in those with the antisocial or borderline personalities, in some psychoses, during manic episodes and in some attention deficit disorders. Often the person can be quite remorseful and embarrassed afterwards.

This happens when the Adult and Parent ego states again become functional and the Child rage dissipates. In Case study 11.1 above, the assault on self was not severe enough to result in a completed suicide. Or, more correctly, it was just lucky that there were others around to help. If there had not been, the suicide attempt could have easily been completed. In addition, it was fortunate that the partner had told him she was ending the relationship over the phone; if she had told him face to face, she could have also been assaulted as well. In cases such as this the suicidal acts are largely an anger management problem.

Pseudo-suicidal

The pseudo-suicidal person is someone who makes suicidal statements, displays suicidal behaviors but is not suicidal. He does not have a "don't exist" decision and his goal is not to kill self. He displays suicidal behaviors and makes suicidal statements but his motive is not to kill self. Instead, he has some other motive. If he does die by his own hand, it is an accident because the suicide attempt was never meant to be completed.

CASE STUDY 11.2: THE PSEUDO-SUICIDAL

Some time ago I was asked to write a report for the coroner about the death of a delightful 23-year-old woman who had been a client of mine some years earlier. In my view, she was a "suicide attempter" or pseudo-suicidal. Her most common pattern was to take medication and then contact her boyfriend who would then come and save her. On this occasion, she did that by sending him an email that she knew he was very likely to get. There was a one-in-a-hundred chance that he would not get it. As it turned out, he never got the email and she died from the overdose.

This woman's goal was never to die by her own hand. She displayed suicidal behavior with the aim of getting others to behave and react in a certain way. This is not commonly said these days because it is considered politically incorrect. Some will view my statements as being unfair and unduly harsh if I use words such as "manipulative" or "attention seeker". There is no doubt that some do make suicidal gestures who are not trying to kill self. In some cases, one only has to look at the method used to see that it is very unlikely to prove fatal. I have had people tell me directly that they have suicidal thoughts for some kind of secondary gain. To try and deny this, or to try and somehow see them in a different light, in the final analysis does these people a disservice. If everyone pretends that their motive is something that it is not, then the real problem is never going to be acknowledged, let alone addressed.

However, there is a view by some in the community that the pseudo-suicidal are simply troublemakers who waste precious healthcare resources. They are viewed with some disdain as attention seekers or manipulators. This view is what needs to be addressed, rather than trying to redefine the pseudo-suicidal as something they are not. These people are no different to any others, and they are doing the best they can with the psychological resources they have available to them at the time. The person who has ongoing depression is doing the best he can day after day with what he has. The individual who believes the only way he can get the feeling of being loved is by pretending to suicide is also doing the best he can with the emotional resources he has at that time.

Indeed, a disparaging view of these individuals can be unwise because it leads some to ignore them or think they will never go through with it. The difficulty with the pseudo-suicidal is that sometimes the act, which is not designed to kill, goes wrong and does kill, as is shown in Case study 11.2. The goal here is to ascertain the motive for the suicidal behavior. Such a motive can be an unsophisticated cry for help, manipulation or attention seeking, or it can be the dramatic and acting-out type of behavior one finds in the hysteric and borderline personalities.

Once the motive is ascertained, the individual gains awareness of it. The goal then is for the individual to use some means other than suicidal gestures to get what they want (such as attention). Those who attempt suicide as a cry for help can learn that there are other ways to ask for help without having to make suicidal gestures. If one denies the existence of such ulterior motives, one can never get to the point of being able to solve the underlying motive for the behavior.

At times one can misdiagnose a person as being pseudo-suicidal behavior when he is in fact suicidal. Some people will make a number of repeated attempts, with none of them being completed. This can result in some concluding that the person is not trying to kill self; if he was, he would have completed an attempt. For the non-suicidal, it is hard to understand the psyche of such a person at the point of making a suicide attempt. Most look at how they complete tasks in their life, even difficult tasks, and expect it to be the same. However, setting out to kill self is not the same as fixing a motor car or baking a complicated recipe for a dinner party.

Even though these are all tasks where a number of things have to be done in the correct order and in a planned way, the end results are obviously quite different, and this will affect the way someone goes about completing and executing the plan for a "successful" outcome. As will be discussed in a later chapter on suicidal ambivalence, all suicidal people are ambivalent. Part of them wants to die and part does not. Thus all suicide attempts are, to some degree, "half-hearted", and this will be reflected in the outcome of some attempts. Because the result of suicide planning is death, rather than a nice-tasting cake, many use alcohol to give them the extra courage they need to go through with the attempt. Many are highly emotional and regressed at the time, and thus their Adult ego states are poorly functioning during the execution of the plan.

As a consequence of these factors, many a suicide attempt is not completed. This does not mean that someone is doing such things in order to get sympathy or because he is not serious and does not really want to die. It does not mean he could be classed as pseudo-suicidal. Instead, he may be very serious about ending his life, but completing the task of taking one's own life is an extremely onerous and emotionally difficult thing to do.

Teenage suicide

If you ask a teenager what will happen if they suicided, most would tell you accurately from their Adult ego state that they would die and their life would cease. However, they are different to adults because their understanding of suicide in their Adult ego state is more fragile than that of the fully grown adult. This highlights the idea of intellectual understanding versus knowing and believing.

For instance, consider superstitions. Most fully grown adults know intellectually that if you walk under a ladder, it does not give you bad luck, but many will avoid doing such a thing. Touching wood, we know in our Adult ego states, does not bring us luck, but many will do it just in case. Many who go to casinos know intellectually they will lose their money but still believe that somehow they will be special and win. People with obsessive compulsive disorder know intellectually that washing their hands 20 times will not make them any cleaner than if they wash them just once, but they will still go ahead and do it anyway. See Figure 11.1.

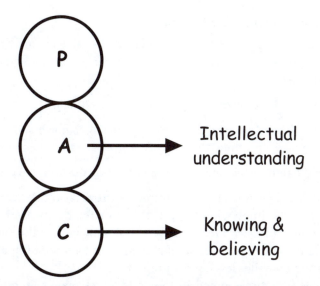

Intellectual
understanding

Knowing &
believing

**Figure 11.1 The dynamics of intellectual understanding
as different from knowing and believing**

All fully developed adults have circumstances in which their Adult ego state intellectual understanding is different from what they believe and know to be true in their Child ego state. If it relates to touching wood or avoiding ladders, it matters very little. However, it can also relate to other matters such as suicide and death. As mentioned before, if you ask a 15-year-old what happens if someone suicides, he would be able to tell you the facts accurately. He would say that the person would die and be buried and that those left behind would feel great grief. However, what he actually knows and believes in his Child ego state may be quite different. He may have all sorts of other beliefs about not really being dead, being able to sit up and still watch his own funeral and so on. Many teenagers are quite egocentric and consider themselves special and the exception to the rule. Many believe that if they did suicide, somehow they would be different to others, or they simply do not think the process through.

Although this can happen with adults, it is more pronounced with teenagers because their Adult ego states are less robust and they have much less life experience. For instance, many have never experienced first-hand the death of a close loved one, whereas most adults have and their understanding of death is therefore more experienced.

Magical thinking about death

I recently spoke with a five-year-old boy who talked about his seven-year-old sister who had died a year earlier. These are some of his comments:

- "When I make my lego, Sarah can see them."
- "When I grow up I am going to be an engineer so I can make a machine that can bring her back from heaven."
- "Sarah comes and visits me in my dreams from heaven."

These are not uncommon comments from a young child, and they give the impression that, in the boy's mind, his older sister is somehow still alive. He certainly is not viewing her the same way an adult would view a deceased person—with a sense of finality. The literature on child development reports the same.

It is sometimes noted in the child development literature that children can develop a death phobia. At about the age of eight years, a child can develop what is sometimes called "eight-year anxiety", which is a pronounced fear of death. As Jean Piaget has shown, prior to age eight, the child is egocentric with magical thinking that is prelogical (Piaget and Inhelder 1969). As a result, up to the age of seven, children often think that death is reversible and that the dead can still see, hear and feel. At about age eight, the child's thinking allows him to understand that death is not reversible and thus he can hit that stage of "eight-year anxiety" when he realizes what is going to happen one day when he dies and when his parents die. In essence, the child has an "existential crisis" and has to come to terms with his own mortality (Mussen, Conger and Kagan 1974).

I have previously mentioned the idea of regression. The psychological process of regression involves a person reverting to an earlier state or mode of functioning. The person stops thinking, feeling and behaving like an adult and begins to think, feel and behave in a more childlike way. This will tend to happen when the person is under considerable stress or when he is highly emotional. In transactional analysis terms, he moves from his grown-up Adult and Parent ego states into the Child ego state part of self. This is supported by research in neuropsychology as cited by Johnston (2009). When people are placed under stress, they are less able to access the prefrontal cortex of the brain which is associated with the more developed functions such as problem solving, decision making and stress management (the Adult ego state). Instead, people tend to access the more primitive part of the brain in the amygdala (the Child ego state).

Teenagers are more prone to regression compared to adults because their Parent and Adult ego states are still somewhat immature and fragile. When they regress, they start to be more influenced by their Child ego state magical thinking about death in a prelogical way. Thus a teenager can decide on suicide and not fully comprehend the consequences of such an act. The finality of death may not be fully comprehended, which makes the decision to suicide easier. Of course, there are many other reasons why teenagers are a higher risk group: their bodies are going through major changes, they are in no-man's-land between childhood and adulthood, they are for the first time considering relationships with the opposite sex, the peer group all of a sudden assumes much more importance than it ever has before and so on. However, I highlight their special propensity to regress because there have been others who have noticed this magical Child ego state thinking about death in the suicidal.

First, Harry Boyd (1972) makes the statement: "My impression is that the suicidal patient does not, on the Child level, really conceive of his death as terminal" (p.87). In addition, Little (2009) talks about the "presuicide fantasy": "suicidal people have transformation fantasies and are prone to magical thinking, like children and psychotics" (p.220). Campbell (1999) also describes fantasies that the suicidal can have about death. He notes the suicidal person expects and understands that his body will die (Adult ego state) but the person can imagine there is another part of himself that can continue to live in a conscious body-less state that is unaffected by the physical death of the body (Child ego state).

These writers are talking about suicide in the general population, including fully grown adults. If adults can regress in these ways so that their Child ego state magical thinking plays a significant role in their presuicidal decisions, then a teenager has more propensity to do so because his Adult ego state is less resilient and more immature. As the stress and emotions increase, the Adult ego state will more easily collapse under the pressure and the Child ego state will assume more influence in the personality. Teenagers as a group tend to be egocentric and narcissistic, and feel they are special and omnipotent and that the general rules do not apply to them. Combine this with the magical presuicidal fantasies and one can end up with quite unpredictable suicidal behavior. This makes teenage suicide a difficult event to predict and assess. Teenagers will tend to act in less predictable ways compared to adults. In addition, if the teenager has made the suicide decision, then the risk is even further heightened. One needs to seek out and assess any presuicide fantasies.

One teenager's statement about suicide

The following comes from a magazine interview with "Sammy", a 16-year-old Australian boy, who talks about his suicide attempts. I have placed in italics the parts I wish to highlight.

> Sammy: I was having a lot of trouble at school. There were groups of popular kids and then there were the "geeks". Some of my so called friends said bad things about me and I got pushed out of the group. I felt… um…real bad about this. At home my mom and dad were fighting. They would shout loudly at night when we were in bed. It made me depressed and sometimes I would cry.

> Interviewer: So what did you do…and then you tried?

> Sammy: I just started feeling badder and badder. It would keep going around in my mind each day and it was like things were bad at school and things were bad at home. I felt like a complete jerk and a failure. Yes a big fat failure. And then it just went through my head, *I might as well go do it*. I started thinking about it a lot.

> Interviewer: What happened then?

Sammy: I was just thinking about *it*.

Interviewer: So you tried the suicide then?

Sammy: A few times I tried *it*.

Interviewer: Do you think that you kind of did not really want to do it? Because you tried a few times and did not succeed may have meant you didn't want to?

Sammy: I think I knew I did not want to *leave*. I thought that on the surface I did but I kind of knew I didn't. I just felt so bad like a loser...a complete loser but *I'd never really realized the significance of what I was doing. I just didn't see it as a serious thing.*

Sammy never actually uses the words "suicide", "death" or "dead". Instead, he talks about going and doing *it*, or he talks about *leaving*. This may indicate a presuicide fantasy in which suicide does not result in a complete death but is viewed as leaving one place to go to another. In interviewing Sammy, one would certainly want to follow up this line of questioning. This is supported by his final comment which seems to show the misunderstanding he has of what he was attempting to do. He reports that he did not realize the significance of what he was doing and thus did not see it as a serious thing. Obviously, killing self is a very serious thing; indeed, it is hard to think of anything more serious. Thus we have a good example of how a teenager can think about suicide and how faulty the thinking can be because the Adult ego state is immature, which allows the Child ego state fantasy to become much more influential in the decision-making process.

On a side note, I stated above when discussing the pseudo-suicidal how some conclude that when a suicide attempt is not completed, that means the person was not serious about killing self. This is demonstrated when the interviewer asks "Do you think that you kind of did not really want to do it? Because you tried a few times and did not succeed may have meant you didn't want to?" As I noted, that may not be the reason because all suicidal people are ambivalent to some degree. Just because a suicide attempt is not completed does not mean the person is pseudo-suicidal. Sammy was probably very serious about it but did not realize the significance of what he was doing.

Another teenager's view of suicide

My personal experience highlights qualities similar to those shown by Sammy in his magazine interview. I made two attempts on my own life when I was about 17 and 18 years old.

In my final year at high school, I used to carry around my creative writing expression book that I had for my English Literature class. I used to love writing, even when I was young. Every week we would be given a creative writing exercise to do. I always kept the writing book with me and would write bits and pieces when I felt it was right. Each exercise was then marked by the teacher and, as I recall, I did quite well. My written expression book in one way was one of my best friends. It was a cathartic journal for me.

One week I did the creative writing task by writing a suicide note. I wrote it just before my first suicide attempt. Obviously, I survived the attempt and then I handed it in for marking by the teacher. I remember her calling me in to see her and said that she refused to mark it. I asked her why and she said it was too personal. I recall being quite surprised at her refusal to mark it. In retrospect, I am surprised that I was surprised.

In one way the suicide attempt had little meaning for me. It was something that I just did, and if I died, I died, and if I didn't, I didn't. In this way, I was similar to Sammy when he mentioned not realizing the seriousness of what he was doing. This is why I was surprised at the teacher's refusal to mark it. I saw the suicide note merely as this week's creative writing exercise and not as a suicide note in the way that a fully grown adult might write one. In my mind, it lacked the serious meaning and implications that the teacher saw in it.

However, as with Sammy, the suicide attempt was done for a reason. The suicide was used as a solution to a problem. At times during that part of my life I felt very, very bad. I felt shut down and robot-like, and I identified with the actor Johnny Depp who played Edward Scissorhands in the movie of that name—in particular, the detachment that he demonstrates in the movie character, which, in technical terms, would be a form of dissociation. Also at the time of the first attempt I thought I had been dumped by my then girlfriend, which I subsequently found out was not the case. However, like Sammy, I felt very low and detached, and thus I chose suicide as a solution to these painful feelings.

I endeavored to gas myself, but the cylinder of gas ran out halfway through when I had lost consciousness. If it had not, then it is quite likely I would have died, and thus it could be viewed as a serious attempt. I was feeling very bad and I saw suicide as a solution. However, that is where my thinking stopped. I knew suicide would stop the pain, but I never actually thought that I would be dead and what that meant. I simply did not think it through. This demonstrates my immature Adult ego state thinking and the illogical thinking of the Child ego state which at that time dominated in the personality, as it did for Sammy.

Since entering adulthood, I have never been suicidal. It is something that I have never thought about in any serious way, and I have certainly never planned such a thing. When I have felt very bad in adulthood, such as with the death of my first-born child, I never even thought about suicide. I have never seen it as a solution to a problem since my late teenage years, meaning one can conclude that I did not make the suicide decision in early childhood. However, I did make two suicide attempts in adolescence, demonstrating a teenager's ability to view suicide as a solution and make a serious suicide attempt without having made the suicide decision in childhood.

Conclusion

As with most human behavior, suicide is not a simple thing. Humans can display suicidal behavior for a variety of different reasons and one single act of suicide can have a number of motives behind it. This chapter has discussed four different groups of people in relation to suicide in order to articulate some of the different motives and reasons behind such actions.

First are those who have no suicidal urges; the idea of suicide is something they never seriously contemplate. Second are those who do behave significantly in suicidal ways. These people make suicide attempts in which they could easily die. Third are those who are not suicidal but who will display suicidal behavior. Their goal is not to die but to achieve some form of secondary gain from publicizing their actions. Finally, we have the teenage suicides. They are identified as a special case because their understanding of death and suicide is particularly immature. This can result in suicide attempts in which the consequences of such actions are simply not fully understood.

Chapter 12

Suicidal Ambivalence

Introduction

One of the difficulties in working with suicide is you cannot see it. If the individual says he has suicidal thoughts or urges, you cannot see them. This can cause difficulty for some because the feelings and thoughts are not clearly defined or observable. This chapter provides a way to make the ambiguous more concrete. It provides a way of understanding suicidal urges and presents them in a diagrammatic form to give a visual representation of what the individual is feeling inside.

All suicidal individuals are ambivalent to some degree. They all have a set of contradictory thoughts and feelings inside. They all have internal dialogue which states "I do want to die" versus "I do not want to die". This is shown in Figure 12.1, in which the Free Child is that part of the personality in which the individual has a drive and urge to stay alive and not die. We all have this aspect to our personality. The suicidal individual also has a contradictory set of thoughts and feelings as is represented by the Adapted Child ego state. This aspect of the personality wants to die in some way or at least does not want to be alive.

If a person is 100 percent "I do want to die", then it won't be too long before he considers a suicide attempt. If a person is 100 percent "I do not want to die", then there would be no suicidal thoughts or urges in the first place. The suicidal individual has percentages of both, with the levels waxing and waning over time. Sometimes it will be 50/50; on other days it might be 60/40 or 30/70. All suicidal people have some desire to stay alive, and it is this that creates a window of opportunity in which the individual can get assistance. Others have noticed this quality of ambivalence. Art Kleiner (2010) studied over 100 suicide notes obtained from coroners. After studying the notes he states: "Were they ambivalent about it? About half the hundred or so letters we saw seemed to have some element of doubt" (paragraph 1).

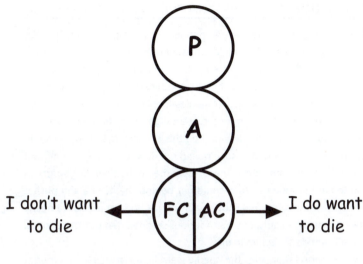

Figure 12.1 Suicidal ambivalence

Understanding the ambivalence

This ambivalence may be reflected in the ratio of suicide attempts to completed suicides. The ratios cited generally range from about 1 in 20 suicide attempts that result in death to about 1 in 100 suicide attempts that result in death (Caruso 2009; Steele and McLennan 1995). When looked at in a purely factual way, that is not a very high "success" rate. To set out to achieve something and only be successful in achieving it 1 in 40 times would not generally be considered a high rate of success. As mentioned before, killing self is not an easy thing to do because the body has many ways of keeping itself alive. Perhaps suicidal ambivalence is another reason why the ratio is so low. Most attempts will reflect this ambivalence and the part of the person that wants to live, and thus the attempt will be "sabotaged" in some way because the person is not fully committed to dying. Most suicide attempts will reflect the person's desire to die and desire to live, and thus most, if not all, suicide attempts will be "half-hearted" in this way.

CASE STUDY 12.1: AMBIVALENT SUICIDAL BEHAVIOR

The man had been treated for depression for many years. This has included being prescribed antidepressant medication. He had a history of three significant suicide attempts. Two of the attempts were both well-planned overdoses with heroin, combined with large amounts of two other types of prescription medication. However, his first attempt was at about age 20 when he thrust an eight-inch sharpened knitting needle into his stomach. He had used this as a shiv in prison and it had two hooks at the end of it, so, if pulled out, it would bring a significant amount of tissue out with it. These hooks meant the operating surgeons had to cut him open so they could get behind the needle and push it out. This was a very significant assault on his body and he very nearly died as a result. Clearly, this was a serious suicide attempt that reflected a significant desire in him to die.

He reports that, after the needle went in, the pain sort of brought him back to his senses and, as he put it, he went into survival mode. He quickly phoned his ex-wife and, fortunately, she got him to the hospital in time. In transactional analysis terms, the Free Child aspect of his personality became operational and he set about keeping himself alive.

This case demonstrates the ambivalent behavior of the suicidal person. First, there was a clear attempt to kill self, followed by some quick-thinking action to save himself. He switched ego states half way through. Initially, he was in a state of mind where the Adapted Child aspect of his personality predominated, which led him to stab himself. The pain produced by the stabbing had a wake-up shock effect, which resulted in a switch in ego states. He switched to Free Child, and thus his drive to stay alive gained more control in the personality.

This ambivalent quality in many suicide attempts can lead to a misinterpretation of the motives of the suicidal person. Some conclude that this contradictory behavior shows he was using the suicide attempt as a means to manipulate his ex-wife. This may not be the case, and one needs to gain more information on the dynamics of their relationship before that conclusion can be made. If there is little sign of such manipulation in the past, then the contradictory behavior may reflect his suicidal ambivalence rather than a manipulative act on his behalf.

Throughout Case study 12.2, the comments made by me are indicated in parentheses. Initially, there is a preamble written by the individual some time after the day of the suicide attempt. That is followed by a brief journal written as the suicide attempt progressed.

CASE STUDY 12.2: DIARY OF A SUICIDE ATTEMPT

Preamble

Confidentiality is a major hot button issue for me…

I work very hard to keep my privacy. I don't have any close friends and especially not at school. I can't trust anyone. If someone gets too close they might find out how crazy I am…

I know it's paranoid, but I have to protect myself. No one else will. This reactivated and exacerbated all of my fears about my privacy being violated, anger towards health professionals who have been sloppy with confidentiality in the past, anger towards people who have used my personal information against me. I had just an overall sense of powerlessness, anger and feeling overwhelmed. I can't put it into words that do it justice so I'm just going to stop trying. Point is I was extremely upset.

I was having cycling panic attacks. I'd taken my maximum daily dose of klonopin and it felt like I hadn't taken a thing. So what next? Clearly the logical step is to take a bunch of painkillers, right? Of course. So I did that.

(Comment: A distressing event has occurred—the breaking of his confidentiality. This leads to a number of conditions such that the suicidal decision can be acted upon:

1. Thinking "I have to protect myself. No one else will".

2. Anger towards others.

3. Sense of powerlessness, anger and feeling overwhelmed.

4. Cycling panic attacks occur.

5. Next logical step is to attempt suicide.

This could be reflective of the suicide decision "If things get too bad, I will kill myself".)

Day of the suicide attempt

This is a series of notes written by a 28-year-old male while he was making a suicide attempt. He had received his file notes from a hospital where he had once been a patient. He felt that some of the things written were unfair and breaking confidentiality.

The suicide attempt involved placing a whole packet of nicotine patches on himself and taking a large quantity of Klonopin, an anti-anxiety prescription medication, together with Motrin, an over-the-counter painkiller.

9–2–09 2:07 pm

having really bad cycling panic attacks

klonopin not helping

I'm really freaking out a ton over this the idea that there careless with the super personal info is just too much to handle

How can I get help when doctor patient confidentiality is a lie

(Comment: At this point the person is angry at the breaking of confidentiality. This has led to the thought that he cannot be helped and that no one can be trusted. These are the conditions necessary for the suicide decision to be acted upon. The Adapted Child aspect of the personality is strong.)

3:36 pm

I've cried so much I don't think I have any more left

taking a 2nd klonopin in 1 day

only done that like 2 times ever bfore

(Comment: At this point the person has decided on the suicide attempt, one and a half hours after the initial angry reaction. In the next two hours, the rest of the medication is taken. One can already see the ambivalence beginning with the statement "only done that like 2 times ever before", which indicates some trepidation at what he is doing and the Free Child becoming stronger.)

5:40 pm

this has escalted extrordinarially yuckily

i dunno what the fuck is going on

how can i get help if i cant trust them

(Comment: Possible anger still present and a restatement of the conditions necessary for the suicide attempt—being able to be helped and not being able to trust anyone—thus indicating that things have reached the point of being too bad.)

6:31 pm

feel so nausiated

i dunno what im doing

(Comment: Confusion indicated and no restatement of the conditions necessary for the suicide decision to be enacted. This could indicate that the Free Child desire to live is becoming stronger.)

> 7:49 pm
>
> I'm such a fucking idiot
>
> i took too much of motrin
>
> put a whole package of nicotine patch on me then i slept for a while
>
> then was like fuck i don't wanna go to the hospital and this isnt enough to kill me

(Comment: The Free Child ego state is now strong enough to lead to direct survival behavior. No restatement of conditions for the suicide decision to be active.)

> took off the patches
>
> make myself vomit up the motrin
>
> i didnt get it al but got out as much as i could
>
> still feel crazy nausiated
>
> when i was vomiting some blod came up
>
> not a ton
>
> but stil I worry some
>
> not like i vomit regurally
>
> hadt done it in years
>
> must be the motirn
>
> dizzily walked ot store ot buy moutwash and salt to rinse
>
> i feel like shit
>
> ovrheating
>
> took off my clothing
>
> don't have a fever
>
> im realyl bloated dunno why
>
> fuck im an idiot
>
> all over this cofidentiality shit

(Comment: Five and a half hours after the episode started, there has been a shift in ego states from the Adapted Child to the Free Child. While under the influence of the Adapted Child, he was stating the circumstances necessary to enact the suicide decision. By the end of the process, the conditions necessary to enact the decision are directly discounted, thus reflecting the more powerful influence of the Free Child in the personality.)

This journal gives some unique insight into the functioning of one individual's mind during a suicide attempt. As indicated, there is a change in the influencing factors in his personality at the time. In reaction to a specific event, initially the self-destructive aspect of the personality, the Adapted Child, predominates in the decision making. As the hours progress there is a slow shift out of that ego state to the Free Child ego state, which results in life-saving decisions occurring. This is an example of the suicidal ambivalence that is experienced by most if not all suicidal people.

Working with suicidal ambivalence

In working with the suicidal client, one can present the idea of suicidal ambivalence so that the client gets a sense of "On the one hand, I want to live, and on the other hand, I want to die". These are the Free Child (FC) and the Adapted Child (AC) ego states, which can be drawn for the client as in Figure 12.1. This will tend to reduce the sense of ambiguity and confusion which the person may be feeling.

This approach of clarifying the suicidal urges and thoughts can be taken further by setting up a two-chair situation. See Figure 12.2.

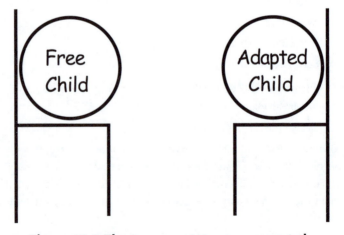

Figure 12.2 The two ego states are separated

Two empty chairs are placed out in front of the client. One chair is the FC and the other is the AC. The person sits in each chair and speaks from that part of self. First, the person may sit in one chair and speak from the AC; he then switches and speaks from the FC ego state chair. This permits the person to actually experience those parts of self, thus allowing an experiential understanding of his suicidal urges. Sometimes the two parts of the personality may even dialogue with each other and, of course, the counselor can also speak to both parts. In the therapy setting, this allows the client to establish a relationship between the two parts of self. Each part is also establishing a relationship with the counselor. What were once intangible thoughts and feelings become clearer, with the obvious therapeutic gains that go along with such self-awareness.

This also forms the basis of one of the more important ways of managing and treating the suicidal individual. As the client and counselor now have a clearer understanding of the suicidal part of the person, the counselor can then start building relational contact with it. The counselor begins to build a relationship with the self-destructive part of the client, his Adapted Child. I cannot stress enough the importance of this. To make good relational contact with the self-destructive part of the client is most therapeutic.

How does one do this? It is, in essence, no different from establishing a relationship between any two people. First, one starts with simple dialogue in which the counselor and the Adapted Child aspect of the client begin talking to each other. They find out what each other thinks and feels, and as they do this, the counselor displays a sense of compassion, empathy and understanding of this part of the client. As the client senses this, he will begin to feel some respect from the counselor, and thus the relational contact or connection between them grows. As the trust grows, the counselor and the AC ego state of the client may begin stating what they think and feel about each other, and at some point there may even be some form of dispute or disruption between them. The counselor facilitates resolution of that dispute and thus the relationship strengthens even more. The counselor would also do a similar task with the Free Child aspect of the client. However, most important is the building of such a connection between the counselor and the self-destructive aspect of the client.

I often use such an approach in conjunction with other techniques that externalize the self-destructive aspect of the client. One is simply requesting the client to project that part of his personality out on to something in his environment. For instance, the client can be asked to give the suicidal part some sort of form. He may be asked to draw it, thus giving it some form, whether that be human or some inanimate object such as a cloud or a block of concrete. Once done, the client has a clearer understanding of this part of self, as does the counselor. The client can then dialogue with it, as can the counselor, and the drawing can be asked to speak itself. In essence, one is doing the two-chair exercise with a drawing rather than with chairs. However, it does add one extra aspect. In the two-chair situation, the client is being the self-destructive aspect of self, which means he cannot sit back and have a look at it. The drawing allows the client to do this and see the AC external to self. This permits further awareness of the self-destructive aspect of the personality and permits an extra dimension to the relationship connection between the AC of the client and the counselor.

Assessing the suicidal ambivalence

With the two-chair exercise as shown in Figure 12.2, the client and counselor can get an idea of the current strength of these two parts of the personality. It can be used to show if the Free Child or Adapted Child is more influential in the personality at that point in time.

The exercise begins with the individual being asked to speak about wanting to live in the FC chair. The request is left open-ended as much as possible. The individual may ask what the counselor is wanting to hear about and to be more specific in that request. As little direction as possible should be given so that when they speak, it is truly coming from the person's Free Child rather than being what the counselor has directed him to talk about. Most often, people will start with why they want to live and create a list of things to live for, but as they are encouraged to talk more, they can start to talk about all sorts of things about living and dying.

As mentioned before, ego states are not roles but actual parts of the personality. Not uncommonly, as people continue to talk in the chair and move into that part of the personality, they begin to experience it first-hand, often with emotions right then and there in front of the counselor. Hence, the counselor gets to see the body language and the level of animation, hear the tone of voice, see all the unconscious nuances and so on. They get to see and "experience" the person being in that aspect of the personality, which provides a far more comprehensive understanding of him than a simple verbal report of what the Free Child or Adapted Child ego states think or say.

If the person in the FC chair finds it hard to think of anything to say or lacks any animation or demonstrative body language, this may mean there is little investment in this part of the personality. If he should then move to the AC chair and speak freely with some vibrancy and energy, this could indicate he has more investment in that part of the personality. Of course, this would be an undesirable situation because the suicidal ambivalence is leaning towards the "I want to die" side. The point of the exercise is to give the person and the counselor an experiential understanding of the where the "energy" is in the client with regard to his suicidality. Besides the increased awareness, it also provides further information on the assessment of suicide risk.

In this method, the person can be afforded the opportunity to move back and forwards between the chairs on a number of occasions. From a risk assessment point of view, the counselor is seeing the person's state of mind at just that point in time, and it will change over time. This assessment method can be used repeatedly over a time period, and on each occasion the results can be checked against previous assessments using the two-chair technique. This affords a suicide risk assessment over time and provides insight into what side of the personality seems to becoming more dominant over time.

However, for the discussion at hand, it also allows the individual to experience first-hand those two aspects of the personality that are in a state of ambivalence. As people do this, they tend to get better at accessing and experiencing those parts of their personality. It's like learning to ride a bike: once the basic skill has been mastered, one only refines the skill more and more as one rides on. As a person masters the basic skill of experiencing these parts of the personality in the chair exercise, he gets better at accessing those ego states and can display them with more ease and with a greater depth of understanding and awareness.

Conclusion

All suicidal individuals are in a state of ambivalence. The decision to die by one's own hand is one of the most profound decisions that can be made. Thus it is not made lightly and there is always an aspect of the person that does not want to go along with such a decision.

This chapter provides a way in which the person can begin to conceptualize and understand his ambivalence and those assisting him can understand it as well. Fortunately, this is quite a simple psychological process, which the vast majority of people are prepared to do. Indeed, most people find it an interesting exercise in self-awareness and are quite cooperative. As we know, people are usually interested in finding out more about themselves and their unconscious aspects.

In the procedure described, the client is afforded an opportunity to gain a clearer understanding of his ambivalence. An experiential suicide risk assessment is permitted as well. Most important, however, relational contact can be established between the counselor and the self-destructive aspect of the client. If that aspect of the client can experience such contact and gain a sense of decreased isolation, then it usually becomes more tempered in its thoughts and feelings. It starts to become more considered and lose its "harsh" edge, just as a person does when he moves from a state of isolation to a feeling of belonging with others.

Chapter 13

Suicide Timelines

Suicidal behavior in context

When a person presents with suicidal urges, one needs to look at those urges in the wider context of his life. One way to do this is to view suicidal urges and attempts on a timeline basis. There are three common timelines of suicidal urges. The first is the acute suicidal crisis shown in Figure 13.1.

The acute suicidal crisis

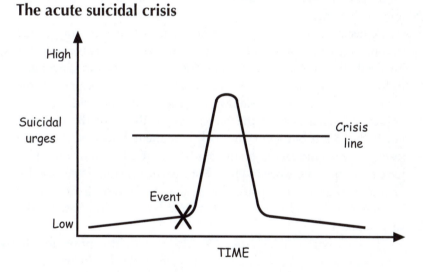

Figure 13.1 An acute suicidal crisis

In this case, the individual is going through life and, for some reason, suicidal urges and ideas rapidly appear. If there is no suicide attempt or completed suicide, then suicidal urges disappear quite quickly. There is an acute suicidal episode. The crisis line is that point at which the individual is a serious suicide risk, when he is close to making a concerted suicide attempt. This scenario most often occurs in reaction to an event such as a marital separation, financial collapse, imprisonment, psychotic episode, loss of reputation and so on.

One good feature of this profile is that when one has feelings that rapidly appear, that often means they can rapidly decrease some time later. As they are relatively new to the personality, these feelings have not had time to become ingrained in the personality. This, of course, is good news for the person, but at the time he is unlikely to appreciate this; if one is suicidal, then one's long-term future looks very bleak, no matter what the facts are. However, it is important information to pass on to the individual and can assist in any counseling. Also, if suicidal thoughts are a reaction to an event, then usually when that event ends, the suicidal thoughts are likely to go away. For instance, if someone becomes suicidal as a result of being arrested, and then he is released on bail, the suicidal feelings may subside because he is out of custody. If the person is suicidal due to a marriage breakdown, as time goes by most people become used to the new situation, perhaps with a new partner, and so the suicidal urges will wane.

A negative of the acute suicidal crisis is that one can get the spontaneous type of suicide attempt, particularly when alcohol is involved. The person simply walks out of his house into oncoming traffic, or jumps into his car and drives into a tree, or goes to the medicine cabinet and swallows all the medication in it. Such unplanned suicides have the increased possibility of the outcome not being death but some form of permanent disability. Also as a result of the suddenness of the suicidal urges, the individual may have no support network in place. For instance, he may have no prior or recent contact with a counselor or an organization that can assist in such a crisis, and he may at that time have no idea how to find such support.

To deal with this situation, it may be a viable option for the person to be hospitalized, put on suicide watch (as in prison) or relocated to some situation where there is a good deal of support, both practical and emotional. If the suicidal crisis is short-term, then this type of approach often helps to prevent the crisis resulting in death or disability. It must be acknowledged, however, that hospitalization is not a panacea. All a hospitalization does is move a suicidal person geographically from one location to another. If the person is quite isolated, then that can indeed be helpful, but it can also make matters worse.

Some people do not want to be removed from their home environment and become even more distressed when this happens.

Some people do not want all the fuss that goes with a hospitalization. In addition, hospitals are buildings full of people. There is a view held by some in the community and some in the hospital system that self-harming and suicidal people improperly use up limited hospital resources. They hold the view that hospitals are meant for "real" patients who are there due to disease, illness or accidents. The culture in some helping institutions can be difficult, depending on the personalities of those who run them, to the extent that the suicidal can be treated with subtle disdain or contempt. This, of course, makes matters worse. Managing the suicidal person is not as simple as just putting them in a hospital to avoid a crisis.

However, if the crisis is short in duration, then some kind of extra supportive care can be most useful, as can a no-suicide contract. The person can make a short-term contract with self not to act on their suicidal urges until the crisis has passed. It should be noted, however, that these are only band-aid solutions and do not deal with the longer-term problem of the individual having made the suicide decision in early life. This person views suicide as a viable solution to a problem, and thus it is quite possible that future circumstances will arise when the suicide decision becomes operational again.

The slowly developing suicidal crisis

Other people can become suicidal over a much longer period of time and not in reaction to a precipitating event. This is shown in Figure 13.2.

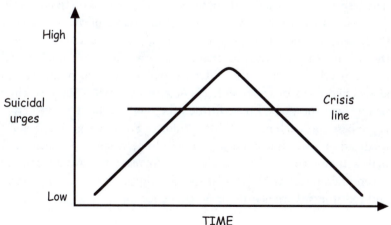

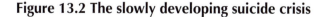

Figure 13.2 The slowly developing suicide crisis

In this instance, the suicidal ideation develops over time and not in a sudden way as shown in Figure 13.1. There is less likely to be an obvious event that precipitates the suicidal feelings; instead, they evolve slowly over time. One needs to be careful not to misdiagnose this as an acute crisis. In the slowly developing suicidal crisis, one can get an event which is the final straw, but the suicidal urges have been developing over some time. For instance, a man reports that he had a fight with his wife and now he has suicidal urges. People do not become suicidal because they have an argument with their spouse. It is more likely that his urge to damage self has been increasing for some time, and the fight was the last straw that pushes him close to the crisis line. In a similar scenario, a teenager has been listening to rock music that could be seen to promote suicide. The teenager starts to report suicidal feelings or may make a suicide attempt. The parents see the music as being the cause. No one has ever become suicidal because of rock music lyrics. In such a case, it is much more likely that the suicidal feelings have been evolving over some considerable period of time and the rock music happens along as the teenager gets close to the crisis line. One needs to make some enquires to make sure that an acute suicidal crisis is not being mistakenly diagnosed, when in reality it is a slowly evolving suicidal crisis.

A slowly evolving crisis is not event-related, and the length of time over the crisis line can vary considerably from weeks or many months even years, before the eventual subsiding of the suicidal feelings. At times these feelings can follow the cyclical nature of depressive episodes and, in these cases, antidepressant medication can be of assistance with managing the suicidality of the person. For those who are not depressed and suicidal, the explanation of why the suicidal urges develop over time can vary from the biochemical to the psychodynamic. The different explanations each suggest an alternative form of treatment. Having worked with many suicidal people over the years, I have formed the opinion that trial and error is the best approach in such circumstances. For some, antidepressant medication can almost be a wonder drug, whereas for others it makes them worse. The same applies to responses to the talking psychotherapies. At times considerable improvement is reported, and for others there is little or no change at all.

One advantage of the slowly developing crisis compared to the acute crisis is that people will tend to seek help of some kind before the crisis line is reached. First, this means there is more opportunity for some form of counseling to result in the crisis line being avoided altogether, which is not the case in an acute crisis. Second, if the crisis line is reached, then the person is more likely to have some form of support network in place so as to avoid a completed suicide.

On the down side, as the suicidal urges have developed over time, that means they become more ingrained in the personality and thus they will disappear less rapidly than they can do in the acute suicidal crisis. Also, in this situation there is less likelihood of the spontaneous type of suicide attempt. The suicides will tend to be better planned and thus more likely to be completed. For instance, the correct amount and type of medication is collected for a completed suicide, rather than an insufficient amount which might just leave the individual disabled in some way.

Hospitalization or suicide watch is less helpful here, as is the no-suicide contract. If an individual is closely watched, then he can simply delay any suicidal actions. How long do you keep a person in hospital for suicidal urges—six months, a year, two years? If the person has felt despairing for the past year, he can last out another few months with little trouble. If the urges have developed over a period of time, they are more ingrained in the personality, and offering a support network will have less meaning for the individual. It will have less impact than for the average individual because the problem is more inside the individual's head than a difficulty with their social milieu.

The chronic suicidal crisis

The timeline of chronic suicidal ideation usually develops over a long period of time (Figure 13.3). Over that period, the person, for whatever reason, just begins to feel worse and worse with depression, despair, shame or whatever feeling it may be. All sorts of medical and psychological solutions to reduce the angst may be attempted but with little success.

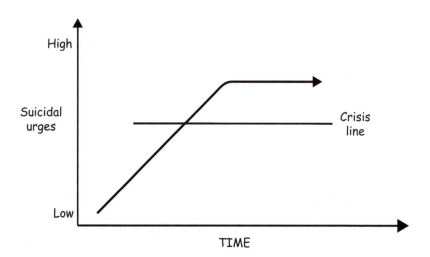

Figure 13.3 The chronic suicidal crisis

This results in a poor quality of life evolving over time and the individual just begins to tire of living; it's just all too hard. This timeline can be more common with someone in the later part of his life or someone who has lived with some form of chronic mental illness for many years. It is likely that at some point this individual will make a very concerted effort to end his life. Indeed, he may do so on a number of occasions.

CASE STUDY 13.1: *TIMELINE OF THE CHRONIC SUICIDAL CRISIS*

A 35-year-old female reports chronic schizophrenic symptoms for the past 15 years. She reports great angst about the hallucinations, delusions, being overweight, medications, psychotherapy, psychiatrists and hospitals. She has not felt any connection to a man for ten years and now has little desire for any connection with a partner. She states that she has had one serious attempt at hanging in the past and that she should be dead. She has tried every type of treatment and sees very little possibility of symptom improvement in the future. She is seriously questioning her quality of life in the long-term future.

This type of suicidal timeline raises all sorts of ethical issues for the helping professional. Is it ethical to tell someone that there is always hope? Are some situations hopeless? If the helping professional says there is always hope, is that to ease the professional's own angst or to help the suicidal person? Most people accept that there are terminal physical illnesses in which there is no hope, but can the same be applied to psychological illnesses? Anyone who works with those who have long-term chronic mental illness and suicidal thoughts will have to come to some form of conclusion about these questions. Of course, one continues to offer support and treatment possibilities but, as with the slowly evolving suicidal crisis, hospitalization is less useful for the same reasons, as is the no-suicide contract.

Conclusion

When meeting a client who expresses suicidal ideation, one needs to understand those symptoms in the wider context of his life. By doing so, one understands better the person and their suicidality, thus making for better management and treatment suggestions. Three alternative scenarios have been described in this chapter, each varying in the length of the suicidal crisis experienced by the person. Generally speaking, the shorter the time, the better the prognosis, at least in the short term. However, it is also noted that, with the rapid onset of suicidal thoughts, there are other dangers such as a lack of pre-existing supports and a tendency to engage in the spontaneous type of suicide attempts. With long-term chronic suicidal urges, one is confronted by a series of ethical dilemmas which do not have any easy or clear answers.

Chapter 14

The No-Suicide Contract

Origin of the no-suicide contract

The no-suicide contract (NSC) originated in the transactional analysis literature and was developed by a few writers including Boyd (1972), Bob Goulding (1972) and Holloway (1973). However, it is the pivotal 1973 article by Drye, Goulding and Goulding (1973)—"No-suicide decisions: Patient monitoring of suicidal risk"—that is usually referred to in the literature as the origin of the NSC.

Theory behind the no-suicide contract

Since the Gouldings presented the idea of the NSC, there has been a huge proliferation in its use and articles written about it. A study by Kroll (2000) questioned psychiatrists about their clinical use of the NSC and 57 percent reported using it in one form or another. American psychologists were researched by Mahrer (1993) on the use of the NSC and 69 percent had used it in the previous 12 months. In the training of nurses, the NSC is officially recognized as a technique to use with suicidal clients (Johnson 1997). As one can see, the NSC is used in a wide variety of fields by a large number of practitioners.

Unfortunately, a large portion of those practitioners do not understand the theory behind the NSC, and thus there is widespread misuse. This misuse and misunderstanding of the theory behind the NSC has led to a plethora of articles and books debating what it is and arguing about its worth. This has occurred in the literature of a number of disciplines including psychology, psychiatry, general practice, counseling and psychotherapy, occupational therapy and particularly nursing and social work e.g. Assey 1985; Egan 1997; Goin 2003; Hipple and Cimbolic 1979; Kroll 2007; Reid 1998; Simon 1999 .

To address this widespread misunderstanding, I have created Figure 14.1—the no-suicide contract iceberg.

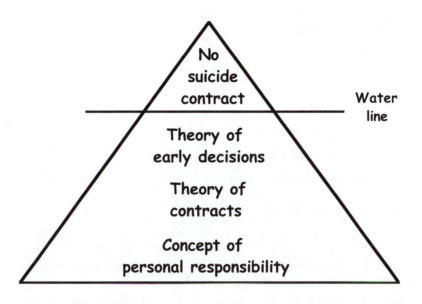

Figure 14.1 The no-suicide contract iceberg

It is presented as an iceberg because what one sees above the water line (the NSC) is just one small part of the whole entity. What people see is the technique of a client making the NSC statement to some kind of mental health professional: "No matter what happens, I will not kill myself, accidentally or on purpose, for *x* amount of time". However, underneath the water line is hidden a large base of theory which the vast majority of practitioners do not understand. Hence it is widely misunderstood and misused, and the literature proliferates because of all the confusion.

For example, Caruso (2010) states:

> No-suicide contracts go by many names, including the following:
>
> • No-suicide contracts
>
> • No-suicide agreements
>
> • No-suicide promises
>
> • No-suicide commitments
>
> • Suicide contracts

- Suicide agreements

- Suicide prevention contracts

- Suicide prevention agreements

- No-harm contracts

- No-harm agreements

- No-harm promises

- No-harm commitments

and many more.

> But regardless of what you choose to call them, no-suicide contracts can be useful tools in helping to prevent suicides. (paragraph 1–2)

Edwards (2007) produced a doctoral thesis titled "No-suicide contracts, no-suicide agreements and no-suicide assurances: An exploratory study of their nature, utilization and perceived effectiveness". Kroll (2007) wrote a journal article on the NSC for the *Psychiatric Times* in which he states:

> Paradoxically, clinicians, especially in those frequent situations in which a strong relationship with the suicidal patient does not exist, instead bank on a peculiar social assumption about human behavior that has its roots in childhood and possibly even in our genes, that promises, commitments, and contracts are binding on each individual even in the face of inconvenience, even when contrary to our strongest urges. It is as if "promises are to be kept" is the 11th commandment by which we guide our lives. (paragraph 3)

Interestingly enough, in the *Transactional Analysis Journal* there have been very few articles written in the past 20 years about the NSC; I could find only two or three. The literature out of which the NSC grew has had very little written about the NSC in the last few decades. The Edwards thesis or the Kroll article would probably not be published in the *Transactional Analysis Journal* because they would not pass the editorial board review process. A no-suicide contract is precisely that: a *contract*. It cannot be a promise or an assurance. In transactional analysis theory, a contract is a specific therapeutic process that is based on a solid body of theory. If one wrote a journal article about the NSC and called it a "no-suicide assurance", it is likely to be rejected by the *Transactional Analysis Journal* editorial board as it would be clear the writer did not understand the theory of contracts.

Hence we end up with the no-suicide contract iceberg. Many have written about and discussed the NSC without understanding the theory underneath. Consider this metaphor. A man who has lived his life in the jungle eventually comes out to civilization. Upon doing so, he sees many new and amazing things, one being the motor car. He observers that a person can get into the car, turn it on and drive it away. He finds this amazing and immediately realizes the potential it has. This motor car allows him to move much further than he has ever done before, much faster then he has ever done before. He quickly obtains such a machine and proceeds to drive it to all the places he needs to go. One day as he is driving, the car starts spluttering, shaking and making funny noises and suddenly stops. He tries to turn the car on again but it does not work. Finally, he gets out of the car and looks at it in bewilderment. He thinks it seemed like a great idea in the beginning, but it's not much good if it just stops working one day. He walks off disillusioned by the whole motor car thing.

Our hypothetical man has only seen the tip of the iceberg: a motor car that works. He does not understand the theory behind it: what is under the water. He does not understand that the motor car requires servicing, it needs water put in it, it needs air in the tires, it needs the oil topped up and so on. As he does not know these things, initially it seems like a great invention, but, of course, eventually it splutters, breaks down and is useless. This is what has happened to the NSC for those who do not understand the theory behind it.

To understand the theory behind the NSC, one must understand the theory of contracts, the theory of early decisions and the Gouldings' concept or philosophy of personal power and personal responsibility. Once done, one is then able to make an assessment of when to use the NSC and when not. The other feature one finds in the research literature about the NSC and debate on the NSC is a one-size-fits-all approach. The NSC is a specific therapeutic option for managing and treating the suicidal person. As with any medical procedure or psychological treatment, its use depends on the particular circumstances of the patient at the time. In some circumstances, the procedure or treatment will be applicable, and in other patient circumstances, it will not. The NSC is the same. It is useful for some patient circumstances and not others. For those circumstances where it is useful, one employs the NSC treatment process for that particular patient at that particular time. In those patient circumstances where it is not useful, one does not use the NSC and does something else. It would seem imperative that any future research on the NSC must have experimental controls for this variable: the circumstances of the client at the time the NSC was used.

Under the NSC iceberg waterline

The theory of early decisions was explained in depth in Chapter 4. The NSC is used in the context of such a theory. Those who talk about the NSC as preventing suicide do not understand how the NSC is related to the theory of early decisions. Goin (2003) illustrates a typical misunderstanding. The 2003 President of the American Psychiatric Association writes an article titled "The 'Suicide-prevention contract': A dangerous myth". She goes on to state: "Increasingly, clinicians refer to the need 'to contract' with patients who they fear might harm themselves. It would be wonderful if contracts truly prevented such tragedies, but there are no reliable or valid data to confirm their effectiveness" (p.3).

A NSC does not cure anything, change anything or prevent anything. Goulding and Goulding (1979) developed the idea of the NSC to buy time so that the early suicide decision could be treated. It was devised as a stopgap measure, not as a way of curing or preventing suicide. If a person has an acute suicide crisis as shown in the suicide timelines in Chapter 13, then an NSC may be seen as a way for the suicide to be prevented. In one sense, it has prevented the suicide in that one crisis, but the longer-term problem still remains. It has not solved the underlying problem in the longer term because the person is still susceptible to acting on their suicidal urges. If one knows early decision theory, then one understands that the NSC is simply used to buy time for the treatment to be applied.

Also under the waterline is the concept of personal responsibility, which is central to the Gouldings' therapeutic approach and their use of the NSC. Indeed, the title of their first book was *The Power is in the Patient* (Goulding and Goulding 1978). They state: "Our main therapeutic principle is that each person is responsible for his or her own actions and feelings, although he or she may be choosing to respond in an automatic, stereotyped way" (p.190). They also state: "This self-responsibility is extremely important from the very beginning" (p.165). One can see that their approach is based on the assumption that people are in charge of their own thoughts, feelings and actions. In this approach, clients are assumed to take responsibility for themselves, how they feel and how they behave. This is no different when the client is making a NSC, and hence we have the quotation about no-suicide and no-homicide contracts from their last major theoretical work on such contracts: "The contract is a statement by the Adult of the client that he will *monitor himself in order to stand guard successfully over his own self-murderous* or other-murderous impulses" (p.55; italics mine). The italicized words highlight the Gouldings' concept of personal responsibility. In an NSC, it is the client who takes charge of his monitoring of self; he is responsible for that.

The criteria of personal responsibility gives the first insight into the circumstances that must exist within the client for the treatment procedure of the NSC to be applicable in his case. If he agrees with the idea of personal responsibility, then it is possible the NSC could be used. If he does not agree and sees some outside cause of his feelings and actions, such as fate, luck or the behavior of someone else, then the NSC treatment procedure will not be suitable for him. For the NSC to be used with a particular person requires that he views self as in control of his suicidal monitoring and his suicidal actions. This does not mean the person is left on his own or isolated. He would be actively encouraged to talk about his feelings and suicidal thoughts with the counselor or helping professional.

The third and final aspect of the NSC that is hidden under the waterline is the theory of contracts. To understand this, one must go back to the basis of contract theory as was presented by Steiner (1971). Each treatment contract has four requirements:

- *Mutual consent.* Both parties agree to the contract. The counselor does not impose the goals or contract on to the client. Nor does the client impose them on to the counselor.

- *Valid consideration.* Both parties are putting something into the relationship. Usually the counselor puts in his skill and expertise and the client puts in monetary payment.

- *Competency.* Both parties must be competent to undertake the goals of the contract. This mainly means that both parties have a functioning Adult ego state and they use that Adult in the contracting process. Thus a client who is intoxicated cannot make an NSC, as is also the case with someone who has significant dementia, is currently psychotic, is eight years old or is significantly intellectually handicapped.

- *Lawful object.* The conditions and goals of the contract must conform to the laws of the land.

To use the NSC with a client, it must conform to these four conditions. If it does not, then it is not a no-suicide *contract* and is something else.

The first important aspect of contract theory, as just described, is mutual consent. The counselor does not impose the NSC on the client. As one reads the literature, one finds this criterion is often broken. At times counselors will give clients ultimatums with an NSC: "Either make the NSC or I won't treat you", "I will hospitalize you", "I will have to increase your medication" and so forth. Clearly, this does not adhere to the requirement of mutual consent. The client is forced to make the NSC or he will have to face the consequences. If the counselor does this with the client, then a treatment contract (in this case the NSC) is not being made, and some other therapeutic technique is occurring between the client and counselor.

CASE STUDY 14.1: MUTUAL CONSENT IN A CONTRACT

An example of how this can occur in the counseling setting is described by White (2010e). Although it does not specifically refer to an NSC, the same process is observable. The woman (A) is describing a series of recent exchanges between her and her therapist. Also included are my comments (T) back to her.

A: What if a therapist had a requirement that in order for me to continue to be able to see them, I had to be back on my psychiatric meds and seeing a psychiatrist regularly? Would this be different than what you have described above? I am a bit confused because while it may have been a goal that I wanted to be better, it was not a goal of mine to be back on meds.

T: It depends on what you do with the therapist's requirement in your own head. If you took the therapist's requirement as a CP demand, then you would very likely be in CC and promise to take them. That is not good as people can so easily switch to RC and the promise goes out the window one way or another. If you took it as an Adult ego state thing from the therapist, then you could make a contract with yourself to take the meds and that contract may work. You say that you don't want to take the meds. That means part of your Child ego state will resent taking them, so that would need to be watched and managed.

A: It makes more sense now. As predicted, I ended up lying about taking the meds and the therapist never knew otherwise. Needless to say, that relationship wasn't very successful. Thanks for the explanation. (Comments section)

For an NSC to be a no-suicide *contract*, the helping professional must not impose or pressure the person into making one. As soon as the professional does that, it stops being a contract and becomes some other kind of therapeutic intervention. In this case study, the "contract" to take the medication became an ultimatum, and thus it cannot be seen as a contract in the first place.

The second important aspect of the contract theory for the NSC is competency. Both parties must have well-functioning Adult ego states because all contracts are made Adult to Adult. For a therapeutic intervention to be a contract, it must involve a statement by the client's Adult ego state that is heard by and responded to by the counselor's Adult ego state. Again, in the literature on the NSC, one sees this requirement regularly violated. Often one sees writers discussing the NSC when clearly what they are discussing is not a *contract*. Indeed, some people refer to therapeutic procedures called a no-suicide promise, a no-suicide assurance or a no-suicide commitment. None of these fulfill the requirements to be a treatment contract and it highlights the difference between a contract and a promise as will be discussed now.

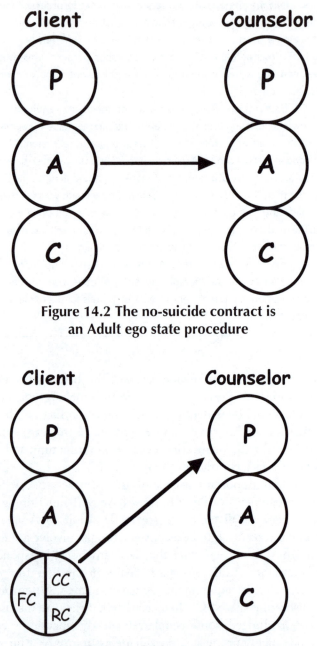

Figure 14.2 The no-suicide contract is an Adult ego state procedure

Figure 14.3 The no-suicide promise or assurance is a Conforming Child ego state procedure

The no-suicide promise, no-suicide assurance or no-suicide commitment

To highlight the difference between a promise and a contract, one simply has to draw some transactional diagrams. The treatment contracting process, such as a no-suicide contract, would be drawn as shown in Figure 14.2.

A promise or an assurance would most commonly be drawn as in Figure 14.3.

As one can see, a promise involves the Conforming Child ego state and not the Adult ego state, and thus is a quite different psychological process with quite different therapeutic implications. What are the therapeutic consequences of asking a client to make a no-suicide promise or no-suicide assurance? To answer this, one needs to examine the psychology of the promise.

If parents ask a child to promise to tidy his bedroom, a number of things could happen. Promises work on the basis of guilt. The child knows that if he breaks his promise, then the parents will feel distressed in some way—disappointed, hurt, let down, betrayed and so on. If the child lets them down, then he knows they will feel distress, and thus the child can feel guilt about "hurting" the parents. The parents are using guilt to get the child to do something he does not want to do. If the child is highly compliant, he will clean his room because the guilt is too much for him to deal with.

When one is in the Conforming Child ego state, it is not hard to switch to the Rebellious Child ego state. This frequently happens at some point with people who enter communication from a Conforming position, as a child does when he makes a promise. If the youngster is not so compliant, this can easily happen as the child realizes he is being manipulated by the parents using guilt.

If the switch to the Rebellious Child ego state occurs, then anger in the child will arise and the child will do one of three things:

- not tidy his room at all and tend to feel angry rather than guilty

- tidy his room and feel resentful

- tidy his room poorly as a passive expression of his anger against the parents.

If one changes the context from cleaning a room to making a therapeutic contract, one can see the potential problems. If the client perceives the counselor to be asking him to make a promise, then the outcomes described above are also likely to occur. Indeed, the counselor may not even be doing that and the client may still perceive him to be requesting a promise and thus the outcomes would be the same regardless. If, when asked to make a promise, the client goes into the Conforming Child ego state in his relationship with the counselor, it is easy for him to switch into the Rebellious Child. Most will do this at some point, so the counselor is wanting to avoid such a dynamic developing in the therapeutic relationship.

In such circumstances, the initial problem often gets lost. The young child may in fact want to have a tidy room, but because he has been made to promise to make it tidy, his initial want can be forgotten. The parents are pressuring him either to comply to or to rebel against their conditions, and thus he moves away from his own Free Child want. If such conflict with the parents continues for an extended period, the child can eventually loose touch with his Free Child and ends up not knowing what he wants.

From a therapeutic point of view, this gains considerable importance, especially when one considers the no-suicide contract. Of all the areas of contracting, this is where promises mostly need to be avoided for the reasons cited above. The desire for the promise is usually generated from the anxiety of the counselor who does not want the client to kill self. Understandable indeed, but to request a client to promise not to kill self is a counterproductive plan of action to take. One does not want an NSC to be made from the client's Conforming Child ego state as happens when it becomes a promise.

A no-suicide *contract* is made from the client's Adult ego state. A no-suicide *promise* or no-suicide *assurance* is made from the client's Conforming Child ego state. They are two quite separate psychological processes with two different likely outcomes. It would seem imperative that any future research on the NSC must exclude those situations where a no-suicide promise, no-suicide assurance or no-suicide commitment is being used.

The no-suicide contracting procedure

An NSC made on the three concepts in the NSC iceberg can be a potent and effective therapeutic intervention. It can be useful for some people to keep themselves alive. Like the hospitalization of the suicidal, however, the NSC is not a panacea. It is like any other therapeutic or medical procedure: for some people in some circumstances it will be useful and for others it will not.

The following steps of the NSC procedure are based on the theories of early decisions, contracts and personal responsibility. How suitable is the person for the NSC procedure? To establish this, one needs to assess the individual on the criteria of personal responsibility and contract theory.

Personal responsibility

Does the person take responsibility for his thoughts, feelings and behaviors, particularly in relation to any precipitating event for the suicidal urges? In the medical and psychological literature, this is sometimes referred to as the locus of control. The Medical Dictionary (2010) defines the locus of control as "A theoretical construct designed to assess a person's perceived control over his or her own behavior. The classification internal locus indicates that the person feels in control of events; external locus indicates that others are perceived to have that control" (paragraph 1).

The more the person has an internal locus of control, the more effective the NSC will be. If he views himself as being at the whim of others' actions, fate, luck or the outcome of a particular event, the less effective an NSC will be. For example, if a man is feeling suicidal about a marital breakdown and says he does not know what he will do if his wife leaves or petitions for a divorce, then he has an external locus of control. He is not accepting personal responsibility for his behavior; instead, he is making it dependent on his wife's actions. An NSC is stating that for a predetermined period of time he will behave in such a way that he will not take his own life, regardless of the outcome of court proceedings, the actions of a spouse and so on.

This aspect of the NSC can be assessed by simple questioning of the individual:

- Are his disappointments in life due to his own actions or to bad luck and timing?

- Does he feel he is in control of what he feels or are his feelings determined by the actions of others?

- Is his behavior determined by hereditary factors or by his choice of how to behave?

- Does he feel he is able to control his life and its outcomes or does he feel such things are due to fate?

Alternatively, there are many simple locus of control tests which can be taken to determine if the person has an internal or external locus of control. Most of these come from the work of Rotter (1966) who developed the Rotter's Locus of Control Scale. The more a person has an internal locus of control, the more he is suited to the no-suicide contracting procedure when required. If he has little sense of personal responsibility or an external locus of control, then an NSC will be less effective and the person will be tending to promise the counselor rather than make a contract with self.

Contract theory

The NSC is made by the Adult ego state of the client. It is a statement by the client to self about how he will behave in the near future. It can be made in the presence of a counselor and very often is, but its primary function is a statement the client makes with himself about his own behavior. The client is not making a promise to anyone or attempting to reassure a counselor because those statements are made by the Conforming Child ego state. If the client is capable of making such an Adult ego state statement, he is suitable for the no-suicide contracting procedure. Some people are not capable of this, as is shown in Case study 14.1. In that instance, the therapist had required the client to make a contract about taking her medication. She was not capable at that point of being in her Adult ego state and making such a contract. Instead, she switched to Conforming Child and stated that she agreed. Almost immediately, she then switched to Rebellious Child and proceeded to lie about taking the medication. She could not make a contract and instead made a promise, in this instance because the therapist was requiring it. In other situations, that may not even be the case. An example of this can be found in Case study 14.2.

CASE STUDY 14.2: *THE NO-SUICIDE PROMISE*

A 30-year-old male, who reports suicidal thoughts, states he has attempted suicide a few times in the past and indicates that at least some of them were quite serious attempts.

Counselor: Are you willing to make a no-suicide contract?

Client: No.

Counselor: Why is that?

Client: Well, it depends who I am making it with. If I am making it as a promise to you, then if I get angry at you, I know I might try and kill myself as a way of getting back at you.

Counselor: Actually, a no-suicide contract is not a promise to me but something that you make with yourself. It is an agreement that you have with yourself.

Client: I feel like it would lock me in too much. The word contract sounds like a legally binding sort of a word and I don't want to feel locked in like that.

In this case, the idea of an NSC is suggested to the client by the counselor. As one can see, the client immediately reframes it and calls it a promise. He refuses to make the contract because he knows he could switch ego states and use his Rebellious Child to try to hit back at the counselor. This is an insightful comment by the client. The counselor then puts it to the client again that the NSC is a contract that he has with self, not a promise to the counselor. However, the client is not in the frame of mind to accept that. At that time he is not capable of making an Adult ego state no-suicide contract. Due to his perception of the relationship with the counselor, he is only capable of making a no-suicide promise at that time and thus an NSC is not made.

Unlike Case study 14.1, in which the counselor is requesting a "take your medication" promise, in this instance the counselor is requesting a no-suicide contract and still the client perceives it as a no-suicide promise. This highlights the need for the counselor to be careful about what sort of statement the client is making: a no-suicide contract or a no-suicide promise. Some clients will even say they are making a no-suicide contract when, in fact, it is a promise. One needs to question the client to see if he is making the statement out of conformity to what the counselor is requesting or making a statement to self about how long he wishes not to act on his suicidal impulses. One needs to make a diagnosis of the Adult ego state or the Conforming Child ego state in the client.

Summary of the steps in the no-suicide contract procedure

Step 1: Preparatory information for the person to make an NSC

The helping professional describes to the person the concept of suicidal ambivalence. Using a technique such as the two-chair exercise (see Chapter 12) allows the person to identify and clarify the two parts of self: the Free Child part which wants to live and the Adapted Child aspect of the personality which wants to die. As was stated in Chapter 12 on suicidal ambivalence, such techniques allow the counselor to establish relational contact with the self-destructive aspect of the person (the AC). To quote from Chapter 12:

> The counselor begins to build a relationship with the self-destructive part of the client, his Adapted Child. I cannot stress enough the importance of this. To make good relational contact with the self-destructive part of the client is most therapeutic.

> How does one do this? It is, in essence, no different to establishing a relationship between any two people. First, one starts with simple dialogue in which the counselor and the Adapted Child aspect of the client begin talking to each other. They find out what each other thinks and feels, and as they do this, the counselor displays a sense of compassion, empathy and understanding of this part of the client. As the client senses this, he will begin to feel some respect from the counselor, and thus the relational contact or connection between them grows. As the trust grows, the counselor and the AC ego state of the client may begin stating what they think and feel about each other, and at some point there may even be some form of dispute or disruption between them. The counselor facilitates resolution of that dispute and thus the relationship strengthens even more. The counselor

would also do a similar task with the Free Child aspect of the client. However, most important is the building of such a connection between the counselor and the self-destructive aspect of the client.

One of the most potent criteria for psychological health is the establishment of relationships. If the individual has reasonable relationships in his life, then psychologically he is better off than if he does not. Indeed, it is generally accepted that it is better to have poor quality attachments than no attachments at all. What is being suggested is that one takes the considerable therapeutic value of relationships and directly addresses the self-destructive aspect of the person. One goes to the very core of the matter such that one is applying the curative powers of relational contact directly with the self-destructive part of the person. One establishes a relationship with the self-destructive aspect of the individual's personality and endeavors to establish some sort of coexistence with it.

In one way, this is a type of no-suicide contract itself. It is not changing the suicide decision but buys time with the self-destructive Adapted Child aspect of the client. If one can establish relationship contact or some kind of attachment with the Adapted Child ego state of the individual, then it no longer feels alone, and nor is it on its own. One rarely sees this done in working with the suicidal. If a relationship is established, its subsequent self-destructive ruminations are changed because it no longer has a sense of aloneness. It has an attachment to someone who wants to stay alive and who wants it to stay alive, and thus we have the type of no-suicide contract. It usually takes only two or three times for the person to sit in the Adapted Child ego state chair for him to get a sense and experience of that aspect of self so that later he can access it easily and quickly. With this done, one can then easily address it in the future and the attachment process can forge ahead.

Step 2: Assessing personal responsibility or locus of control

If the individual has a belief in his own personal responsibility for his actions, thoughts and feelings, or demonstrates an internal locus of control, one can proceed with the contracting process. If the person has primarily an external locus of control, the contracting procedure halts.

One then determines if more action needs to be taken, such as some kind of suicide watch, and goes back to relational building in Step 1.

Step 3: Determining the ego state

One determines if the person is making a no-suicide contract from the Adult ego state or a no-suicide promise from the Conforming Child ego state. If he is diagnosed as being in the Adult ego state, then the client can make a no-suicide contract. If the person is not able to adequately stay in the Adult ego state in the contracting process, then the procedure halts. One then determines if more action needs to be taken, such as some kind of suicide watch, and goes back to relational building in Step 1.

The person then makes the contract, which can be stated a number of ways:

- "No matter what happens, I will not kill myself, accidentally or on purpose, for x amount of time."

- "No matter what happens, I will not act on my suicidal thoughts and urges for x amount of time."

Some prefer the second form of wording as it acknowledges there are suicidal urges and that the person is choosing not to act on them for a period of time. To my mind, either is acceptable.

The third aspect of the NSC is the theory of early decisions as cited earlier in this chapter and in depth in Chapter 4. This aspect is not necessary for the NSC procedure to continue, but determines more the course of action the counselor will take with regard to the NSC. If one views suicidal behavior as being based on the suicide decision, one can proceed with some kind of treatment for that decision. An example of this is shown in Chapter 15 on redecision therapy. In this case, the NSC contract is viewed as a stopgap measure only, which allows the person time to receive treatment so that the suicide decision is changed. Once done, the person is at less threat of suicide as he is no longer heavily influenced by that suicidal aspect of his personality. Thus the long-term threat of suicide is reduced. If one is of the view that suicidal urges cannot be "cured", then those people will be seen as always having an elevated longer-term suicide risk and will need to be managed in a similar way whenever self-destructive urges manifest.

Refusal to make a no-suicide contract

It is generally regarded that if a client refuses to make a no-suicide contract (as in Case study 14.2), this indicates he is at significant current risk of making a suicide attempt. This certainly can be the case, but it is not so in all instances, as discussed in Chapter 9. Some people will refuse for other motives. They may wish to present themselves as more suicidal than they actually are, in order to achieve something such as a hospitalization or further psychological investigations; they may exaggerate psychological symptoms for some kind of financial gain, or they may currently suffer from Munchausen syndrome.

Others can refuse from a simple rebellious position. They may have been in the mental healthcare system for some time and developed a rebellious and reactionary attitude. They seek to fight the system and thus will identify instances in which the system requires them to conform, such as with taking medication. Some will stop taking medication as an act of defiance against the health system with which they are currently involved. Some will refuse to make a NSC for the same reason.

Escape hatch

Another reason for refusal, which does not necessarily indicate elevated suicide risk, comes from the idea of suicide as an escape hatch. The whole concept of suicide as an escape hatch is an interesting one in itself.

The term "escape hatch" and its relationship to suicide was coined by Bill Holloway (1973) who wrote a number of monographs in the early 1970s. The term is an interesting one and a very apt choice by Holloway. An escape hatch is usually a good thing. It provides a way to get away from danger or undesirable circumstances. Most people like to have an escape hatch because it makes them feel safer, more comfortable and better able to deal with any current difficulties.

However, the way it is presented in the literature by writers such as Boyd and Cowles-Boyd (1980) and Holloway (1973) is in a negative frame of reference. They see it as necessary to close the suicide escape hatch. They acknowledge that suicide can be seen as an escape hatch that allows one to escape from very undesirable stress or feelings of depression, for example, but, of course, they see suicide as a very poor method of escape. They would suggest other means by which the person can escape from the emotional pain. It is safe to say that this is a commonly held view and a view held by myself.

Inherent in the concept of suicide as an escape hatch is the idea that suicide is a solution to a problem. Some do not like this idea at all and will argue vehemently that suicide is not a solution. They argue that suicide does not solve problems because the person is dead and therefore has no knowledge of the problem being solved. If suicide is seen as an escape hatch, that implies the person is escaping from some problem. This is a view that I agree with in part. Suicide does solve problems in the sense that if, for example, the person is faced with divorce and then dies, he does not have to face it.

Those who work with the suicidal would most often see closing the suicide escape hatch as a worthwhile thing. I would agree with this, but it needs to be considered in another light as well. It is not as simple as it initially seems. This demonstrates another dimension that must be taken into account when working with the suicidal person.

Below are two examples of the suicidal escape hatch and the way in which it can serve a positive psychological function.

CASE STUDY 14.3: SUICIDE AS AN ESCAPE HATCH

A 29-year-old woman writes about the option of killing herself:

Having the option there in the back of my head actually serves to help me. It doesn't help once the danger is more immediate. When it starts making messes. But on a day to day basis it is nice.

It helps with the more minor bad things like "yes this situation is bad, but it's not quite bad enough to kill myself over, which if it does get worse is an option."

Most of the time I have a method picked out. I'm very protective of the method of the moment. I feel like sharing it corrupts it.

There have been times where I felt my method had been corrupted or somehow made unusable. And it immediately has pushed me into a depression, often times making me want to die more. I've had times where I became suicidal because I felt my option to kill myself was ruined. Feeling that option is taken away from me makes everything feel like it is crumbling around me.

It's such a strongheld belief that I will kill myself eventually, I just don't know when. It might be at 90. It might be at 25. A threat to that belief I have trouble handling.

I visualize the method in my head a lot though during times of stress. It's soothing.

This case example demonstrates some of the positive functions her thoughts of suicide serves and illustrates the notion of suicide as an escape hatch. Her last statement sums this up. The thought of suicide can soothe her in times of stress. So why would she want to give up that way of self-soothing by making an NSC?

CASE STUDY 14.4: THE SUICIDE FANTASY AS STRESS RELIEVER

A 40-year-old female describes what she does at home sometimes.

She sits in a chair in her living room and can see the drawer in her kitchen that has many pills in it. It gives her a sense of security or relief somehow. She reports that the pills give her a sense of security for whenever everything just gets too bad.

She imagines putting the pills into little piles and taking one and then two and so forth. She has created a ritualized suicidal fantasy that gives her a sense of solace and relief because it reminds her that she has an escape hatch should she require it one day.

She states:

The pills are a comfort because they give me a sense of choice when I am in that place.

What happens when those pills beckon me?

When my eyes go back to the drawer time after time

What do I imagine when I'm staring at it

Thinking about the pills inside

And the oblivion they could bring to my mind.

As in Case study 14.3, this woman has developed a way of self-soothing by using a suicide fantasy. It is used as a stress reliever. The idea of suicide as an escape hatch has obvious clinical implications.

First, one needs to be aware that closing the suicide escape hatch with an NSC can, in fact, make the situation worse. In such circumstances, the client needs to be able to see other ways of easing the pain (alternative escape hatches) before the counselor suggests closing the suicide escape hatch with an NSC.

Thus we arrive at the point at hand: why some people may refuse to make a no-suicide contract and not be at current high risk. The person may feel that his method of escape is being taken away from him as indicated in Case studies 14.3 and 14.4. Indeed, in Case study 14.2, the man states precisely: "I feel like it would lock me in too much." Thus he refused to make a NSC, not because he is currently at risk but because to make it would make him feel more distress.

Conclusion

The no-suicide contract can be a useful tool for some people to deal with their suicidal urges. It is not a panacea, nor is it appropriate for everyone or every circumstance. This chapter describes the conditions necessary for the NSC to be deemed an appropriate therapeutic procedure. If these conditions are met, then the no-suicide contracting procedure has been described. If it is deemed not appropriate, one then returns to attachment building with the Adapted Child or self-destructive aspect of the individual's personality.

Suicidal people are anxiety-producing for those around them, including helping professionals. This probably explains why the NSC has engendered such a large volume of debate and discussion. The helping professional's anxiety has unknowingly changed the original no-suicide contract into a promise, assurance or commitment. In his desire to be able to go home and not worry about the suicidal person, the counselor seeks such promises and commitments that will reassure him of the person's safety. In using the NSC, one needs to be clear of the difference between the no-suicide contract and the no-suicide promise. In addition, the refusal to make an NSC does not necessarily indicate an increased risk of suicide at that time. People can refuse to make a NSC for other reasons.

Chapter 15

Redecision Therapy

This chapter will describe the process by which an individual can redecide his early decisions, including the suicide decision. Obviously, it is a productive thing to do if the person can make such a decision less influential in his personality. A comprehensive description of redecision therapy would take a whole book in itself. This chapter examines only the actual redecision process, which gives insight into how the therapy functions and illustrates further the nature of early decisions, including the suicide decision.

This approach was originally developed by Goulding and Goulding (1979) who also developed the idea of the no-suicide contract. The basic process is as follows.

1. Contract for change

The client and counselor discuss the difficulties and define the problem. For example, the person is having suicidal ruminations, is thinking about suicide and has done some planning for a suicide attempt. The client has made a no-suicide contract, which buys some time to work on changing the suicide decision made in childhood. The client makes a contract to change his early suicide decision to one of wanting to live and not die by his own hand.

2. Diagnosis of early decision

The counselor diagnoses the problem in terms of the decision the person made in childhood. Goulding and Goulding (1979) state that the young child can make a variety of decisions and have classified twelve:

- don't
- don't exist
- don't be you
- don't be a child

- don't grow up
- don't succeed
- don't be important
- don't be close
- don't belong
- don't be well
- don't think
- don't feel.

In cognitive behavioral therapy terms, these are thinking errors. The theory of early decisions provides an explanation of how such thinking errors originate.

These are summaries of the decisions a child can make in response to adverse parenting in childhood, as explained in Chapter 4. First, the child is placed in circumstances that he finds distressing and difficult. This is called the early scene, which we all have—those events that occurred in our childhood which we recall as painful memories and from which we made decisions about self and life. These were discussed in Chapter 9 when examining the "Bad Day at Black Rock" method of diagnosing the suicide decision. An example is shown in Case study 15.1.

CASE STUDY 15.1: AN EARLY SCENE

I was about ten years old and was in the washroom doing some laundry with my sister. My mom was sitting at the table next to the kitchen. I heard this loud noise and lots of swearing and shouting. It was my dad in the garage. He came into the house from the garage and walked by my mom saying "F..." and "S..." to her. I looked up from the laundry as the door was open and I could see my dad walk into the door way. He saw me there and he picked up a telephone book and threw it at me. It hit my right shoulder so that it turned me around a bit. It hurt real bad. He then just walked off, he didn't say anything or do anything more. I thought "That's weird". It was always so confusing. No one ever said what was going on. My sister said nothing, but I felt sorry for her, and my mom said nothing. It was treated like it never even happened.

But I knew my dad hated me. He said many times that I looked like his father and he always hated his father. He was always so angry and he hated me so much. I knew he didn't want me. He told me that. I was unwanted and unlovable, so I wanted to die. (White 2010b)

Figure 15.1 shows a drawing this man made of the event in his "Bad Day at Black Rock" exercise. As one can see from the case study, this man made the "don't exist" or suicide decision in reaction to the events that occurred in this scene.

Figure 15.1 A "Bad Day at Black Rock" scene

3. Recreating the early scene

After the treatment contract has been defined and the diagnosis of the decision has been made, the counselor sets up a two-chair situation for the client to recreate the early scene once again. The counselor invites the client to recall that early scene, to relive it and re-experience it. As the client does this, he will move more into his Child ego state, and start to feel and think as he did when he was ten years old in the laundry that day.

It should be noted that this is not role playing. As the client becomes more involved in the dialogue between the two aspects of his personality, he again, psychologically, becomes that ten-year-old boy. He will start to act like and talk as the young boy did at that time all those years ago. Psychologically, he is in the scene once again, not just role-playing the scene. This forms the scientific basis of redecision therapy, which comes from psychopharmacological research in the area of state-dependent learning.

In state-dependent learning, when a person learns something in a chemically altered state, he can recall that learning better if he is in the same chemically altered state. For instance, if a man learns the words to a new song when he is drinking beer, a week later he will have better recall of those words if he is under the influence of beer than if he is not intoxicated. The learning he did is dependent on the psychological state he was in at the time.

The boy in Figure 15.1, was in a highly emotional and physiologically aroused state when he made the suicide decision in the scene. When he regresses into that scene, he will find that he recalls all sorts of things which he thought he had forgotten. More importantly, if he gets into the same state of physiological arousal he was in that day, then he is in a better position to "relearn" what he learned the first time. His redecision, or new learning, in the same state of arousal will have more impact than new learning in a different state, such as in a fully logical Adult ego state frame of mind. Recreating the early scene is therefore important in the redecision method. Fortunately, it is not hard to do. One can use the two-chair technique to permit regression in order to achieve the same emotional and physiological state of arousal as occurred when the first set of state-dependent learning was achieved.

Usually, the person remains in his chair and another chair is placed in front of him as in Figure 15.2. The extra chair will be the Critical Parent ego state chair.

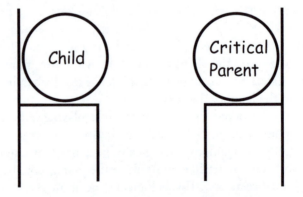

Figure 15.2 The two-chair exercise

In his chair, he is asked to talk from the Child ego state position. He is asked to be that part of his personality and dialogue from it. When he moves to the second chair, he is asked to talk from the Critical Parent aspect of his personality. In the Child ego state chair, he will be himself as the ten-year-old who standing in the laundry. When he moves to the second chair, he will be the father who now represents part of his own Critical Parent ego state. All the anger, being told he was hated and the throwing of the phone book, which the father originally directed at the boy, now forms part of his own Parent ego state. An example of the two-chair dialogue follows in a summarized form.

Client in Child ego state chair:

"I have always looked up to you, umm, you were my father and I just wanted you to, umm, just show me that you liked me. I tried to, to…help you, do chores at home, make, make things…that you may like."

Client in Critical Parent ego state chair:

"You were just standing there looking dumb, you should know that is bad. Who cares anyway…tell someone who cares…"

Client in Child ego state chair:

"You know I can't tell mom she, she…is just scared of you. I just tried to do good things for you…so we could be friends and help each other. I am just confused."

Client in Critical Parent ego state chair:

"You're disgusting… I never wanted you. I'm just angry at you."

Client in Child ego state chair:

"Please don't say that…umm… What do you want me to do for you?"

This is the type of dialogue that allows the client to re-experience the early scene, become those aspects of the personality that are in conflict, and recreate the same physiologically aroused state he was in when the original learning occurred. After this dialogue continues for a while, the counselor then moves to the fourth part of the redecision process in which the client makes his redecision.

4. The redecision

To explain this, one must look at the various parts of the Child ego state. See Figure 15.3.

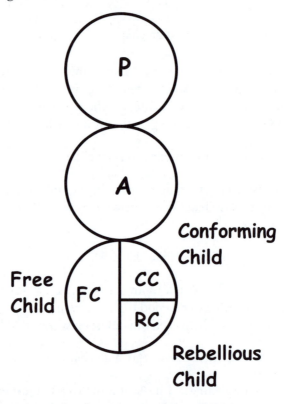

Figure 15.3 The three parts of the Child ego state

In the Child ego state dialogue above, the client is in his Conforming Child ego state. He is pleading, explaining himself, trying to be good, trying to get his father to behave another way and taking the anger. This will support his early suicide decision because this is how it played out in the original early scene. As a consequence, the counselor is wanting the client to change from this ego state at some point.

To do this, the counselor uses what are called heighteners. The counselor asks the client to say or do certain things so that there is likely to be shift in ego states. In essence, the counselor is wanting the client to shift ego states from Conforming Child to Rebellious Child. If this happens, then one reaches the point of redecision. The counselor heightens for the client what he is doing by asking the client to say things to the Critical Parent chair. For example, in summarized form:

> Counselor to client, who is in the Child ego state chair:
>
> "Tell your father that he is right and you should have been doing something else so as to not make him mad. Tell him that."
>
> Client in Child ego state chair:
>
> [Usually a short period of silence as the client contemplates what is being requested.]
>
> "I'm not going to say that."
>
> Counselor to client, who is in the Child ego state chair:
>
> "Well, that is what you are doing. I am just asking you to verbalize your behavior."
>
> Client in Child ego state chair:
>
> "I won't say that."

The vast majority of clients will not do what the counselor requests at this point. A few will and do start to tell the Critical Parent that they are bad and should die. If that happens, the counselor stops the process because it will reinforce the early decision, and then moves on to something else.

The vast majority of clients refuse because they are not willing to verbalize such self-defeating thoughts and feelings. The client feels organismic disgust at such a task. By refusing to do what the counselor suggests, the client is moving into the Rebellious Child position. Then the counselor tries to get that rebellion in the client to shift to the Critical Parent in the chair.

Counselor to client, who is in the Child ego state chair:

"What are you willing to say to your father?"

Client in Child ego state chair:

"Umm… I don't know but I know that I don't want to agree with him."

Counselor to client, who is in the Child ego state chair:

"If you are not going to agree with your father, what are you going to do? He threw the phone book that hurt you!"

Client in Child ego state chair:

"Well, he shouldn't have treated me like that."

Counselor to client, who is in the Child ego state chair:

"So tell him in the chair there."

Client in Child ego state chair:

"I don't have to seek your approval any more. You should not have thrown it at me, it hurt. I am not disgusting and I can feel good about myself and stay alive! I don't need to kill myself to give you what you want!"

The point of redecision has just been achieved. The client is in the process of making a decision that counters his early suicide decision and relearns what was his prior state-dependent learning. He has rebelled against it, usually with some potency, which can be found in the anger of the Rebellious Child ego state. He has moved from the Conforming Child ego state to the Rebellious Child ego state, and thus the first stage of the redecision has been made. This is shown diagrammatically in Figure 15.4.

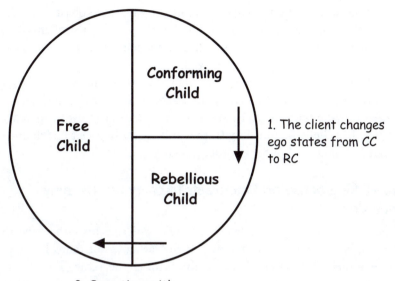

1. The client changes ego states from CC to RC

2. Over time with reflection, trying new contracts of relating the client finally shifts to FC and the redecision is complete

Figure 15.4 The two steps in the redecision process

He has revisited the early scene in which the original suicide decision was made. He has dialogued with the parent figure, moved into Rebellious Child ego state and made a redecision while in that same scene. All that remains is for him to continue the process by which he will eventually move into the Free Child ego state. Sometimes at this point the client will say he needs to do it again so he can convince himself more. The response to that is it's not about convincing self of the new decision; instead, he needs to sit with the new decision, feel the feelings about that and then complete the process as follows.

5. Bringing the client back to the here and now

The client gets back into his Adult ego state and out of the prior state of heightened arousal. He leaves the regressed Child ego state of the early scene. The counselor ends the two-chair exercise and removes the chair. The counselor asks the client questions about what he is thinking, what sense he makes of it and so on. These questions will bring the client back into the Adult thinking mode. The client and counselor intellectually process what happened, with the counselor giving feedback on what he observed.

At this point, the counselor can perhaps explain a bit of the process to the client. The main point is about feeling what the Child felt as it made the new decision—when it rebelled against the parent figure. The client should sit with that and reflect on what he felt and what he thought about it in order to experience it.

6. Making behavioral contracts to carry out the new decision

The client may make a contract that, when he sees his father again, he will behave and feel differently. If the father is not there, he may have some other parent figure who is doing the same. The client makes a contract to begin relating to these people in more healthy ways. This allows the client to experience first-hand the consequences of his redecision. This may feel good but it may also cause some distress, which can constitute the content of later sessions in which subsequent redecisions are made around the same issue.

As these behavioral experiments happen, the client begins to shift slowly into the Free Child ego state, and the new decision becomes the norm. As this happens, the suicide decision becomes less potent in the personality, and the person starts to think that suicide is not a viable solution to problems. The directive to die inside his head wanes over time. For a strong early decision, this process make take six months to achieve. For less dominant decisions, the process can be much shorter. When this is the case, sometimes the suicidal urges can diminish quite substantially in a reasonably short space of time.

7. Ongoing relational contact with the self-destructive aspect of the client

As the individual goes through this process of initial redecision, the shift to Rebellious Child, followed by subsequent redecisions and the shift to Free Child, the counselor is regularly addressing the Adapted Child ego state that has the suicidal urges. The importance of this was mentioned in Chapter 14 and it also allows an ongoing appraisal of how potent the suicidal urges are in the person. As the

Adapted Child senses the contact with the counselor and develops an attachment, this significantly facilitates the shift to the Free Child and the end point of the redecision process.

Conclusion

The seven steps of the redecision process are:

1. contract for change

2. diagnosis of early decision

3. recreating the early scene

4. the redecision

5. bringing the client back to the here and now

6. making behavioral contracts to carry out the new decision

7. ongoing relational contact with the self-destructive aspect of the client.

Through this process the suicidal person can truly address his suicidal urges and make them significantly less influential in his decision making. As a youngster, the person makes the early decision that suicide is a viable solution to problems and highly distressing feelings. As he enters adulthood, this decision simply sits in his psyche and he is quite often unaware of it. When certain circumstances arise, the decision becomes operational and the individual begins to have suicidal thoughts and urges. At this point, the NSC can be useful as it buys time for the redecision therapy to occur. If effective, the longer-term problem is solved because the early suicide decision is altered. Any future events that may cause the suicide decision to become operational have little effect because the original decision is altered.

Epilogue

The study in this book of understanding, assessing and supporting the suicidal individual is complete. Perhaps just one last thing needs to be said regarding this topic.

Suicide holds an infamous place in the psyche of us all. It is anathema to us because we all have such a will to live. We see very young children relentlessly strive to survive illness, and our bodies are designed with a myriad of mechanisms to survive terrible assaults of all kinds. We are also acutely aware of death and that each and every one of us dies sooner or later.

When we are confronted with the death of a loved one, we often reflect on our own lives and mortality. If that death is due to old age, accident or disease, we may not like it but we can understand it and we eventually accept it. We can put it down to "that's life" or bad luck. However, suicide is different. When we see a member of our own species die by his own hand, especially a young member, that is much harder to understand and accept. Indeed, we know that many of our species kill themselves each and every day. We find this much more difficult to reconcile in our own minds.

There is one other thing that makes suicide exceptional in our minds. It shows that some of our species do kill themselves, which reminds us that we can also. This frightens most people: "If others can do it, then perhaps I can." Maybe Freud was right and each of us does have a Thanatos or self-destructive urge in our very core. When we see or hear of suicide, it reminds us that we also have such urges in our own psyches, and we find that perturbing. If we were pushed to the very limit of our physical and psychological resources, would we indeed take the solution of suicide?

Stopper Analysis

Questionnaire

This questionnaire is a forced choice questionnaire. You answer "True" or "False" to all the questions.

_____ 1. I nearly always plan my work several weeks in advance.

_____ 2. When others talk a lot, I usually just "turn them off".

_____ 3. I feel uncomfortable when people silently look at me.

_____ 4. I rarely do anything just for the fun of doing it.

_____ 5. I sometimes "go blank" when asked to solve a problem.

_____ 6. I try hard at most things I do.

_____ 7. I have never really decided what I want to do with my life.

_____ 8. I seem to be more of a follower than a leader.

_____ 9. I don't visit very much with family and friends.

_____ 10. I tend to distrust people until I really know them.

_____ 11. People I work with usually make their own plans in what they do.

_____ 12. Sometimes others don't understand my instructions.

_____ 13. There have been times when I wished I could just "disappear".

_____ 14. I have been accused of being too serious.

_____ 15. I don't seem to be as smart as many people I know.

_____ 16. I like to keep several projects going at the same time.

_____ 17. I often put off making major decisions.

_____ 18. I have some difficulty in seeing myself as successful.

_____ 19. I sometimes feel "left out" of family and other groups.

_____ 20. I have some difficulty telling my family how much I love them.

_____ 21. I use a systematic method of measuring other's work place performance.

_____ 22. I sometimes mentally practice what I am going to say to others.

_____ 23. Sometimes I feel like I am unloved by others.

_____ 24. I enjoy serious or dramatic TV programmes more than comedies.

_____ 25. I don't read much educational type material.

_____ 26. I have changed careers or jobs several times.

_____ 27. I sort of take life as it comes rather than make detailed plans.

_____ 28. I often feel inadequate to other people.

_____ 29. I don't like group settings like church or social clubs.

_____ 30. I feel somewhat uncomfortable around people who are quite affectionate.

_____ 31. I am consider a "stickler" for results rather than details.

_____ 32. I like to argue or discuss controversial subjects.

_____ 33. I think I was an unwanted or unplanned child.

_____ 34. I am not very good at telling funny stories or jokes.

_____ 35. Self-discipline is sometimes difficult for me.

_____ 36. I am not content to live with average success.

_____ 37. I don't like to have my time structured for me.

_____ 38. I often "give in" to others rather than take care of my own wants.

_____ 39. I don't think much about my ancestors or cultural heritage.

_____ 40. I don't give praise or recognition unless it is deserved.

Scoring

1, 11, 21, 31	Total of falses _____	Others are incapable of doing things.
2, 12, 22, 32	Total of trues _____	Does not listen to others.
3, 13, 23, 33	Total of trues _____	Don't exist.
4, 14, 24, 34	Total of trues _____	Don't be a child.
5, 15, 25, 35	Total of trues _____	Don't think.
6, 16, 26, 36	Total of trues _____	Don't make it.
7, 17, 27, 37	Total of trues _____	Don't do anything.
8, 18, 28, 38	Total of trues _____	Don't be important.
9, 19, 29, 39	Total of trues _____	Don't belong.
10, 20, 30, 40	Total of trues _____	Don't be close.
	Grand total _____	

Count up the number of "False" responses to questions 1, 11, 21, 31 and place the number in the scoring sheet. For all other scores, add up the relevant number of "True" responses and record the total of each in the appropriate place.

Total up all the scores to get the grand total.

Any total of 3 or 4 indicates that at some time the person may have made that decision.

If the grand total is more than 20, this indicates the presence of the "Don't exist" decision, even though it may not show up in the individual "Don't exist" score.

This questionnaire comes from Bob Avary (1976) and is reprinted with his permission.

References

Akechi, T., Okamura, H., Kugaya, A., Nakano, T. *et al.* (2000) 'Suicidal ideation in cancer patients with major depression.' *Japanese Journal of Clinical Oncology 30*, 5, 221–4.

Alderman, T. (1997) *The Scarred Soul: Understanding and Ending Self-Inflicted Violence.* Oakland, CA: New Harbinger Publications.

Allen, J.R. and Allen, B.A. (1978) *Guide to Psychiatry: A Handbook on Psychiatry for Health Professionals.* New York: Medical Examination Publishing Co., Inc.

American Psychiatric Association (1994) *Diagnostic and Statistical Manual of Mental Disorders (Fourth edition).* Washington, DC: American Psychiatric Press, Inc.

Assey, J.L. (1985) 'The suicide prevention contract.' *Perspectives in Psychiatric Care 23*, 99–103.

Australian Psychological Society (1999) *Suicide: An Australian Psychological Society Discussion Paper.* Melbourne: Australian Psychological Society.

Australian Psychological Society (2010) *Understanding and Preventing Suicide in Young People.* Available at www.psychology.org.au/publications/tip_sheets/preventing_suicide/, accessed on January 3, 2010.

Avary, B. (1976) *Transactional Analysis for Management.* Odessa, TX: Bob Avary & Associates.

Beautrais, A.L. (2001) 'Australian research.' *LIFE: Living is for everyone.* Available at www.livingisforeveryone.com.au/Library.aspx?PageID=55&ItemID=1095, accessed on January 3, 2010.

Beck, A.T. (1967) *Depression: Clinical, Experimental and Theoretical Aspects.* London: Staples Press.

Beck, A.T., Brown, G. and Steer, R.A. (1989) 'Prediction of eventual suicide in psychiatric inpatients by clinical ratings of hopelessness.' *Journal of Consulting and Clinical Psychology 57*, 2, 309–310.

Beck, A.T., Steer, R.A., Kovacs, M. and Garrison, B. (1985) 'Hopelessness and eventual suicide: A 10-year prospective study of patients hospitalized with suicidal ideation.' *American Journal of Psychiatry 142*, 559–63.

Berne, E. (1964) *Games People Play: The Psychology of Human Relationships.* New York: Grove Press.

Bowlby, J. (1971) *Attachment.* Harmondsworth: Pelican.

Boyd, H.S. (1972) 'Suicidal decisions.' *Transactional Analysis Journal 2*, 2, 87–8.

Boyd, H.S. and Cowles-Boyd, L. (1980) 'Blocking tragic scripts.' *Transactional Analysis Journal 10*, 3, 227–9.

Cameron, L. (1988) *Talking TA.* Perth: WPATA Publications.

Campbell, D. (1999) 'The Role of the Father in the Pre-Suicide State.' In P. Perelberg (ed.) *Psychoanalytic Understanding of Violence and Suicide.* London: Routledge.

Carr, S. and Francis, A. (2009) 'Childhood maltreatment and adult personality disorder symptoms in a non-clinical sample.' *Australian Psychologist 44*, 3, 146–55.

Caruso, K (2009) *Suicide Statistics.* Available at www.suicide.org/suicide-statistics.html, accessed on December 7, 2009.

Caruso, K. (2010) *No-Suicide Contracts: What They are and How You Should Use Them.* Available at www.suicide.org/no-suicide-contracts.html, accessed on March 29, 2010.

Clark, D.C. and Fawcett, J. (1992) 'Review of Empirical Risk Factors for Evaluation of the Suicidal Patient.' In B. Bongar (ed.) *Suicide: Guidelines for Assessment, Management and Treatment.* New York: Oxford University Press.

Clark, D.C. and Horton-Deutsch, S.L. (1992) 'Assessment in Absentia: The Value of the Psychological Autopsy Method for Studying Antecedents of Suicide and Predicting Future Suicides.' In R. Maris, A.L. Berman, J.T. Maltsberger and R.I. Yufit (eds) *Assessment and Prediction of Suicide.* New York: Guilford Press.

Collins, J.K. (1991) 'Research into adolescence: A forgotten era.' *Australian Psychologist 26*, 1, 1–9.

Commonwealth Department of Human Services and Health (1994) *Handbook for Medical Practitioners and Other Health Care Workers on Alcohol and Other Drug Problems.* Canberra: Australian Government Publishing Service.

Cooper, J. and Kapur, N. (2004) 'Assessing Suicide Risk.' In D. Duffy and T. Ryan (eds) *New Approaches to Preventing Suicide: A Manual for Practitioners.* London: Jessica Kingsley Publishers.

Cutajar, M.C., Mullen, P.E., Ogloff, J.R.P., Thomas, S.D. *et al.* (2010) 'Suicide and fatal overdoses in child sexual abuse victims: A historical cohort study.' *The Medical Journal of Australia 192*, 4, 184–7.

Dalton, V. (1999) 'Suicide in prison 1980 to 1998: National overview.' *Trends and Issues in Crime and Criminal Justice.* Canberra: Australian Institute of Criminology.

Drye, R.C., Goulding, R.L. and Goulding, M.M. (1973) 'No-suicide decisions: Patient monitoring of suicidal risk.' *American Journal of Psychiatry 130*, 171–4.

Edwards, S. (2007) *No-Suicide Contracts, No-Suicide Agreements and No-Suicide Assurances: An Exploratory Study of Their Nature, Utilization and Perceived Effectiveness.* Dissertation. Perth: University of Western Australia.

Egan, M.P. (1997) 'Contracting for safety: A concept analysis.' *Crisis: The Journal of Crisis Intervention and Suicide Prevention 18*, 17–23.

Eyland, S., Corben, S. and Barton, J. (1997) 'Suicide prevention in New South Wales correctional centers.' *Crisis: The Journal of Crisis Intervention and Suicide Prevention 18*, 4, 163–9.

Favazza, A.R. and Rosenthal, R.J. (1993) 'Diagnostic issues in self-mutilation.' *Hospital and Community Psychiatry 44*, 2, 134–40.

Frankl, V.E. (1959) *Man's Search for Meaning.* Singapore: Washington Square Press.

Garlow, S.J., Rosenberg, J., Moore, J.D., Haas, A.P. *et al.* (2007) 'Depression, desperation, and suicidal ideation in college students: Results from the American Foundation for Suicide Prevention College Screening Project at Emory University.' *Depression and Anxiety 25*, 6, 482–8.

George, N. (2008) *Gatekeeper Suicide Prevention Training Workshop Handouts.* Curtin University of Technology, Perth: Telethon Institute for Child Health Research.

Goin, M. (2003) 'The "suicide-prevention contract": A dangerous myth.' *Psychiatric News 38*, 14, 3.

Goulding, R. (1972) 'New Directions in Transactional Analysis: Creating an Environment for Redecision and Change.' In C.J. Sager and H.S. Kaplan (eds) *Progress in Group and Family Therapy.* New York: Brunner/Mazel.

Goulding, R.L. and Goulding, M.M. (1978) *The Power is in the Patient: A TA/Gestalt Approach to Psychotherapy.* San Francisco, CA: TA Press.

Goulding, M.M. and Goulding, R.L. (1979) *Changing Lives through Redecision Therapy.* New York: Brunner/Mazel Publishers.

Gratz, K.L. and Chapman, A.L. (2009) *Freedom from Self-Harm: Overcoming Self-Injury with Skills from DBT and Other Treatments.* Oakland, CA: New Harbinger Publications.

Green, B. (2009) *Deliberate Self-Harm: Breadth and Scope*. Available at http://priory.com/psych/DSH.htm, accessed on December 26, 2009.

Hassan, R. (1996) 'Social factors in suicide in Australia.' *Trends and Issues in Crime and Criminal Justice 52*. Canberra: Australian Institute of Criminology.

Hawton, K. and van Heeringen, K. (2009) 'Suicide: The risk factors.' *The Lancet 373*, 9672, 1372–81.

Hayes, L.M. (1995) *Prison Suicide: An Overview and Guide to Prevention*. Washington, DC: US Department of Justice, National Institute of Corrections.

Hipple, J. and Cimbolic, P. (1979) 'Contracts to Stay Alive and Get Well.' In J. Hipple and P. Cimbolic (eds) *The Counselor and Suicidal Crisis: Diagnosis and Intervention*. Springfield, IL: Charles C. Thomas.

Holloway, W.H. (1973) *Shut the Escape Hatch: Monograph IV. The Monograph Series*. Medina, OH: Midwest Institute for Human Understanding.

Humphry, D. (1991) *Final Exit: The Practicalities of Self-Deliverance and Assisted Suicide for the Dying*. New York: Penguin Books.

Jenet, R. and Segal R. (1985) 'Provoked shooting by police as a mechanism for suicide.' *The American Journal of Forensic Medicine and Pathology 6*, 274–85.

Johnson, B.S. (1997) *Psychiatric Mental Health Nursing*. Philadelphia, PA: Lippincott-Raven Publishers.

Johnston, S. (2009) 'Anger and its management from a Buddhist psychologist's perspective.' *Psych News Newsletter: The Australian Psychological Society*, November 2009, 10.

Kleiner, A. (2010) *Suicide Notes*. Available at www.well.com/~art/suicidenotes.html, accessed on February 7, 2010.

Kroll, J. (2000) 'Use of no-suicide contracts by psychiatrists in Minnesota.' *American Journal of Psychiatry 157*, 1684–6.

Kroll, J. (2007) 'No-suicide contracts as a suicide prevention strategy.' *Psychiatric Times 24*, 8.

Little, R. (2009) 'Understanding the psychodynamics of suicidal clients.' *Transactional Analysis Journal 39*, 3, 219–28.

Mahrer, J. (1993) *The Use of No-Suicide Contracts and Agreements with Suicidal Patients*. Dissertation. Palo Alto, CA: Pacific Graduate School of Psychology.

McArthur, M., Camilleri, P. and Webb, H. (1999) 'Strategies for managing suicide and self-harm in prisons.' *Trends and Issues in Crime and Criminal Justice*, August 1999. Canberra: Australian Institute of Criminology.

McCormick, P. (1971) *Guide for Use of a Life Script Questionaire*. San Francisco, CA: Transactional Publications.

McNeel, J.R. (1980) 'The early demand.' *Transactional Analysis Journal 10*, 1, 47–8.

Medical Dictionary (2010) *Locus of Control*. Available at http://medical-dictionary.thefreedictionary.com/locus+of+control, accessed on April 14, 2010.

Midgley, D. (1993) 'Character disorder: A TA perspective.' *ITA News*, Summer, Number 36, 4–6.

Miller, K.M., Sayers, M., Jones, J., Follett, D. and Ministerial Council for Suicide Prevention (2005) *Information and Support Pack for those Concerned about Someone who is Distressed or Suicidal*. Perth: Ministerial Council for Suicide Prevention.

Moscicki, E.K. (1995) 'Epidemiology of Suicidal Behavior.' In M.M. Silverman and R.W. Maris (eds) *Suicide Prevention: Toward the Year 2000*. New York: Guilford.

Mussen, P.H., Conger, J.J. and Kagan, J. (1974) *Child Development and Personality*. Harper: London.

Newcombe, R. and Woods, S. (2010) *How Risky is Ecstasy? A Model for Comparing the Mortality Risks of Ecstasy Use, Dance Parties and Related Activities*. Available at www. drugtext.org/library/articles/newcombe.htm, accessed on January 7, 2010.

Perroud, N., Uher, R., Marusic, A., Rietschel, M. *et al.* (2009) 'Suicidal ideation during treatment of depression with escitalopram and nortriptyline in Genome-Based Therapeutic Drugs for Depression (GENDEP): A clinical trial.' *BMC Medicine 7*, 1–14.

Piaget, J. and Inhelder, B. (1969) *The Psychology of the Child*. New York: Basic Books, Inc.

Reid, W.J. (1998) 'Promises, promises: Don't rely on patients' no-suicide/no-violence "contracts".' *Journal of Practical Psychiatry and Behavioral Health 4*, 316–18.

Reilly, P.M. and Shopshire, M.S. (2002) *Anger Management for Substance Abuse and Mental Health Clients: A Cognitive Behavioral Therapy Manual*. Rockville, MD: Center for Substance Abuse Treatment, Substance Abuse and Mental Health Services Administration.

Rotter, J.B. (1966) 'Generalized expectancies for internal versus external control of reinforcement.' *Psychological Monographs 80* (Whole No. 609).

Shioiri, T., Nishimura, A., Akazawa, K., Abe, R. *et al.* (2005) 'Incidence of note-leaving remains constant despite increasing suicide rates.' *Psychiatry and Clinical Neurosciences 59*, 226–8.

Simon, R.I. (1999) 'The suicide prevention contract: clinical, legal, and risk management issues.' *Journal of the American Academy of Psychiatry and the Law 27*, 445–50.

Steele, A.A. and McLennan, J. (1995) 'Suicidal and counter-suicidal thinking.' *Australian Psychologist 30*, 2, 149–52.

Steiner, C. (1971) *Games Alcoholics Play*. New York: Grove Press.

Stewart, I. and Joines, V. (1987) *TA Today*. Nottingham: Lifespace Publishing.

Stone, S. (2009) *The Silent Scream, Can It Be Stilled?* Available at http://sarahsfleeces. wordpress.com/2009/09/22/the-silent-scream-can-it-be-stilled/, accessed on December 26, 2009.

Stone, S. (2010) *How the Silent Scream Was Stilled (self harm part 2)*. Available at http:// sarahsfleeces.wordpress.com/2010/01/06/how-the-silent-scream-was-stilled-self-harm-part-2/, accessed on January 7, 2010.

Temby, I. (1990) 'Neglected to death.' *Criminology Australia*, July/August, 19–20.

Treatment Protocol Project (2004) *Management of Mental Disorders (Fourth Edition)*. Sydney: World Health Organization Collaborating Centre for Evidence in Mental Health Policy.

Thomas, A., Chess, S. and Birch, H.G. (1968) *Temperament and Behavior Disorders in Children*. New York: New York University Press

van Wormer, K. and Odiah, C. (1999) 'The psychology of suicide-murder and the death penalty.' *Journal of Criminal Justice 27*, 4, 361–70.

Wada, K., Murao, J., Hikasa, K., Ota, T. *et al.* (1998) 'A clinical analysis of the suicidal ideation of outpatients with major depression.' *Sheishin Igaku 39*, 1077–82.

White, T. (1986) *How Kids Grow Up and Leave Home: Two Years Old, Four Years Old and Adolescence*. Perth: T.A. Books.

White, T. (1991) *Staying Alive: A Handbook on the No-Suicide Contract*. Perth: T.A. Books.

White, T. (1995) 'Born unwanted: The developmental effects of denied abortion.' *TA Times Newsletter*, August 1995, 9–10. Available at www.ynot1.com.au/magazines/ Born%20unwanted.pdf, accessed on February 2, 2010.

White, T. (2010) *Question Time*. Available at http://graffiti99.blogspot.com/2010/02/ question-time.html, accessed on February 24, 2010.

White, T. (2010a) *Life Script Analysis 1*. Available at http://graffiti99.blogspot. com/2010/02/life-script-analysis-1.html, accessed on May 7, 2010.

White, T. (2010b) *Life Script Analysis 3*. Available at http://graffiti99.blogspot. com/2010/02/life-script-analysis-3.html, accessed on May 7, 2010.

White, T. (2010c) *Life Script Analysis 2*. Available at http://graffiti99.blogspot. com/2010/02/life-script-analysis-2.html, accessed on May 10, 2010.

White, T. (2010d) *Life Script Analysis 4*. Available at http://graffiti99.blogspot. com/2010/03/life-script-analysis-4.html, accessed on May 10, 2010.

White, T. (2010e) *Contracts and Promises*. Available at http://graffiti99.blogspot. com/2010/04/contracts-and-promises.html, accessed on April 12, 2010.

Wilkinson, R. and Marmot, M. (1998) *Social Determinants of Health: The Solid Facts*. Geneva: World Health Organization.

Woollams, S. and Brown, M. (1978) *Transactional Analysis*. Ann Arbor, MI: Huron Valley Institute Press.

World Health Organization (2009) *Suicide Prevention*. World Health Organization Mental Health. Available at www.who.int/mental_health/prevention/suicide/ suicideprevent/en/, accessed on November 15, 2009.

Further Reading

More on transactional analysis can be found in the book *TA Today* by Stewart and Joines (1987).

Further reading on suicide, self-harm and transactional analysis can also be found at the following locations:

www.ynot1.com.au

http://graffiti99.blogspot.com

http://graffiti99.blogspirit.com

These include a regularly updated catalogue of articles and comments, as well as some cutting-edge thinking on these three areas.

Alternatively, one can also find more on transactional analysis in the book *Talking TA* available from the writer here.

Any comments or questions on suicide, self-harm and transactional analysis can be directed to Tony White at:

Western Institute

136 Loftus Street

North Perth, 6006

Western Australia

Australia.

Email: agbw@bigpond.com

Subject Index

Note: Page numbers in italics refer to figures.

abortion, denied, developmental effects 51

abuse
  emotional, in childhood 47–8
  physical, in childhood 9, 43–4, 47–9, 82
  rational, in childhood 51–2
  sexual, in childhood 9, 47–8, 82, 153
  of substances 98

accidents
  and suicide 16–18, 17, 18, 40, 107, 155
  see also high-risk behavior

adaptability, in children 54, 55

Adapted Child (AC) ego state 31, 206, 210–13, 210, 236–7, 252–3

adolescence, and suicide pacts 66

adolescents
  as poor risk-takers 105–6
  and suicide 56

Adult ego state 25, 31, 113, 142, 196–7, 251–2
  and no-suicide contracts 229, 230, 234

Adult in the Child (A1) ego state see Little Professor (A1) ego state

alcohol 10, 22, 108, 196, 216

and regression 110–12, 110, 111–12

ambivalence, suicidal 204–13, 205
  assessing 212–13
  diary 207–10
  understanding 205–10
  working with 210–12

American Psychiatric Association 114
  DSM-IV (1994) 64, 125, 192–3, 193–4

amygdala, access 69, 100, 199

anatomy, knowledge of surface 89–90, 90

anger 50, 70, 155–6

anorexia nervosa, and suicide statistics 9

anxiety 70, 109, 198, 242

At-Risk Management System (ARMS), in prisons 106, 184–5

attention seeking 84–6, 195

Auschwitz, psychological consequences 36

Australia, statistics 97, 120–1, 124

Australian Psychological Society 96, 107, 112

automatic responses 44

"Bad Day at Black Rock" exercise 162–73, 163, 167, 169, 171, 245

Berne, Eric, Games People Play (1964) 21

bipolar disorder, and suicide statistics 9

bodily dismorphic disorder, and suicide statistics 9

bodily mutilation, in context 75–6
  see also self-harm

bodily needs, newborn children 27–8

body language, and no-suicide contract 177–8

bombers, suicide 14, 15

borderline personality 116–18, 193

brain, access 69

breast augmentation surgery, and suicide statistics 9

bulimia, and dissociation 78

Cannon, Walter, fight or flight response to stress 69

car accidents
  and suicide 16–17, 17–18, 47–8
  suicide made to look like 10

castration 75

change
  sucidal gestures 41

child development, theories 102, 151, 198

Child ego state
  and early decision-making 42–4
  early scene recreation 245–7
  excluded 79
  flight response 155–6
  function 31–2
  intellectual understanding 197
  and irrational demands 50–1

and parents 52
and redecision therapy
   248–51, *248*
reexperiencing 103
and regression 199–200
structure 25–6
talking about suicide
   144
childhood abuse *see* abuse
childlike behavior 25, 71,
   100
children
   development theories
      102
   newborn, ego states
      26–30, *27*
   personal resources 54–6
   rational and irrational
      demands by parents
      49–52
   responsibility for, as a
      protective factor 101
   suicide decisions 37–41
   support for decisions
      52–3
   temperament qualities
      54–6
chronic suicidal crisis
   219–21, *220*
circumcision 75
clinical depression 128–9
cognitive behavioral
   therapy (CBT) 37
cognitive conclusions,
   determining 153–4
command hallucinations
   115–16, 192
Commonwealth
   Department of
   Human Services and
   Health, reasons for
   drug use 108–9
complacency, and suicide
   decisions 55–6
compulsive behavior 28,
   83–4, 197

Conforming Child (CC)
   ego state 31, *230*,
   231–2, 234, 248–51
consent, mutual, and
   no-suicide contracts
   228–9
counseling
   amenability to change
      54
   for new Parent ego state
      tapes 63–4
   response to stress 71–2
   for self-harm 81
   two-chair situation
      210–13
counselors
   legal obligations 185
   as a protective factor
      135–6
criminals, dysfunctional
   Parent ego state 24
crises
   acute suicidal 215–17,
      215
   slowly developing
      217–19, *217*
   and suicide statistics 9
Critical Parent (CP) ego
   state 31, 246–7, *246*
criticism, parental, and
   suicide decision 154–5

daydreams, and suicide
   158, 159–60
death penalty, and "suicide-
   murder" 19
decision-making
   automatic responses, and
      Electrode (P1) ego
      state 29–30
   early 36, 42–57, *42*, 69
   suicide 35–56, *60*, 150,
      151–2, 154–8
deliberate suicide risk
   (DSR) 187–9
delusions
   contamination of Adult
      ego state 113

and *folie à deux* 64–5
God 15
depression
   chronic 135
   correlation with suicide
      9, 56
   cycle *128*, 129
   degree of depression and
      suicidality 130–1
   key symptoms 125–7
   timing and structure of
      depressive episodes
      127–8, *128*
   types 128–30
Diagnostic and Statistical
   Manual of Mental
   Disorders *see* DSM-IV
   (1994)
diary, of a suicide attempt
   207–10
dissociation, and Free
   Child (FC) ego state
   78–9, *78*
domestic violence 19, 70
dominant party, in
   relationships 65–6
"don't exist" interviews
   152–62
drinking games 108
drug addiction, and self-
   harm 83
drug use 107, 108–12, 121
DSM-IV (1994),
   American Psychiatric
   Association 64, 125,
   192–3, *193*–4
DSR (deliberate suicide
   risk) 187–9
dynamics of intellectual
   understanding *197*
dysthymia 128, 129, 130

early decisions
   determining events 153
   and no-suicide contracts
      226, 238
   process 42–57

early decisions *cont.*
    suicide thoughts and
        actions based on 19,
        30, 36
    suppression of feelings
        169, 170–1
    for survival 37–8
    very early decisions
        171–3
ego states 21–34, *21*
    determining for no-
        suicide contracts
        238
    functional 30–2, *30*
    and the newborn child
        26–30, *27*
    and psychosis 113–14
    see also Adapted Child;
        Adult; Child;
        Conforming
        Child; Critical
        Parent; Electrode;
        Free Child;
        Little Professor;
        Nurturing Parent;
        Parent; Rebellious
        Child ego states
Electrode (P1) ego state
    29–30, 44
emotional abuse, in
    childhood 47–8
emotional responses
    12–13, 43–4, 176–7
Eros 16
escape hatch, suicide as
    239–42
Europe, suicide statistics 9
executions, voluntary 19

factitious disorder 82
family support 66–7, 101
fantasies, suicide 40, 175,
    199, 201, 241
fight response 69, 70, 71,
    72, 156–7
fighting spirit, and suicide
    decisions 55, 56

Final Exit (Humphry)
    (1991) 145–6
flight response 69, 70,
    71–2, 72–3, 146,
    155–6
florrid phase, of psychosis
    115
folie à deux 64–7
Frankl, Viktor, *Man's
    Search for Meaning*
    (1959) 36
Free Child (FC) ego state
    31, 78–9, *78*, 206,
    210–13, *210*, 251, 252
freeze response to stress
    69, 70
Freud, Sigmund 16, 254
functional ego states 30–2,
    30

gain, secondary 118–19,
    139
gangs, and self-harm 77
gender, and risk assessment
    99
genital mutilation 75
gestures, suicidal 40–1
God
    command hallucinations
        115–16
    delusions 15
guilt 10, 231

habitual thinking errors 44
hallucinations 113,
    115–16, 192
hatred, self-harm as self-
    82–4
health, and psychological
    stability 132
heaven 15, 100, 116, 142
heighteners, and redecision
    therapy 249
high-risk behavior 103–4,
    105
high-risk groups 35, 95,
    119–24

hopefulness, as a protective
    factor 101
human attachment 131–8
Humphry, D., *Final Exit*
    (1991) 145–6
hurt, and suicide 41

ideation, suicidal 97, 130
imitation, and Parent ego
    state 58, 60–1, 62–3
impulsive acts 192–4
information
    accuracy of client
        98–100
    from parents 47
insurance, non-payment of
    life policies 10
intellectual understanding
    dynamics *197*
Intermittent Explosive
    Disorder 192–3, 193–4
interviews, "don't exist"
    152–62
introjection process 63–7
irrational demands
    interpretation by
        children 52–3
    by parents 49–52

Langer's lines 89–90, *90*
life script questionnaires
    152–62
Little Professor (A1) ego
    state 28–9, 29–30, 42,
    53, 82
locus of control 233–4,
    237–8
Longitudinal Study, New
    York 54

magical thinking 28,
    40, 100, 103, 162,
    198–200
manipulation
    of boyfriend 118–19
    and self-harm 84–6

marriage
  as an addition to suicide
    risk 137–8
  and delusional belief
    systems 65
  and likelihood to suicide
    131–8
martyrdom, and suicide 15
mental health care, as a
  protective factor 101
mental health problems,
  factor in suicide 9
mental illness
  history of 112–18
  in prisoners 121–2
messages, suicidal, from
  parents 38
modeling
  and imitation 58, 60–1,
    62–3
  parental behavior 22,
    23–4
Munchausen syndrome
  82, 88
murder, as suicide 19
mutilation 75–7

narcissism 29, 40, 106, 142,
  200
"nature" aspect of
  childhood 54–6
neglect
  emotional 157, 158
  parental 42, 43, 55–6
neuropsychology 69, 199
neurotic depression 128
New York Longitudinal
  Study 54
newborn children, ego
  states 26–30, 27
no-harm contracts see
  no-suicide contracts
  (NSCs)
no-suicide assurances 230
no-suicide contracts
  (NSCs)
  as an Adult ego state
    procedure 230

contracting procedure
  232–8
iceberg 223
mutual consent 228–9
origin 222
promises, assurance and
  commitment 230–2
refusal to make 174,
  239–42
theory 222–9
no-suicide promises 230,
  235–6
no-suicide statements
  173–80
non-suicidal, the 191
notes, suicide 41, 139–44
NSCs see no-suicide
  contracts (NSCs)
nurturing, and self-harm
  82
Nurturing Parent (NP) ego
  state 31

pacts, suicide 64–7
Parent ego state
  function 31
  modeling and imitation
    58, 60–1, 62–3
  modifying tapes 63–4
  regression 141
  structure 22, 23–4, 23,
    59
  and suicide notes 141,
    142
  talking about suicide
    144
Parent in the Child (P1)
  ego state see Electrode
  (P1) ego state
parental behavior
  anger 155–6
  and Child ego state 52
  criticism of children
    154–5, 158, 159–60
  punishment of children
    47

rational and irrational
  demands 49–52,
    52–3
suicidal 59, 61, 62
suicidal messages 38
passivity 56, 145, 157–8
peer groups, and self-harm
  77
penile subincision 75
personal responsibility 227,
  233–4, 237–8
personality
  antisocial, in prisoners
    120
  borderline 116–18
  features of DSRs 187–8
  structure of the
    regressed person
    68, 101
  structures for psycotic
    individuals 113
  theory of 21–6, 21
physical abuse, in
  childhood 9, 43–4,
    47–9, 82
planning suicide 145–6
police, suicide by being
  killed by 19
*Power is in the Patient,
  The* (Goulding and
  Goulding) (1978) 227
practitioners, healthcare
  12–13
predictors of suicide 125–6
prefrontal cortex, access 69
prelogical thinking 28, 103
preverbal issues, in adults
  28
prisoners, as a high-risk
  group 119–24
prisons, At-Risk
  Management System
  (ARMS) 106, 184–5
protective factors
  counselors as 135–6
  reduction of 101–3

proximity, need to
maintain geographical
133
pseudo-suicide 194–6, 201
psychiatric disorders, and
suicide statistics 9
Psychiatric Times 224
psychological attachments
131–2
psychological dysfunction,
and childhood
mistreatment 35–6
psychological environment,
difficulty of changing
in adulthood 38
psychological motives, for
self-harm 74
psychological stability, and
health 132
psychoses 29, 35–6,
113–14
psychotic depression 129
psychotic disorder, shared
64–7
punishment
of children by parents 47
self-harm as self- 82–4
suicide used as 39

qualitative measures,
suicide risk 150–80
quantitative measures,
suicide risk 95–149
questionnaires, life script
152–62

rational abuse, in
childhood 51–2
rational demands
interpretation by
children 52–3
by parents 49–52
reaction intensity, in
children 54, 55–6
reality, detachment from
and self-harm 77–9

Rebellious Child (RC) ego
state 32, 145, 231–2,
234, 249–51
redecision therapy 243–53
bringing client back to
the here and now
251–2
contract for change 243
diagnosis of early
decision 243–5
early scene 244–5, *245*
making behavioral
contracts 252
recreating the early
scene 245–8
the redecision 248–51,
251
self-destructive aspect
of client, ongoing
contact 252–3
regression
and drug use 110–12
and human attachment
134
of Parent ego state *141*
and schizophrenia 114
and stress 68–9, *68*
and teenagers 199
tendency and degree
100–3, *101*
two-chair exercise
246–7
relationships
dominant and
submissive parties
65–6
importance 237
problems and desire to
hurt 143
repetition compulsion 37
risk assessment
quantitative measures
95–149
qualitative measures
150–80
risk, deliberate 183–90
risks, taking 16–18

Rotter's Locus of Control
Scale 234
running away, and suicide
71

schizophrenia 9, 29, 113,
114–16
Seasonal Affective
Disorder (SAD) 130
secondary gain
lack of 118–19
and suicide risk 139
secret suicide 183–90
self-defeating behavior 16
self-destructive aspect
establishing a
relationship with
237
ongoing relational
contact 252–3
self-destructive behavior
16–20, 51, 254
self-harm
definition 74
harm minimization
89–90
motives 76–87
non-suicidal 74–5
separate from suicide
74–5
trichotillomania 156
self-reporting, reliability
issues with 98–100
self-soothing 241
Serbia, suicide statistics 9
sexual abuse, in childhood
(CSA) 9, 47–8, 82, 153
shared psychotic disorder
64–7
single people, and
likelihood to commit
suicide 131–8
skin cuts 89–90, *90*
social support, as a
protective factor 101
soldiers, actions not suicide
14

Somatic Child (C1) ego
 state 27–8, 43, 44
statistics
 depression and suicidal
  thoughts 150
 disclosing suicide secret
  183–4
 on suicide 9–10, 12–13,
  35
status, suicide to achieve
 15
stigma, of suicide 10
Stopper Analysis
 questionnaire 152
stress
 fantasy for relief of 241
 flight response 146
 reactions to high 68–73
 self-harm for relief of
  80–1
submissive party, in
 relationships 65–6
substance abuse 98
substance use, history of
 106–12
suicidal ambivalence
 204–13, *205*
 assessing 212–13
 diary 207–10
 understanding 205–10
 working with 210–12
suicidal command
 hallucinations 192
suicidal crisis
 acute 215–17, *215*
 chronic 219–21, *220*
 slowly developing
  217–19, *217*
"suicidal ideation" 97, 130
suicidal impulsive acts
 192–4
suicidal messages, from
 parents 38
suicide
 by being killed 18–19
 decisions 35–56, *60*
 definition 14–20

as a flight response 71
 pacts 64–7
 planning 145–6
 statistics 9, 9–10, 35
 supported 64–7
 timing 114–15
suicide attempts, previous
 history and risk 138–9
suicide behavior, in context
 215
suicide contracts *see*
 no-suicide contracts
 (NSCs)
"suicide-murder" 19
suicide notes, and suicide
 risk assessment
 139–44
suicide risk, deliberate
 187–9
suicide, secret 183–90
suicide timelines 215–21
superstitions 196–7
support, for childhood
 decisions 53–4
supported suicide 64–7

talking about suicide
 144–5
technicalities, and no-
 suicide contract 179
teenage suicide 196–203
teenagers, and suicide
 pacts 66
temperament, qualities in
 childhood 54–6
tension, self-harm for relief
 of 80–1
terminology 12
Thanatos 16, 17, 254
therapeutic relationships,
 as a protective factor
 135–6
thinking
 in child development 28
 habitual errors in 44
 magical 28, 40, 100, 103,
  162, 198–200

prelogical 28, 103
thoughts, suicidal 97–8
time, buying 226, 237, 243,
 253
time span, and no-suicide
 contract 178–9
timelines, suicide 215–21
timing, of suicide 114–15
transactional analysis
 21–34
*Transactional Analysis
 Journal* 224
transactions 32–4, *32,
 33, 34*
transference "cures" 63–4,
 135–6
Treatment Protocol Project
 113, 114, 115, 117, 128
trichotillomania 156
two-chair exercise 245–8,
 246

"voluntary executions" 19

wars, and suicide statistics
 9
women, as second-class
 citizens 53
World Health
 Organization (WHO),
 suicide statistics 9

Author Index

Abe, R. 139
Akazawa, K. 139
Akechi, T. 126
Alderman, T. 80
Allen, B.A. 138
Allen, J.R. 138
American Psychiatric
    Association 64, 77, 82,
    114, 125, 192, 226
Assey, J.L. 222
Australian Psychological
    Society 96, 98, 107,
    112
Avary, B. 152

Barton, J. 123
Beautrais, A.L. 95
Beck, A.T. 17, 125, 126,
    130
Berne, E. 21
Birch, H.G. 54
Bowlby, J. 132
Boyd, H.S 199, 222, 239
Brown, G. 125
Brown, M. 26

Camilleri, P. 119
Campbell, D. 199
Carr, S. 35
Caruso, K. 205, 223
Chapman, A.L. 77
Chess, S. 54
Cimbolic, P. 222
Clark, D.C. 124, 183
Collins, J.K. 105
Commonwealth
    Department of
    Human Services and
    Health 108
Conger, J.J. 198
Cooper, J. 35, 95, 98, 101

Corben, S. 123
Cowles-Boyd, L. 239
Cutajar, M.C. 153

Dalton, V. 120, 184
Drye, R.C. 222

Edwards, S. 224
Egan, M.P. 222
Eyland, S. 123

Favazza, A.R. 77
Fawcett, J. 124
Follett, D. 77, 183, 184
Francis, A. 35
Frankl, V.E. 36

Garlow, S.J. 130
Garrison, B. 125
George, N. 35, 124
Goin, M. 222, 226
Goulding, M.M. 37, 39,
    47, 54, 173, 222, 226,
    227, 243
Goulding, R.L. 37, 39, 47,
    54, 173, 222, 226, 227,
    243
Gratz, K.L. 77
Green, B. 81

Hass, A.P. 130
Hassan, R. 35
Hawton, K. 9, 10, 124, 125
Hayes, L.M. 183
Hikasa, K. 126
Hipple, J. 222
Holloway, W.H. 222, 239
Horton-Deutsch, S.L. 183
Humphry, D. 145

Inhelder, B. 25, 103, 198

Jenet, R. 19
Johnson, B.S. 222
Johnston, S. 69, 199
Joines, V. 21
Jones, J. 77, 183, 184

Kagan, J. 198
Kapur, N. 35, 95, 98, 101
Kleiner, A. 204
Kovacs, M. 125
Kroll, J. 222, 224
Kugaya, A. 126

Little, R. 199

McArthur, M. 119
McCormick, P. 152
McLennan, J. 13, 97, 205
McNeel, J.R. 162
Mahrer, J. 222
Marmot, M. 132
Marusic, A. 130
Medical Dictionary 233
Midgley, D. 120
Miller, K.M. 77, 183, 184
Ministerial Council for
    Suicide Prevention 77,
    183, 184
Moore, J.D. 130
Moscicki, E.K. 98, 116
Mullen, P.E. 153
Murao, J. 126
Mussen, P.H. 198

Nankano, T. 126
Newcombe, R. 104, 107,
    108, 121
Nishimura, A. 139

Odiah, C. 19
Ogloff, J.R.P. 153
Okamura, H. 126
Ota, T. 126

Perroud, N. 130
Piaget, J. 25, 103, 198

Reid, W.J. 222
Reilly, P.M. 37
Rietschel, M. 130
Rosenberg, J. 130
Rosenthal, R.J. 77
Rotter, J.B. 234

Sayers, M. 77, 183, 184
Segal, R. 19
Shioiri, T. 139
Shopshire, M. S. 37
Simon, R.I. 222
Steele, A.A. 13, 97, 205
Steer, R.A. 125
Steiner, C. 227
Stewart, I. 21
Stone, S. 86

Temby, I. 120
Thomas, A. 54
Thomas, S.D. 153
Treatment Protocol Project
    113, 114, 115, 117,
    127, 128

Uher, R. 130

van Heeringen, K. 9, 10,
    124, 125
van Wormer, K. 19

Wada, K. 126
Webb, H. 119
White, T. 51, 132, 144,
    163, 164, 167, 168,
    169, 171, 172, 228, 245
Wilkinson, R. 132

Woods, S. 104, 107, 108,
    121
Woollams, S. 26
World Health Organization
    (WHO) 9